Modern Judgements

DICKENS

MODERN JUDGEMENTS

General Editor: P. N. FURBANK

Dickens   A. E. Dyson
Henry James   Tony Tanner
Milton   Alan Rudrum
Walter Scott   D. D. Devlin
Shelley   R. B. Woodings
Swift   A. Norman Jeffares

IN PREPARATION
Matthew Arnold   P. A. W. Collins
Freud   F. Cioffi
Marvell   M. Wilding
O'Casey   Ronald Ayling
Pasternak   Donald Davie and Angela Livingstone
Pope   Graham Martin
Racine   R. C. Knight

Dickens

MODERN JUDGEMENTS

edited by

A. E. DYSON

MACMILLAN

Selection and editorial matter © A. E. Dyson 1968

MACMILLAN & CO LTD
Little Essex Street London W C 2
and also at Bombay Calcutta and Madras
Macmillan South Africa (Publishers) Pty Ltd Johannesburg
The Macmillan Company of Australia Pty Ltd Melbourne
The Macmillan Company of Canada Ltd Toronto

Printed in Great Britain by
WESTERN PRINTING SERVICES LTD
Bristol

Contents

Acknowledgements

Angus Wilson, 'Charles Dickens: A Haunting', from *Critical Quarterly*, II, 2 (1960); Professor C. B. Cox, 'In Defence of Dickens', from *Essays and Studies*, 1958; 'The Young Dickens', from *The Lost Childhood and Other Essays* (Eyre & Spottiswoode Ltd, Viking Press Inc.; © Graham Greene 1951); A. E. Dyson, '*The Old Curiosity Shop*: Innocence and the Grotesque'; 'Sons and Fathers', from *Dickens: From Pickwick to Dombey* (Chatto & Windus Ltd, Basic Books Inc.; © Steven Marcus 1965); J. Hillis Miller, '*Martin Chuzzlewit*', from *Charles Dickens: The World of His Novels* (Harvard University Press; © the President and the Fellows of Harvard College 1958); Kathleen Tillotson, '*Dombey and Son*', from *Novels of the Eighteen Forties* (The Clarendon Press); Mark Spilka, '*David Copperfield* as Psychological Fiction', from *Dickens and Kafka* (Indiana University Press); '*Bleak House*', from *The Maturity of Dickens* (Harvard University Press; © Monroe Engel); W. J. Harvey, 'Freedom and Causality', from *Character and the Novel* (Chatto & Windus Ltd, Cornell University Press); Humphry House, '*Hard Times*', from *The Dickens World* (Oxford University Press); Lionel Trilling's introduction to *Little Dorrit*, from *The Opposing Self* (Oxford University Press); John Gross, '*A Tale of Two Cities*', from *Dickens and the Twentieth Century* (Routledge & Kegan Paul Ltd, University of Toronto Press); Dorothy Van Ghent, 'On *Great Expectations*', from *The English Novel, Form and Function* (Holt, Rinehart and Winston Inc.); Robert Morse, '*Our Mutual Friend*', from *Partisan Review* (Mar 1949), vol. XVI, no. 3; James Wright, 'Afterword to *The Mystery of Edwin Drood*'; the Epilogue from *Charles Dickens: His Tragedy and Triumph* (Professor Edgar Johnson and Victor Gollancz Ltd).

General Editor's Preface

LITERARY criticism has only recently come of age as an academic discipline, and the intellectual activity that, a hundred years ago, went into theological discussion, now finds its most natural outlet in the critical essay. Amid a good deal that is dull or silly or pretentious, every year now produces a crop of critical essays which are brilliant and profound not only as contributions to the understanding of a particular author, but as statements of an original way of looking at literature and the world. Hence it often seems that the most useful undertaking for an academic publisher might be, not so much to commission new books of literary criticism or scholarship, as to make the best of what exists easily available. This at least is the purpose of the present series of anthologies, each of which is devoted to a single major writer.

The guiding principle of selection is to assemble the best *modern* criticism – broadly speaking, that of the last twenty or thirty years – and to include historic and classic essays, however famous, only when they are still influential and represent the best statements of their particular point of view. It will, however, be one of the functions of each editor's Introduction to sketch in the earlier history of criticism in regard to the author concerned.

Each volume will attempt to strike a balance between general essays and ones on specialised aspects, or particular works, of the writer in question. And though in many instances the bulk of the articles will come from British and American sources, certain of the volumes will draw heavily on material in other European languages – most of it being translated for the first time.

P. N. FURBANK

Introduction

EVERYTHING in this volume, with one exception, has been written since 1949; much of it dates from 1959. During this period, Dickens's reputation has been not established, but recognised. No-one pretends any longer that he is unread, or that his readers are too lower middle class to count. From the tone of bemused patronage in which intellectuals would mention him in the earlier part of this century, we have passed to more fruitful bemusement at the range and complexity of his work. Students settle down to him with lively expectations of symbolism. Our modern anxieties, enigmas and literary experiments are seen foreshadowed in his work.

But the idea that 'nobody' reads Dickens was so prevalent only a few years ago that it seems a logical place to start from. His reputation during his lifetime is not in question: 'Whether our great-grandchildren do or do not read Mr Dickens', George Stott wrote in 1869, 'they will all have to recognise that their great-grandfathers certainly did.' The demand for his work, said Trollope in *St Paul's Magazine* in 1870, exceeds that 'for the work of any other writer in our language'. With Dickens's death in 1870, sales showed no falling off. During the twelve years following, over four million copies were sold.[1] By 1891 the sales were four times greater than they had been in 1869; about 330,000 copies were sold each year. Between 1900 and 1920 there were thirteen complete editions, and innumerable versions of individual works. By 1944 no less than sixty different editions of *A Tale of Two Cities* had been published in Great Britain alone. In 1948 the Everyman Library reported that the book with the highest annual sale was *David Copperfield*. At the same time Dickens was read and discussed in

[1] For these, and many other facts, I am indebted to George H. Ford's *Dickens and his Readers: Aspects of Novel-criticism since 1836* – a highly readable account, published in 1955, and now available in paperback.

most parts of Europe, Asia and America. In France and Germany he
has been particularly admired (though in Germany with some loss of
interest since the First World War). Among other European countries
favourable to his reputation, Spain, Italy, Holland and Denmark stand
out. He was always a great favourite in Russia, under the Tsars and
under the Soviets. Most other communist countries find him congenial, including China, where, it seems, he even accords with the
Thought of Mao Tse-Tung. For serious critical discussion and attention, the U.S.A. has long led the world. No other English writer,
except Shakespeare, has been so widely and enthusiastically read.

It is against facts such as these that one has to test the mystical conviction of certain intellectuals twenty or thirty years ago that 'nobody'
read Dickens. Their view rested on the authority of a tradition which
was started in his lifetime – notably by G. H. Lewes, James Fitzjames
Stephen and Walter Bagehot – and which passed, by way of Leslie
Stephen's tepid account in the *Dictionary of National Biography* and the
faint praise of Saintsbury, into the hostility of Leslie Stephen's daughter,
Virginia Woolf, and the Bloomsbury Group. I can remember being
told myself in the early 1940s that nobody read Dickens, and feeling
sorry – though I should have remembered that a set of his works
sponsored by a popular newspaper in the 1930s had found its way into
my own home, and presumably into a great many more. Even as a
boy, I half realised that 'nobody' in this context had a special meaning,
and should be taken more as a rebuke than a fact. Yet, even on this
enlightened showing, it ran into difficulties; could 'nobody,' even in
the grandest circles, include Gissing and Morris, Swinburne and
Hopkins? – an amazing spectrum of admirers in themselves. Indeed,
was Henry James nobody? After his famous youthful attack on *Our
Mutual Friend* he had come round, after all, to writing of Dickens in
French Poets and Novelists (1884):

> In intensity of imaginative power, the power of evoking visible objects
> and figures, seeing them themselves with the force of hallucination
> and making others see them all but just as vividly, they [Dickens and
> Balzac] were almost equal. Here there is little to choose between them;
> they have no rivals but each other and Shakespeare.

Kipling enjoyed Dickens, and so did Bennett; Conrad thought him
the first among English novelists, confessing that he had read *Bleak
House* 'innumerable times', and found 'the very weaknesses more

precious to me than the strengths of other men's work'. Bernard Shaw ranked most of the novels after *Hard Times* among the world's great subversive literature, and wrote to Frank Harris in 1919:

> Your ignorance of Dickens is a frightful gap in your literary education. He was by far the greatest man since Shakespeare that England has produced in that line. Read *Little Dorrit*, *Our Mutual Friend* and *Great Expectations*. Until you do, you will not have the very faintest notion of what the name Dickens means.

Chesterton was no less enthusiastic, and his brilliant, erratic little book (*Charles Dickens*, 1906) remains a work to read.

Foreign admirers also include impressive names. Turgenev thought Dickens the greatest nineteenth-century English novelist; so did Tolstoy, who wrote (very sensibly, and without prescience of Professor L. C. Knights): 'All his characters are my personal friends – I am constantly comparing them with living persons, and living persons with them, and what a spirit there was in all he wrote.' Tolstoy linked Dickens with Dostoevsky, among artists of the highest type. Dostoevsky himself, of course, would read only *David Copperfield* and *Pickwick Papers* during his imprisonment – or so the story firmly goes.

II

How, then, has any reverse impression ever flourished? – to trace this, we must return to the start. Dickens's first success came through journalism. *Sketches by Boz* appeared in February 1836, and won him modest fame as a rising young man. Reviews were chiefly favourable. Boz, wrote Hogarth in the *Morning Chronicle*, is 'a close observer of characters and manners, with a strong sense of the ridiculous and a graphic faculty of placing in the most whimsical and amusing lights the follies and absurdities of human nature. He has the power, too, of producing tears as well as laughter. His pictures of the vices and wretchedness which abound in this vast city are sufficient to strike the heart of the most careless and insensitive reader.' By August, Dickens was writing of the great success of his book, and his publishers had every reason to share his delight.

Real fame came, however, with *Pickwick Papers* (1836–7) – that strange venture which began as a series of sporting prints which

Seymour was to draw and Dickens was to illustrate with a commentary, and which got off to such a disastrous start. Little did Seymour, or Chapman & Hall the publishers, realise what energy they were loosing. It took Dickens very little time to decide that the priorities were askew and that his own inventiveness must be senior partner in the affair. 'I thought of Mr Pickwick', he records, and Mr Pickwick was launched, a sportsman very remote from Seymour's original plan. Alas, the first issue fell flat, selling only 400 copies. Chapman & Hall began to panic, and Seymour by then detested the project with all his heart. He was a desperately unhappy man for many reasons, and, after illustrating the first issue of *Pickwick*, he blew his brains out; his last plate for the venture, 'The Dying Clown', was found in his studio after death.

Undeterred, though anxious, Dickens now found a new illustrator, and thought of Mr Weller; failure turned into success on an undreamed-of scale. From the initial sale of 400, circulation rose to 40,000. The critics were rapturous, and everywhere in England *Pickwick* was talked of; 'Not having heard of Dickens', wrote Miss Mitford in June 1837, 'seems like not having heard of Hogarth, whom he resembles greatly, except that he takes a far more cheerful view, a Shakespearean view, of humanity.' This first, great success of Dickens was to remain the favourite of the reading public throughout his lifetime and for many years after his death. '*Pickwick* has been to us very much what *The Rape of the Lock* was to the poets of the last century', wrote a *Westminster Review* critic in 1864. Sometimes in the 1850s, when readers urged Dickens to return to the Pickwick manner, and seemed oblivious to his far more complex and costly later achievements, he might slightly have regretted this first-born child. But never, one feels, seriously; 'if I were to live a hundred years', he had confided to his publishers in November 1836, 'and write three novels in each, I should never be so proud of any of them as I am of Pickwick'. There was no recantation of this.

Nicholas Nickleby (1838–9) had a comparable success (50,000 of the monthly part sold on the first day), and was again very generally praised (Dr Arnold was to complain later, however, in the *North British Review* of 1845, that *Pickwick Papers* and *Nicholas Nickleby* had brought about 'a decrease of manly thoughtfulness' at Rugby). But before *Nicholas Nickleby*, though in the later stages of publication the two overlapped, Dickens had astonished his public with a wholly

different kind of book. *Oliver Twist* (1837–8) was as grim and menacing
in its theme as *Pickwick* had been cheerful; it shone a startling light on
the sins of the criminal and the Pharisee alike. Now, for the first time,
Dickens ran into some hostile criticism concerning his 'realism'. 'I
don't like that low, debasing style', said Lord Melbourne, 'I shouldn't
think it would tend to raise morals'. Henry Fox declared the novel
'painful and revolting', and Thackeray also objected to it: parodying
Oliver Twist along with other Newgate novels, he remarked that the
'discerning reader' is 'sick of the hideous scenes of brutal bloodshed
which have of late come forth from the pens of certain eminent wits'.
The challenge to Dickens's new style took two directions; the first,
that such scenes did not happen, and Dickens was inventing them, or
at the very least exaggerating; the second, that if they did happen,
they should not be written about. 'I know there are such unfortunate
beings as pick-pockets and street walkers,' said Lady Carlisle, 'but I
own I do not much wish to hear what they say to one another.' Of
these two indictments, Dickens's main resentment was against the first.
When writing prefaces to later editions of his novels, he was frequently
concerned to assert the social reality of the evils depicted there. If
anything, he said, he had understated – and this because he agreed
that certain realities never could be put into print. His novels, like his
journalism, were meant for the family; the problem was to stir the
conscience of his readers without disgusting them, to present social
evils vividly and truthfully, yet to steer clear of obscenities in word
and deed. His problem was, in short, for a novelist, very normal and
central; though forced into the *avant-garde* of social realism by moral
seriousness, he could scarcely be expected to write books that no-one
would buy. He fully agreed, moreover, with his readers' scruples, and
would have been horrified by the notion that his books could initiate
anyone into crime, sin, sadism or lust. Though he never sympathised
with Lady Carlisle's languid plea for total protection, and his response
to the later prudery of the 1860s was to be Mr Podsnap and Mr
Podsnap's 'young person', his writings always were intended as household words. It is important for us in the 1960s to remember, in this
connection, that a writer's licence to depict the full range of obscenity
and violence, even supposing that he wishes to, is very recent; if we
except pornography, and one or two celebrated classics of the 1920s
and 1930s, it virtually belongs to the last ten years. It depends, too, on
the loss of Dickens's typical reader to television, and the growth of

a new audience of 'Eng. Lit.' students and middle-class sophisticates in his place. The result is the highly feverish situation at present prevailing, from which the novel will recover, no doubt (if it recovers at all), only by rediscovering some degree of reticence as the norm. The extraordinary achievement of Dickens was to go as far as he did towards social realism in the early Victorian climate without becoming feverish, and without giving widespread offence. It was his remarkable and unusual gift to be able to depict the most warped and criminal people in a manner horrifyingly vivid to a sensitive adult, but unlikely to harm a young person, or a reader only partly engaged with the book. Dennis the hangman is a creation of fantastic horror: obsessed with his art in even casual conversation, and dressed wholly in the clothes of people he has killed, he would not be out of place in *The Naked Lunch*. Yet his evil is in no way forced upon the reader through sick evocation. No-one is more likely to become a psychopathic killer through reading *Barnaby Rudge*.

After *Oliver Twist*, Dickens's fame reached a new peak with *The Old Curiosity Shop* (1840), where he proved that he could make the nation weep as well as laugh. By the time Little Nell died, 100,000 copies were being sold, and America had also dissolved into tears. There were always some, it is true, who remained dry-eyed, and some who detected sinister undercurrents to the ordeal. 'He gloats over the girl's death as if it delighted him', said Fitzjames Stephen; 'Nell was simply killed for the market', said Ruskin, 'as a butcher kills a lamb.' But most readers saw no need for such cynicism; they had already responded, long before little Nell's sufferings overwhelmed them, to the tremendous zest of the tale. This was Dickens's first novel to be issued in weekly instead of monthly parts, and though he groaned at the discipline, he was later to submit to it again; *Barnaby Rudge*, *Hard Times*, *A Tale of Two Cities* and *Great Expectations* were also issued in weekly parts.

The next novel, however, started a reverse in his fortunes. The idea of *Barnaby Rudge* had been long in his mind, and its pre-publishing history was already a stormy affair. He had major disagreements with both Macrone and Bentley – the very title *Barnaby Rudge* is one to make publishers tremble – and, in the course of these, amid enforced delays and threats of litigation, his sense of the novel had somewhat soured. But after the triumph of *The Old Curiosity Shop* he turned back to the few pages already drafted, and decided upon *Barnaby*

Rudge (1841) as the next serial for his periodical *Master Humphrey's Clock*. This was his first historical novel, with London of the later 1770s as its setting and the Gordon Riots as the climax towards which everything moves. Of all his novels it was the least generally successful either in his own lifetime or afterwards, and work on it seems to have given him more than usual pain. In my own view, it is a very great novel, and an advance in sheer artistry on everything that had gone before. Sales, however, were not encouraging; from 70,000 copies at the start – a very hopeful number – they fell to 30,000 before the end.

After this, there was the first real pause in Dickens's career, during which he made his famous tour of the U.S.A. When he returned and started publishing again, it was to face the first (and last) great crisis in his career. The reception of *Martin Chuzzlewit* (1843–4) was, in comparative terms, a disaster; it began by selling only 20,000 copies, and this number obstinately refused to improve. Crabb Robinson pronounced it an unpleasant book, 'so generally disgusting are the characters and incidents of the tale', and this view was widely, if uneasily, shared. Depressed and alarmed by the reception, Dickens decided to remove his hero to the U.S.A. and to involve him in episodes of bitingly satiric force. This enraged America without much helping the circulation; sales rose to 23,000, but still failed to soar. Perhaps it was as well for Dickens's morale that *A Christmas Carol*, published at Christmas 1843 while *Martin Chuzzlewit* was still appearing, met with such conclusive acclaim. He made very little money from this first Christmas tale, owing to errors of costing, but he learned that his real audience had not gone away. Even Thackeray was won over, and commented: 'Who can listen to objections regarding such a book as this? It seems to me a national benefit, and to every man or woman who reads it a personal kindness.' But the reception of *Martin Chuzzlewit* was still not assisted, and in retrospect this remains hard to understand. It contains, after all, two of Dickens's greatest 'immortals', and offers abundant compensation in vitality for any apparent lack of shape. Later, it caught up in popularity, and by 1870 was exceeded in sales only by *Pickwick Papers* and *David Copperfield*. At the time of the failure Dickens was annoyed and bewildered. 'I feel my power now more than I ever did', he wrote in November 1843, and again, 'I think *Chuzzlewit* in a hundred points immeasurably the best of my stories.' He was inclined to blame the poor reception wholly on reviewers, but the truth, perhaps, is that all great artists have at some time to stand the test of public caprice. It may be that readers were still hankering after Mr Pickwick and that it took *Martin Chuzzlewit* to exorcise that genial ghost.

With *Dombey and Son* (1847–8), Dickens's novels became more painful to write and more difficult for the reader; and, most critics would now agree, of even greater stature and power. The tide of public fidelity turned, and though there were no more dramatic successes (except for the Christmas books and stories), sales rose steadily for the remainder of his life – from *David Copperfield* (1849–50) at 25,000 and *Bleak House* (1852–3) at 35,000, to 50,000 copies of *Edwin Drood* (1870) at the time of his death. Sales of all the earlier novels also continued; Dickens lived to see his 'favourite child' (*David Copperfield*) second only to *Pickwick* in public regard.

III

Yet by the 1850s, though Dickens's hold on his readers was established, the volume of hostile criticism started to grow. There were several reasons for this, even apart from the vicissitudes natural to an established author. There were more competitors now on the scene – notably Thackeray, the Brontës, George Eliot and Trollope – and the taste for a new, analytical realism was being fed. Ironically, the increasing respect during this period for the novel as an art-form told against Dickens; he was repeatedly accused of slapdash and improvisation in the very years when his artistry matured. And here it is important to remind ourselves that Dickens was indeed an artist, and a fully conscious one, even though he valued his hold on an audience and his dedication to moral purposes beyond any aesthetic purposes *per se*. Some critics have been misled, I fancy, by Forster's comment:

> What I had most indeed to notice in him, at the very outset of his career, was his indifference to any praise of his performances on the merely literary side, compared with the higher recognition of them as bits of actual life, with the meaning and purpose on their part, and the responsibility on his, of realities rather than creatures of fancy.

This is too crude to be even a half-truth, though one sees what Forster means; naturally a writer will be angry if his insight into life is dismissed as mere fantasy and his moral seriousness as fancy run wild.

But literature *is* an art, and all writers know it; the more wounding charge must be that a novelist offers 'bits of actual life' and no more than this, as though he were a journalist choosing to report in a fictional mode. As early as the 1840s, Dickens criticised Thackeray for being too little an artist; and it is Thackeray who is reported to have said, much later, 'I am played out. All I can do now is bring on my old puppets . . . But, if he lives to be ninety, Dickens will still be creating new characters. In his art that man is marvellous.' Trollope also wrote, in 1870, 'It is fatuous to condemn that as deficient in art which has been so full of art as to capture all men.' Today, the misguided notion that Dickens lacked artistry is no longer dangerous – every essay in this present volume testifies to the reverse. It was, however, a dangerous criticism in the 1850s, when new criteria of 'realism' and 'naturalism' were distorting many critics' understanding of art itself. The new tendency was to see the novel simply as a fictional account of social and psychological observations – and this, pernicious in itself if art is lost sight of, is never more so than when social and psychological observations are assimilated to a postulated *zeitgeist* or a progressive 'norm'. Trollope and George Eliot, in their very different fashions, satisfied the new taste for sociology and the prevailing *zeitgeist*. The profundity of Dickens's social vision remained hidden from those who stumbled over the conventions of his art.

But the other great factor which told against Dickens at this time was his pessimism; during the high Victorian years between the Great Exhibition of 1851 and the Second Reform Bill of 1867, his view of reality darkened all the time. This offended many of his distinguished contemporaries, including Trollope, who was always happier with *laissez faire* economics, self-help, conspicuous wealth and middle-class Podsnappery than Dickens could ever bring himself to be. We have to remember that Dickens was carrying on fiercely radical campaigns in his journalism – *for* sanitation and basic welfare services, *against* Palmerstonian patriotism and the Crimean War – at the time when Trollope was satirising radical journalism in *The Warden* (1855) and other books. But even more important in its implications, and in its unacceptability to Trollope and the many who thought like him, was the nightmare vision that Dickens was coming to have of nineteenth-century capitalism – its inborn cruelties, its incompatibility with virtue, its drift towards squalor, its inherent contradictions – so many years ahead of his time. It is no accident that from our present viewpoint we see Dickens chiefly as a modern – a prophet of twentieth-century anxieties and enigmas no less than a literary innovator in the line of Kafka, Eliot and Proust. The late novels, in particular, are among the most subversive accounts of our present-day society that we have even yet been offered. It is not simply the juxtaposition of William Dorrit, Mrs Clennam and Merdle; or Pip, Miss Havisham and Magwitch; or Bella Wilfer, the Veneerings and Silas Wegg which leaves this impression; it is the interaction of these characters with a score or so others, in contexts as richly realised in detail yet as morally ambivalent as any that even modern literature can show.

IV

The situation by the early twentieth century, then, was this: Dickens's popular audience continued to grow, and many creative artists acknowledged his greatness, but in élitist circles he was thought to be Victorian, discredited and unread. This alone can account for the mingling of caution and astonishment with which his return to full favour came about. Even Orwell seems surprised to find how good he is, while Humphry House's *The Dickens World* (1941), admirable in content, is very seriously marred by its patronising tone.

The year 1939 was significant for Dickens's reputation, on account of two important essays (both too long to reproduce here): Edmund Wilson's 'Dickens: The Two Scrooges', and George Orwell's 'Charles Dickens'. The first of these was read to students in the University of Chicago, and is now to be found in *The Wound and the Bow* (1941). Wilson begins by asserting:

> Of all the great English writers, Charles Dickens has received in his own country the scantiest serious attention from either biographers, scholars, or critics.

The habit of sneering at Dickens is brought home to Bloomsbury, which 'talked about Dostoevsky', but 'ignored Dostoevsky's master, Dickens'. Wilson finds very little in previous Dickens criticism to interest him (though he praises Gissing, and also T. A. Jackson's book of two years before). What he does himself is to relate Dickens's biography fairly closely to the novels – particularly Dickens's sufferings for a few months at the age of twelve in a blacking factory, which he regards as traumatic. Much of the darker side of Dickens's vision is attributed to this experience – the paranoid fears and obsessions, the bizarre human relationships, the preoccupation with squalor – though Wilson recognises, also, that Dickens's gloom deepened as he grew older and matured with his conscious analysis of men and affairs. There was the particular dilemma presented to Dickens's radicalism by his powerful negative intuitions – his contempt for organised religion, despair of democracy, mistrust of power, fear of violence in individuals and in the mob. Wilson endorses Shaw's view (which has since become orthodox) that Dickens's novels grew in social insight after *Bleak House*. He calls attention (and attention has, indeed, been given) to such symbols as the fog in *Bleak House* and the marshes in *Great Expectations*. He concludes by finding a manic-depressive cycle in Dickens, which can be traced equally in his life and his art.

Also in 1939, Orwell wrote his essay 'Charles Dickens' (now available in *Inside the Whale* and in his *Collected Essays* (1961), as well as elsewhere). This is almost Johnsonian in its masculine judiciousness, its resolute sobriety, its massive alternations of praise and blame; it is an exploration of mid-Victorian problems in the light of the 1930s, and Orwell's personal homage to a very great man. Orwell starts by noting Dickens's predicament as a member, though a highly subversive one, of the middle-class puritan *bourgeoisie* – that class ubiquitous in mid-Victorian England through all its spectrum, from the Podsnap ascendancy to William Dorrit's last-ditch gentility. Orwell's chief interest is in Dickens as a novelist of 'problems', but he blames him, oddly, for producing too few solutions to these. Oddly, because Dickens's main problems were so personally familiar to Orwell: did Orwell also not mistrust power, democracy, education, and combine strong faith in the decency of many ordinary people with despair for decency in politics, economics and society at large? Orwell blames Dickens's supposed failure to find solutions upon two main factors – his artistry, which created characters and situations that fit only uneasily into plot and action (their proper home is eternity), and his inability to carry political analysis through to the end. Dickens was not finally able, says Orwell, to see through private property and come down on the side of total social change. Yet Orwell *does* understand Dickens's intense dread of mob violence, and his political scepticism; looking back, one is inclined to feel that it was Orwell's analysis, not Dickens's, which stopped short. His essay is dated 1939, but would it have come out like this a few years later? It is interesting, with this in mind, to consider a paragraph from Humphry House's *The Dickens World*:

> A plain thesis can be extracted from the book [*A Tale of Two Cities*]: the aristocrats deserved all they got, but the passions engendered in the people by misery and starvation replaced one set of oppressors by another. One aristocrat can be rescued to repent and live in the decent quietude of England; one individual can assert his goodness against the double evil of the rest. But the concentration of emotion is never on Charles Darnay; it is all on the wild frenzy of people who have committed everything to violence. Dickens hated and feared such violence; there is not a sign of approval or defence of it; he attributes every kind of monstrous wickedness to its leaders; but he projects into his treatment of it his own feelings of desperate impotence in the face of the problem of political power.

This is a synopsis, and a very succinct one, of a late Dickens novel. If we replace Charles Darnay with (say) Boxer, and remove the escape clause, does it not equally describe *Animal Farm*?

But Orwell's essay transcends its weaknesses; the insights are powerful, and the final tribute testifies to Dickens's relevance in a world, and a crisis, far different from his own. Orwell is talking of the 'faces' that he imagines for certain great writers:

> Well, in the case of Dickens I see a face that is not quite the face of Dickens's photographs, though it resembles it. It is the face of a man of about forty, with a small beard and a high colour. He is laughing, with a touch of anger in his laughter, but no triumph, no malignity. It is the face of a man who is always fighting against something, but who fights in the open and is not frightened, the face of a man who is *generously angry* – in other words, of a nineteenth-century liberal, a free intelligence, a type hated with equal hatred by all the smelly little orthodoxies which are now contending for our souls.

Humphry House's *The Dickens World* was published two years after these essays by Wilson and Orwell, in 1941; it is now available in paperback, and remains a book that all students of Dickens should read. Like Orwell's essay it suffers a little from the assumption that Dickens's fiction is almost a department of his journalism and that he was in constant search, throughout his novels, for 'solutions': this means that he is berated both for failing to produce solutions, and for producing solutions that appear to House irrelevant or 'tame'. House sets Dickens in the context of Victorian thought with admirable clarity, and for this reason if for no other he remains classic (it may be as well, though, to mention at this point two other works, not specifically related to Dickens, which are even more valuable as 'background' for his novels – G. M. Young's *Portrait of an Age* and Asa Briggs's *Victorian People*). On practical matters also, House is lucid; he delves into the time-schemes of the novels (very fascinating, this), and their historical sources, and is full of illumination on the exact nature of Dickens's feelings about religion, philanthropy, political economy, communications (stage-coach *versus* train) and the rapid flux of the times. He is also interesting on the conjunction of Dickens's deep hatred for the so-called 'wisdom' of ancestors (here, if nowhere else, Dickens agreed with Bentham) with his rejection of all the modern creeds and panaceas – nonconformity, catholicism, utilitarianism, *laissez faire*, organised charity, trade unionism, militant patriotism, podsnappery and a score or so more. But the fault in House's book is that it stays in this area; it relates Dickens's deeper vision of evil and chaos too little to the force of his works. There is an irony, of sorts, in House's title; it is precisely not Dickens's world, the created world of the novels, that he writes about, but the mid-Victorian world as it appears in Dickens's books. He scarcely comes to terms with Dickens as an artist; his Dickens is essentially the editor of *Household Words* (1850–9) and *All the Year Round* (1859–70).

v

This brings us to the period covered by this anthology, where all I can hope to offer is a very brief guide. First, the mountains: and the Everest is Edgar Johnson's splendid two-volume biography, *Charles Dickens: His Tragedy and Triumph* (1952). This is fuller and richer than Forster's biography (though it does not supersede Forster), and it is interspersed with chapters of criticism on the individual works. Dickens has been exceptionally lucky in a biographer who is intensely readable as well as exhaustive, as though some touch of the Inimitable has rubbed off on himself. For bibliography, most students will find all that they need in Ada Nisbet's valuable contribution to *Victorian Fiction: A Guide to Research* (ed. Lionel Stevenson, 1964). For an account of Dickens's methods of work and publication, a very useful volume is *Dickens at Work*, by John Butt and Kathleen Tillotson (1957). For an account of Dickens's reputation there is the excellent work I have already acknowledged and leaned heavily upon, George H. Ford's *Dickens and his Readers: Aspects of Novel-criticism since 1836* (1955; now available in paperback). For nineteenth-century background, two stimulating recent books are *Dickens and Crime* (2nd ed. 1964; also available in paperback) and *Dickens and Education* (1963; also available in paperback), both by Philip Collins; Kathleen Tillotson's *Novels of the Eighteen-Forties* (1954; now available in paperback) must be mentioned as well. For general background, there are the two little masterpieces of compressed history which I have already mentioned: G. M. Young's *Portrait of an Age* (1936; now available in paperback) and Asa Briggs's *Victorian People* (1954; now a Pelican). For further anthologies of critical essays on Dickens, I particularly recommend *The Dickens Critics*, edited by George H. Ford and Lauriat Lane, Jr (1961), which contains many of the best critical essays from Edgar Allan Poe to Angus Wilson. There is also a collection of new essays, one on each of the major novels, written by well-known younger critics and edited by John Gross and Gabriel Pearson: *Dickens and the Twentieth Century* (1962).

A very massive project currently in preparation is the Pilgrim edition of *The Letters of Charles Dickens*, edited by Madeline House and Graham Storey. The first volume (1820–39) has recently been published and there are nine or ten further volumes to come. A scholarly new edition of Dickens is also projected by the Clarendon Press; it started under the joint editorship of Kathleen Tillotson and the late John Butt. (Perhaps I can confess here that in my own reading of Dickens, I always turn to one of the great Chapman & Hall Illustrated Library editions of the last century. The large, clear print and the spreading of the longer novels over two volumes is to my mind essential – mean print, cramped layout, poor paper, seem wholly at odds with his work.)

In criticism there have been many books and articles, a selection of which will be found in my short bibliography (pp. 281–2). The present anthology represents a cross-section: my general aim has been to choose something on each of the major novels (with two exceptions), whilst also representing most of the kinds of critical attention now being given to his work. It is perhaps symptomatic that the two exceptions are *Pickwick Papers* and *Nicholas Nickleby*; these are fairly central to C. B. Cox's general defence of early Dickens, but modern critics have less to say of them, in detail, than of later works. Their zest and gusto keeps them evergreen, but their particular virtues seem less in need of commentary of our present kind.

What, then, *are* the main kinds of current criticism? First, I suppose, biographical; Dickens's life has come in for much attention, and it is now normal to see connections between the vast world of the novels and the novelist's life. This no longer takes the form of crude assertions that Mrs Nickleby 'is' Dickens's mother and Mr Micawber his father; it is the perception, rather, that real people and relationships are very frequently the raw material for art. Thus, Mr Micawber may be seen as a comic version, and William Dorrit a tragic one, of the kind of person suggested by John Dickens. This does not disguise either the immense creative distinctiveness of these two characters, or their immense dissimilarities from one another as well as from their real-life original. It is a formula which allows us to acknowledge the distinctive tug upon them of Dickens's unmistakable fantasy, and at the same time to relate them to other characters in the novels – Harold Skimpole for instance – for whom a different real-life original was the starting-point.

Biographical criticism shades in one direction into historical criticism, and modern critics are now very aware of the mid-Victorian scene. But in the other direction it shades imperceptibly into psychological criticism, which has also proved a potent lure. Perhaps it is inevitable that the known frustrations and tragedies of Dickens's life should loom large to us, and that pondering certain recurring themes and obsessions in the novels, we should relate these in one manner or another to his personal experience: to his precocious and sensitive years as a child in Rochester, while the family prospered; his traumatic months in the blacking factory at the age of twelve, when its fortunes collapsed; his father's imprisonment for debt in the Marshalsea, and his mother's indifference to her son's wounded feelings; his unrequited passion for Maria Beadnell; his unexciting and deteriorating marriage; his extraordinary idealisation of his sister-in-law Mary Hogarth, and grief at her death; his crippling responsibilities for a prodigal father and wastrel brothers; his desperate and unhappy affair, much later in life, with the young Ellen Ternan; his compulsive walks, travels, amateur theatricals; his sensational public readings in the 1860s (undertaken against all medical advice), which certainly shortened his life. These aspects of his life, and the dark moods of his later years, recorded in letters, reveal a stranger and fiercer man than the public persona of Victorian days. They have also alerted critics to the depths of psychological insight underlying characters once dismissed as 'caricatures' and situations once thought too dramatic or melodramatic for truth. But at the same time we have become more aware, through close reading, of his sheer exuberance – the exuberance which produced the biggest corpus of great writing in English (Henry James is the only rival) and a still larger corpus of journalism and correspondence, all within the framework of a most exacting and tireless public and private life. To call his profoundly warring moods 'manic-depressive' may be marginally illuminating, but what other 'manic-depressive' interests us like this? The inadequacy of psychological clichés and biographical speculations to account for genius cannot fail to strike us. It may even be that biographical knowledge is fated to lose importance (though not, of course, all importance) for the literary critic, in direct proportion to the greatness of the art.

Of more lasting importance, then, than biographical criticism is our new recognition of the nature and stature of Dickens's art – a recognition often to be found, of course, in the same critics who write best of his life. It was, I think, Masson who first called Dickens a poet, and Taine who developed the idea. In 1872 Robert Buchanan said:

> . . . the world decided long ago that Dickens was beyond all parallel the greatest imaginative creator of his generation, and that his poetry, the best of it, although written in unrhymed speech, is worth more, and will probably last longer, than all the verse-poetry of this age, splendid as some of that poetry has been.

This notion of Dickens as a poet has become still more fruitful in the light of symbolist theories, and since the breakdown of any rigid distinction between poetry and prose. While Dickens's detractors have sometimes used it as a stick to beat him with (his most rhetorical flights, they say disapprovingly, can be scanned as iambics), the more flattering implications have also been grasped. Attention has been drawn to the highly individual speech rhythms of his characters – Mrs Gamp and Pecksniff are as distinctive in speech as Falstaff or Edmund – and also to the extraordinary vigour of syntax and imagery throughout his prose. The opening chapters of nearly all the novels written after *David Copperfield* are nearer in technique to *The Waste Land* and

Ulysses than they are to *Emma* or *Barchester Towers*. It is not only the elaboration of syntax, the proliferating images and symbols, the heightened rhetoric which seem 'poetic' but, more basically, the haunting evocations of the prose. Graham Greene talks of Dickens's 'secret prose', which gives us 'that sense of a mind speaking to itself with no-one there to listen'; *Great Expectations*, he says, is written in 'delicate and exact poetic cadences, the music of memory, that so influenced Proust'. There are, too, the underlying myths and arche-types, the suggestions of dream and nightmare, the teasing resonances; the intimations of some unity beyond the plot. Many of Dickens's recent critics have found anticipations of Kafka, in his symbolism, and in the experiences of anxiety and enigma which the symbols create. Kafka is, indeed, the purest example of this technique, in that he brings symbolism into a final ascendancy over plot by a degree of suggestive-ness which precludes any normal resolution of 'meaning', any normal perception of cause and effect, of beginning, middle and end. Dickens is still a long way, of course, from sharing conscious purposes such as Kafka's, but it takes no great critical hindsight to notice his close approach to Kafka's actual effects. If we define Dickens's own tech-nique, with deliberate caution, as an undercurrent of symbolism adding resonance to the plot, we come close to what may have been the most important single innovation in the novel's modern history – an inno-vation pervasive in literature since Dickens's death. Its influence may be found not only in Kafka himself, and indeed not only in an im-pressive range of masterpieces from (say) *The Sacred Fount* (though almost any James novel would do) through *A Passage to India*, *The Great Gatsby*, *1984* and *Pincher Martin* to nearly every major British and American novel of the 1960s, but also in a whole host of impressive achievements in the second rank; there are some, such as Rex Warner's *The Aerodrome* and Graham Greene's *The Ministry of Fear*, where one is hard put to say whether *The Trial* or *Bleak House* has had the more immediate influence.

In another medium, Pinter's handling of dialogue, situation and character seems much indebted to Dickens, whose other great affinity was, of course, with the stage. 'Every writer of fiction', he said, 'although he may not adopt the dramatic form, writes, in effect, for the stage.' Ruskin's famous aside about Dickens's habit of speaking 'in a circle of stage fire' has been much quoted; and though the use of this, for praise as well as for blame, raises intricate problems, it contains

a notable element of truth. Certainly the nearness of Dickens's art both
to poetry and to drama suggests its range and universality; he was very
far from isolating the novel as a separate, and limited, genre.

Allied to these considerations, and possibly even more basic, is the
highly distinctive quality of inventiveness and fantasy in Dickens's
work. On this central theme there is no space here to do more than to
record my impression; which is that the vividness and magnitude of
his created world, its variety, exuberance, and total particularity, are
equalled in literature by Shakespeare and by no-one else. To comparisons with Shakespeare, criticism is constantly returning; and the
impressiveness of this is not lessened by the ultimate dissimilarity of
their work. Of the many general and detailed comparisons, two strike
me as particularly important – the *number* of 'characters' created by
Dickens and Shakespeare who have passed into universal folk-lore,
and the hold which both writers have continued to exercise on a great
popular audience as well as upon the best critical minds. There is, also,
one's sense that no two other writers from previous centuries would
have been less surprised (or, it can safely be assumed, less overawed)
by Freud and Jung; their insight into humanity is comprehensive in
the highest degree. But the final comparison between them comes
back, from whatever starting-point, to magnitude; they are both
creators on the vastest scale.

The present danger for Dickens studies follows from this, and is
familiar to Shakespeareans; as critical interest grows and develops,
certain aspects of his genius tend to be wrenched, in isolation, into
lop-sided schemes. The tendencies this way are already visible; to
Dickens the Entertainer and Dickens the Ring Master, we have seen
added Dickens tortured by *angst*, soured by politics, crushed by tragedy,
maddened by satire – trapped in a manic-depressive cycle, or inventing
the twentieth century well ahead of its time. The inevitable reaction
against these isolated Dickenses has also announced itself. Barbara
Hardy begins her recent essay on *Martin Chuzzlewit* (in *Dickens and
the Twentieth Century*) by asserting that 'many of the recent interpretations by close and serious critics' leave her wondering whether
she has read the same book; she allows, for instance, that J. Hillis
Miller's chapter (reprinted here) illuminates 'many aspects of the work',
but finds its vision of disintegration too subtle to be true. A. G. Hill
also protested, in a review of recent books on Dickens in the *Critical
Quarterly*, that 'many of his admirers must surely by now feel a little

uneasy at the way his books have been made to reflect the pressures and perplexities of the twentieth century rather than the realities of the nineteenth'. To which, I am myself inclined to answer, 'Yes, but: even supposing there is some degree of exaggeration, is this not an easy price to pay?' Of course Dickens *was* a great social realist, and a mid-Victorian; and critics such as Gissing usefully return us to this truth. But he was one of the greatest writers of any period: Gissing found him relevant to the 1890s, Orwell to the 1930s; it is not surprising that so many critics find him relevant today. Our modern critical insights, especially those deriving from the symbolists, are demonstrating, more precisely and analytically than ever before, a greatness that has always been *felt*. They are also demonstrating that Dickens and his period were, after all, modern. His novels are not 'made' to reflect the pressures and perplexities of the twentieth century, they do reflect them; the pressures and perplexities of mid-Victorian England are indeed our own.

My final comment is a simple one; Dickens seems to me one of the supreme tests of literary taste. If readers have a theory of literature which will not accommodate him, so much the worse for their theory; if they have an outlook on life which is offended by him, so much the worse for themselves. We hear endless cant these days about 'life-enhancement' from embittered puritans; but if 'life' means anything that is penetrating in observation, unquenched in sympathy, angered by cruelty, courageous in protest, zestful in creation, unflagging in energy – gaily outward-looking, yet seeing to the heart of man and society – then Dickens is life. He is a supreme test of literary taste for this simple reason: that however much we may dislike this or that aspect, this or that emphasis, we can hardly quibble with genius on so fantastic a scale.

A. E. DYSON

Chronology of Dickens's Works

1833   'A Dinner in Poplar Walk' (reprinted in *Sketches by Boz* as 'Mr Minns and his Cousin'), in the *Monthly Magazine*.

1834–5 *Sketches by Boz*, printed as 'Sketches of London' and 'Scenes and Characters', in the *Monthly Magazine*, *Morning Chronicle*, *Evening Chronicle* and *Bell's Life in London*.

1836   Collected *Sketches by Boz*, in two volumes, published by John Macrone.

1836–7 *The Posthumous Papers of the Pickwick Club*, in monthly numbers, issued by Chapman & Hall.

1837   First number of the journal *Bentley's Miscellany*, edited by Dickens.

1837–8 *Oliver Twist*, in *Bentley's Miscellany*; published in three volumes by Richard Bentley in 1838.

1838–9 *Life and Adventures of Nicholas Nickleby*, in monthly numbers, issued by Chapman & Hall.

1839   *Sketches by Boz*, first complete edition, published by Chapman & Hall.

1840–1 *Master Humphrey's Clock*, in weekly numbers, incorporating *The Old Curiosity Shop* (1840) and *Barnaby Rudge* (1841), with linking papers. The two novels were published in single volumes without *Master Humphrey's Clock* by Chapman & Hall in 1841.

1841   *The Pic Nic Papers*, by 'Various Hands', edited by Dickens, with preface and opening story 'The Lamplighter', published by Henry Colburn.

1842   *American Notes for General Circulation*, two volumes, published by Chapman & Hall.

1843–4 *Life and Adventures of Martin Chuzzlewit*, in monthly numbers, issued by Chapman & Hall; published complete in 1844.

1843   *A Christmas Carol in Prose*, published by Chapman & Hall.

1845   *The Chimes*, published by Chapman & Hall.

1846   *The Cricket on the Hearth*, *Pictures from Italy* (first printed in the *Daily News*), and *The Battle of Life*; all published by Bradbury & Evans 'for the author'.

1846–8 *Dealings with the Firm of Dombey and Son*, in monthly numbers, issued by Bradbury & Evans 'for the author'; published complete in 1848.

1848   *The Haunted Man and the Ghost's Bargain*, published by Bradbury & Evans.

1849   *The Life of Our Lord*, written for Dickens's children, and unpublished until 1934.

1849–50 *The Personal History of David Copperfield*, in monthly numbers, issued by Bradbury & Evans; published complete in 1850.

1850   First number of the journal *Household Words*, edited by Dickens.

1851–3 *A Child's History of England*, in *Household Words*; published complete by Bradbury & Evans in 1853.

1852–3 *Bleak House*, in monthly numbers, issued by Bradbury & Evans; published complete in 1853.

1854   *Hard Times*, in weekly numbers in *Household Words*; published complete by Bradbury & Evans in 1854.

1855–7 *Little Dorrit*, in monthly numbers in *Household Words*; published complete by Bradbury & Evans in 1857.

1859   First number of the journal *All the Year Round*, edited by Dickens, and incorporating *Household Words*. *A Tale of Two Cities*, in weekly numbers in *All the Year Round*, and in monthly numbers; published in one volume in 1859.

1860   *The Uncommercial Traveller*, in seventeen papers in *All the Year Round*; published in one volume in 1860.

1860–1 *Great Expectations*, in weekly numbers in *All the Year Round*; published in one volume by Chapman & Hall in 1862.

1864–5 *Our Mutual Friend*, in monthly numbers; published in two volumes by Chapman & Hall in 1865.

1870   *The Mystery of Edwin Drood* (unfinished), issued in monthly numbers; published by Chapman & Hall.

1871   *Christmas Stories*, collected from *Household Words* and *All the Year Round*.

ANGUS WILSON

Charles Dickens: A Haunting (1960)

I HAD hoped, free of any creative nag, to prepare an objective, docu-mented assessment of Dickens' significance for the modern novelist. A novel of my own has refused to give me either the time or the detachment required; yet the itch to analyse, if only in outline, the constant and haunting pressure of Dickens' created world upon my imagination has persisted despite all the pull of my own fantasy. I make, then, only a half-apology for offering the following short 'thinking aloud'; it is I suspect the only sort of critical contribution that a novelist, untrained in literary scholarship, can make which may justify his amateur intrusion – a contribution unashamedly subjective.

Dickens first exerted a strong hold over me when I was a somewhat sophisticated boy of eleven. I had already laughed at but failed to understand *Pickwick Papers*. I had felt the pursuing breath of Quilp upon Nell's innocent neck and the awful eyes of Fagin intruding into Oliver's illusory rural safety, as too terrible to bear. But now at eleven I was enough detached from the terrors of childhood to support such horrors and yet still to feel the full force of their reality. Dickens already had the power of 'taking me back' in emotion; he also hinted, as obscurely as my then sophistication could support, at hidden adult sins. I remember particularly the double force of the passage describing the luring of poor Florence Dombey by Good Mrs Brown. It was a terror familiar from nurses' lips to me as to all children of comfortably off families; and, I suppose, in the earlier twenties, there was still the possibility of lost well-dressed children being brutally robbed by old hags. But then came the old woman's mention of her harlot daughter, Alice Marwood, and all its hints of a mysterious adult world of sex and crime. In the combination of fading childhood fears and impinging adolescent knowledge it was the right passage at the right age. But the intense haunting of my imagination by scenes and characters from Dickens' novels has continued and developed into my middle age; nor has some experience of the craft of novel writing exorcized this possession, although it has often increased my admiration for his technical powers and on occasion explained my dissatisfaction with some of his weaker artistic devices.

Jane Austen, too, possesses and haunts me for many hours every week; as do other writers. But although I can feel the sad, rather hypochondriacal piety of Fanny putting up so gallant a fight against the lively, tough desperation of Mary Crawford's will; or again can participate with Emma in her struggle to accept with good grace the humiliations her spoiled vanity has brought upon her; I can always step out of Miss Price or Miss Woodhouse, can leave Mansfield's lawns and Hartfield's shrubberies to see the novels from outside as total works, as significant invented tales; – and this I can do without losing the emotions I have participated in. With Dickens it is, more often than not, quite otherwise. As I pull myself away from the gales and the waves and from Steerforth's dead head leaning upon his arm as in his schooldays, other images may take its place – of Daniel Peggotty's neat London lodging ready for Emily as he tramps the ports of Europe to find her, or of Mrs Steerforth and Rosa alone in their Highgate garden looking down over London's lights in hatred and misery – but the 'inside' feeling obstinately refuses to give place to an outside view. There are novels of Dickens, as I shall suggest, that on various serious levels seem to me wholly satisfactory works of art. But their obsessive power does not derive from their total statements; it seems to come impressionistically from atmosphere and scene which are always determinedly fragmentary.

That this places him – save for a work like *Hard Times* that has been equally shaped and impoverished by discipline – outside the significant tradition suggested by Dr Leavis is a matter of regret, I think, for both sides. It is no assistance to Dickens' reputation to pretend that could he have married his genius to a more completely disciplined artistry without reducing its force, we should not all be the richer. It is also disturbing that the most suggestive and sincere literary criticism of our time should have to guard its moral health so desperately that it can find no place for the heterodoxy of Dickens' masterpieces. Perhaps the misuse of such brilliance may qualify him for the place of Lucifer – but

admiration; as the analyses of the class structure of *Little Dorrit* or *Our Mutual Friend* fascinate the Marxist. But neither can explain the power of his novels any more than the prefiguration of Joycean linguistic experiments with the dialogue of Jingle, Mrs Gamp, or Flora. That he should have spoken so directly to our age is evidence, I think, of his exceptionally sensitive response to the depths of his own time; for he undoubtedly heard overtones that were not to be commonly received for half a century. But prophecy, even intuitive prophecy, is not literary greatness; and our harping upon these prophetic excellencies seems a little provincial.

I used the word 'heard' purposely because Dickens' greatest natural gift was his ear. Those who think that his ear was a naturally distorting one have only to be referred to Mayhew to see how authentic was the working-class note which Dickens caught. Nevertheless to dismiss him as a great mime is one of the least satisfactory attacks made by his detractors. Indeed he was incapable of the sustained mime required for an 'I' narration that went outside himself, as the disastrous voice of Esther Summerson all too clearly announces. Nevertheless he had a marvellous ear; but, I believe, an only just less marvellous eye. Certainly a combination of the two that is possibly unique in the English novel. Jane Austen had as good an ear, so for some voices had George Eliot; but Jane Austen's eye appears to have been no more than adequate, while George Eliot's vision, so naturally clear, is too often dissipated in discursive thought.

In his early works, of course, his eye and his ear both desert him when the wealthier classes cease to be objects of irony and are intended to suffer real emotions. From Sir Mulberry Hawk and Lord Frederick onwards passion in the nobility or the upper middle classes is bad theatrical melodrama. But just as *Dombey and Son* saw the first really well observed relics of the Regency upper class in Cousin Feenix and Mrs Skewton; so the same book said farewell to ranting in the last, stilted words with which Edith turned upon the man who had wronged her. The Dedlocks in their tragic hours have an altogether greater realism.

Apart from this limited failure in the early novels, it is difficult to see when Dickens' eye and ear ever failed him. The people whom we hear and see may not always be to our taste as they were to the taste of Victorian readers; but I do not doubt the authenticity of, for example, either Dora's playfulness or Agnes' moralizing.

Is this all – a miraculous eye and ear – that accounts for the atmospheric genius, the encircling magic of Dickens? I do not think so. Edmund Wilson and Lionel Trilling have at various times traced through the symbolic unities of individual novels. I have no doubt at all that if we must assess Dickens' greatness on the basis of any artistic unity, it is to this deeper level rather than to the more conventional technical or moral surfaces that we must go. *Little Dorrit* in its working out of symbol and in its unity of atmosphere is surely the most perfect of his books. It is here rather than in the more conventionally unified novels that Dickens competes with *Emma* or *Middlemarch* or *The Secret Agent*. To seek his greatness in *Hard Times, David Copperfield*, or *Great Expectations*, is to judge him by as alien a measure as to assess Lawrence's greatness by *Sons and Lovers* – the conventional mistake of all who fail to see the point of Lawrence.

Yet this great unity of symbolism, which, infusing the realism of speech and vision, creates that unspoken 'atmosphere' which is Dickens' form of communication, is not to be found only in individual novels. There are certain situations, images, and symbols that recur throughout his work. These, it is, that account to me for the haunting quality of his world; their obsessive power over him finds an equally obsessive need in that large number of serious contemporary readers who are so possessed by him.

These situations, images and symbols, changing their relationships as he grew older, may be found in nearly all his work, great, ordinary, or feeble. So comparatively poor a book as *Pictures from Italy* illustrates this excellently. Mr Sacheverell Sitwell, who contributes the preface to the New Oxford edition of this work, points to a characteristic piece of humour as the link between the improbable subjects of Vesuvius, Leonardo, Papal ceremonies, etc. and Dickens, the familiar novelist. It is a good example of his humour; an English gentleman tourist at the back of a huge crowd that watches the Pope's Feeding of the Poor who calls out, 'Can any gentleman, in front there, see mustard on the table? Sir, will you oblige me? Do you see a mustard pot?' It is indeed a fine piece of Mr Podsnap or, to be kinder, Mr Meagles abroad. Yet to see only this as a characteristic in the book is to allow only for Dickens' ear. There are indeed a hundred examples as excellent of his eye's power. More striking than either, however, is the journey he makes around northern Italy on a winter visit from Genoa (or home with Kate, Georgina, and the children) on his way to England (home, conviviality, boon companions, the Inimitable at his liveliest, etc.). It is one of the haunting passages of Dickens, with coaches at night, strange alighting passengers, stranger inns and towns seen through night's darkness, and so on. Here in these somewhat ordinary essays of a tourist-novelist we are brought into the heart of Dickens' atmosphere. Why?

The answer lies, I believe, in the fundamental and complex meanings of 'travelling' and 'home' that lie deep in Dickens' world. Only Mr Jack Lindsay, to my knowledge, has traced the importance of the wanderer in Dickens' work; and he has limited his analysis by confining it to the lost boys or children of the early works who tie up so conveniently with the blacking-factory trauma. To extend the search over the whole of Dickens' work may tell us a little more of his obsessive strength.

We must begin, surely, with *Pickwick Papers*. In *Oliver Twist*, *The Old Curiosity Shop*, *Dombey*, and *David Copperfield*, he relived his childhood terrors, but *Pickwick Papers* is something deeper connected with his youth. This masterpiece which changed by the outpouring of his vision of life from a hack writer's notes to the English *Don Quixote* surely represents the ideal world as his youthful heart conceived it, before even childhood terrors had been allowed to mar it, let alone the despairing vision of his middle years. Of course evil is there in Dodson and Fogg, but it isn't very serious; like Jingle, one feels, these lawyers might have been changed by true virtue. That true virtue surely is the ethic of the New Testament personified in Mr Pickwick, and exemplified by the feasts and social occasion which throughout Dickens' work may stand for the reign of love on earth. This sort of New Testament Christianity, with its hostility to dogma and ceremony, and its dislike of ostentatious piety and works, is far away from any religion now revered, whether Catholic or Quaker. Nor can it be assimilated to any humanism though it may seem akin to it; for, in fact, the Redemption was central to Dickens' belief. As a humanist without transcendental beliefs, I cannot share it, but I agree with Mr Fielding in believing it to be vital to our understanding of Dickens' work.

The whole history of Dickens' novels is the story of the attempt, often near to despair but never wholly forsaken, to retain something of the vision of *Pickwick Papers* against the inflow of the knowledge of evil's power. It centres around and is at its most powerful in scenes that concern the wanderer, 'home', the feast of fellowship. As Dickens grew more complex, each of these essential symbols came to be filled with ambiguities which alone sufficed to reflect the subtle interaction of good and evil which he observed. By fusing them with such moral subtlety, he was able to maintain a more conscious simplicity on the surface of his books, and so retain the 'humors' of his characters that were his great means of popular appeal.

Some examples must suffice to illustrate what I mean. After *Pickwick Papers* and the power of love, he regressed, as I have said into childhood. There 'home', the ideal world of love, may be either the family party or the rural retreat. Into such perfect happiness Fagin's, or Squeers's, or Ralph's, or Quilp's menacing, jovial hideousness may suddenly be thrust. Quilp's arrival at the ladies' fish tea is a kind of humorous parody of the awful invasion. Stagg, the sinister blind man (with his blackmailing secret), forerunner of Rogue Riderhood, finds Mrs Rudge in sweetest rural seclusion. The wanderers seek a home: Oliver and Nell. Yet Nell looks forward to later works, because she also leaves what home she has because it is menaced. The picaresque wanderings of Nicholas and Martin need less of our attention, they are derivative; indeed not a little of the weakness of these two books comes I think from the fact that this important symbol is lost in the conventional figures of the eighteenth-century picaresque hero. Nevertheless in Jonas' flight we have the precursor, though in an unsubtle form, of the murderer in flight. At the time of *Martin Chuzzlewit* we may see that though Dickens could already identify himself with the murderer, he had not yet realized that the murderer was also the victim, nor had he associated this fugitive figure with 'home'.

The pattern may be found in all his middle books. What, one wonders, would he have made of Walter Gay, had he but kept to his resolution of making that young wanderer a 'bad' person? Would he have been a sort of Pip or a Charlie Hexam, and had such a figure been tied to the concept of 'wandering' and of Florence's 'prison' home and Uncle Sol's 'home of love' might not something more potent and subtle than Mr Carker's Jonas-like flight have been given to us? Perhaps Dickens was not yet ready for it. Steerforth, the Stavrogin angel-devil whose charm so dominates the novel, first ties the murderer (seducer) wanderer to the 'home'. Peggotty's boat is the exact type of the house of fellowship and love, so different from the prison world of Rosa and his mother, who had smothered James Steerforth. The first visit of Steerforth *chez* Peggotty brings him to exactly one of those evenings of fellowship and feasting that are central to Dickens' gospel kingdom. Fleeing from the smothering fires of Highgate, Steerforth must destroy the Peggottys' world. Everything in the novel, I think, that connects with this has an extra force. For example how horrifying is the entrance of Littimer upon exactly another such love feast of innocents, the party of David for Traddles and the Micawbers. We have to go forward to *Great Expectations* to see the feast so horribly blasphemed, but by then it is not an intrusion of evil among the innocents, but the demonstration of evil in youth and innocence themselves by the cynical Mr Jaggers. The last profanation of the innocents' feast follows the pattern of that of Jaggers very exactly. But Jasper's motives seem more evil than those of Jaggers, who only used the occasion to try to point a moral lesson to Pip.

To enumerate every example of the conjunction of these themes would only be tedious for the ardent Dickens reader. Lady Dedlock runs from a prison home, thinking herself to be suspected of murder; and in so doing she kills herself and to all intents and purposes destroys Sir Leicester. Yet the most powerful ambiguities of home and prison, murderer and victim, love and hatred, occur in *Little Dorrit* and *Our Mutual Friend*, and in my opinion it is in these two last completed novels that Dickens makes a more haunting and subtle communication than in any of his work. In *Little Dorrit* indeed the central figure of the wanderer, Arthur Clennam, who returns to his prison home gives the novel a unity of mood which makes it the most impressive of all Dickens' work.

It would be easy to ally this pursuit-flight and home-prison theme solely to our modern dilemma. Dickens, like many of his contemporaries, came almost to despair of social progress in his own age. However, he never wholly rejected the idea of progress; he never sought a religion that consigned this world to vanity or to the evil one; though nostalgic about his childhood, he never romanticised the past to compensate for his disillusionment with the present. He would have been unhappy with the social views of Mr Eliot or Professor C. S. Lewis today. On the other hand, in his last novels his refusal to renounce man's achievement permitted him no progressive complacency; I suspect that he would have found even the moral stoicism of C. P. Snow too determinedly unregarding of the power of evil. Dickens' dilemma – that of a simple New Testament Christian who found little evidence of the Kingdom around him – is in great degree that of the modern humanist who sees man's nature lagging behind his achievements. The parallel may well be an underlying cause of the revival of his reputation today. Yet the fugitive-wanderer, the prison house, the blazing log and the convivial feast seem subtle enough symbols of the human dilemma to give his spell of lasting power.

C. B. COX

In Defence of Dickens (1958)

In his famous defence of Dickens, first published in 1906, G. K. Chesterton argued that at the turn of the century Dickens's reputation had suffered because criticism was analytic, self-conscious and descriptive in approach, and therefore was unfitted to deal with the comic simplicity of a Mantalini or a Micawber. Chesterton forecast that as time went by, Dickens would be recognized as the greatest of the Victorian novelists, standing above Thackeray, Charlotte Brontë, George Eliot and Thomas Hardy. Chesterton's prophecy has not yet come true. Modern critics are usually still analytic, self-conscious and descriptive in their treatment of literature, and they prefer the novels of George Eliot and Henry James, who possess these very same qualities, to the exuberant writings of Dickens.

It is significant that the two best-known recent studies of Dickens should be Edmund Wilson's essay, 'The Two Scrooges' and Humphry House's *The Dickens World*. Wilson's essay is mainly a description of Dickens's emotional conflicts, and a series of speculations about their influence on his work. Humphry House's book is a brilliant analysis of the relation between Dickens and his times, with detailed studies of Dickens's attitudes towards contemporary economic and social problems. Neither of these works deals at any length with what Chesterton calls the comic simplicity of Dickens. The same is true of the recently published *Dickens at Work*, by John Butt and Kathleen Tillotson, which contains a very interesting study of Dickens's methods of composition.

Modern critics often fail to do justice to Dickens because they place too much emphasis on the importance of a certain type of intelligence. In Dr Leavis's *The Great Tradition*, novels are judged by the success with which they give a dramatic reconstruction of the processes of the mind. The great novelist investigates the contemporary situation with a quality of insight which separates him from the mass of his fellow men. Great novelists are 'significant in terms of the human awareness they promote; awareness of the possibilities of life'. *Clarissa* is thus preferred to *Tom Jones*, and *Middlemarch* to *David Copperfield*. *The Great Tradition* is a book of highly perceptive criticism because its method of approach applies to George Eliot, Henry James and Joseph Conrad, the novelists with whom Dr Leavis deals, but its method does not do justice to writers such as Dickens. That Dickens is often muddled, imprecise, and sentimental and that he is an unequal writer, no one can deny; but he is successful because through his comic art he shows the profound importance of the most commonplace human relationships. His apparent simplicity expresses an understanding of life just as compelling as that shown in the works of George Eliot or Henry James. There are comic characters and episodes scattered in profusion throughout Dickens's work which demonstrate his insight into the human heart; it is these characters and scenes which still entitle Dickens to his place among the great English novelists.

Modern critics often fail to appreciate the underlying effects of Dickens's humour. For example, the precise physical details which he uses to describe his characters have more than picturesque importance. When we meet a stranger for the first time, a complex impression of his character is immediately given to us by the lines on the face, the gait, the tone of voice, a sort of 'aura' we all carry about with us. A novelist such as George Eliot builds up our sense of her characters through a series of dramatically significant scenes; only gradually is Rosamund Vincy's true nature revealed. Dickens had the power of imagining odd physical details or habits which *immediately* give a sense of 'aura' to the reader: we feel we know Sam Weller or Betsy Trotwood just as well as we know Casaubon or Margaret Schlegel. Dickens's choice of significant details also builds up a rich sense of personality. Of Miss Tox in *Dombey and Son*, Dickens writes: 'She was much given to the carrying about of small bags with snaps to them, that went off like little pistols when they were shut up . . .' This immediately conjures up a picture of people jumping with surprise and alarm whenever Miss Tox is present; the picture gives an impression of Miss Tox's personality, of her fluttering incompetence and her continual nervous embarrassments. It fits in with the description of the baptism service for Paul Dombey, when she was so nervous that she kept her Prayer-book open at the Gunpowder Plot, and occasionally read responses from that service.

Dickens's usual practice is to repeat these significant details over and over again as the character reappears in the novel. This leads to the static quality of his characters, and to our feeling of dissatisfaction when Micawber is transformed into a successful magistrate. He has betrayed that essence which characterized him in all his doings in England. That Dickens's comic characters do not develop has often been adduced as a weakness in the novels, but in one sense the character of a typical adult *is* static; he responds over and over again in the same way to the same situations.

This is true of Pickwick, whose adventures reveal further underlying meanings of Dickens's comic art. When discussing Pickwick, Chesterton claims that 'his soul will never starve for exploits or excitements who is wise enough to be made a fool of'. Pickwick has a 'god-like gullibility', and is at his greatest when most deceived. In literature, the great and virtuous man is often a fool. Parson Adams, Uncle Toby, Don Quixote and Prince Muishkin are foolish because their enthusiasms, their kindliness, their visions, all reflect an ignorance of the cunning and deceit which constitute so much of human life. They have become so absorbed with their own sense of values and their own ideals that they have forgotten that other men are not moved by the same impulses. Pickwick is the most successful example of this form of commitment in Dickens's work. His wisdom lies in his faith in kindliness and in that joy in life which no vanity or self-interest can impair. At Dingley Dell in his zest for life he slides on the ice and even dances. As he parades about the room he smiles on his partner all the while 'with a blandness of demeanour which baffles all description'. We may laugh, but at the same time we must admire the greatness in him. Neither vanity nor weariness can damp his love of life and his kindness. A touch of this mixture of wisdom and folly is seen in the optimism of Micawber, in the devotion to the stage of Crummles, and in the fantastic imagination of Mr Dick. Dick's brains may be a little touched, but, as he flies his kite on peaceful summer days, he evinces a god-like serenity.

Dickens's treatment of this type of fool introduces into his comedies a profound sense of the human predicament in the universe. We react towards Pickwick in two almost contradictory ways. On one level he is absurd, and yet on another he is a symbol of the greatness of man. This contradictory feeling that there is both a fundamental absurdity and a fundamental glory in human experience is the unifying element in Dickens's work, the essence of that vision which makes him a great novelist. It is seen in a very simple form in his treatment of certain strange weddings in his novels. The wedding of Mr Weller, Senior, was brought about because he was persuaded by a touter to buy a marriage licence, and so thought it appropriate to find a bride to go with it. Barkis's wooing of Peggotty is famous for the odd phrase, 'Barkis is willin'', with which he declares his intentions. Wemmick invites Pip to go for a morning walk, and takes with him a fishing-rod. They arrive at a church, and Wemmick, pretending he has just thought of the idea, puts down his fishing-rod and nips in to marry Miss Skiffins. In each case the laughter is not merely directed at the way these people's idiosyncrasies make them different from the normal. As with all Dickens's caricatures, their greatness is that their apparent oddity hides something which, on a deeper level, is typical of all human experience. Many people will remember that on their wedding-day they felt a slight sense of surprise to find themselves involved in such an important event. On one level Dickens's humour suggests how infinitely absurd are all human pretensions. All our pomp and cere-mony seem ridiculous before the vastness of the universe and the length of time, and we remember how the most petty and foolish considera-tions become involved with all our most important actions; yet on another level life is seen as deeply significant. The kindliness and integ-rity of Mr Weller, Peggotty and Wemmick demonstrate Dickens's faith in the value of human life. Is the dignity of a wedding an absurd show or an eternal sacrament? Wemmick taking a fishing-rod to his wedding represents the human comic misfortune of being placed in a world in which we understand nothing of our situation, and in which man is a creature of odd habits and needs, yet endowed with great powers of love.

A simple example of this paradox is to be seen in the description of the parting between the Pickwickians and the Dingley Dell party after the festivities at Rochester:

> As the Pickwickians turned round to take a last glimpse of it [the carriage], the setting sun cast a rich glow on the faces of their entertainers, and fell upon the form of the fat boy. His head was sunk upon his bosom; and he slumbered again (ch. 4).

This might be compared to the end of Charlie Chaplin's *Modern Times*, as the two wanderers depart along the road towards the setting sun; but Dickens's picture is the finer because the comic element is emphasized so strongly. The setting sun symbolizes the glory of life which is ever passing away, and over which one might sentimentalize; but the fat boy restores proportion to the picture, for man is a strange comic figure, caught between two worlds of glory and absurdity.

These contradictory feelings can result from one finely comic scene, or from a series of alternating episodes which demonstrate the two sides of the picture. The sense that man is absurd is often linked to a feeling that human life is a matter of confusion upon confusion; that in one's contacts with other people there is never any certainty, and that all experience is an enigma. Man's comic misfortune is to be placed in a world which he can never understand and which defies all his attempts to impose order. After Pickwick, Winkle and Snodgrass have been left stranded on the way to Dingley Dell, they are still in possession of the horse which had pulled the chaise. They approach a little road-side public house, which has 'one or two deformed hay-ricks behind, a kitchen garden at the side, and rotten sheds and mouldering out-houses, jumbled in strange confusion, all about it'. The scene seems to represent the decay of all civilized order. The Pickwickians try to leave the horse with a red-haired man who is working in the garden, but he answers in unencouraging monosyllables. He and his wife are certain Pickwick has stolen the horse, and they go back into the house, banging the door behind them. Pickwick says: 'It's like a dream . . . a hideous dream. The idea of a man's walking about all day, with a dreadful horse that he can't get rid of!' This scene gives the impression that all human relationships are comically confused. What contact can we really make with other people? Our confidence that we understand the world about us is likely to lead to comic misfortune. Particularly to the mind of the child there often comes this sense of fear that he does not understand his relation to society or to the world. Is there really an order, or is everything chaos?

Chesterton believed that Dickens's characters are mythical personages like Father Christmas or Punch, living statically in a perpetual summer of being themselves. It is also true that their experiences often seem to have the quality of myth or allegory, to represent, perhaps, well-known experiences in the human mind. The scene with the red-haired man seems typical of all human confusion, and of the sense we all have sometimes of being lost in an incomprehensible world.

Dickens's treatment of this scene gives originality to this common experience. He enjoys Pickwick's predicament with obvious zest, and his humour provides a compensating attitude. He is determined to delight in life whatever its meaning may or may not be. Even if human life is lost in confusion, he will continually celebrate the animated scene. The ability to be amused at one's own misfortunes is a healthy response, leading to acceptance of a courageous stoicism, and this is often central to Dickens's works.

The sense of being lost in universal confusion, of human life as swept by mysterious forces which no one can understand, is often expressed in isolation from the comic treatment so far described. Episodes of this kind contrast with those passages in which Dickens pictures the value of integrity and benevolence. Just as the humour reveals a contradictory sense of absurdity and glory, so these episodes balance Dickens's strong awareness of evil against his faith in goodness and the 'good life'. The feeling of comic bewilderment at the mystery of the universe often turns, at such times, into fear and horror at the inexplicable strength of evil. More successful than the well-known melodramatic outpourings are certain short dramatic scenes in which evil is shown to run unchecked through all society. When David Copperfield prepares to escape to Dover, he asks a youth to carry his trunk on his cart. The youth steals both the trunk and a half-guinea, and accuses David of being a thief. In answer to the child's remonstrances, the youth departs shouting: 'Come to the pollis! come to the pollis!' David's fear typifies that sense we all have at certain times of being alone in an alien society. The frustration David feels in his attempts to overcome the youth's lack of sympathy enacts the common experience of evil grown too powerful for our resources. It is typical of Dickens to depict a happy family background as the one successful antidote for such experiences of desolation. As David journeys to Dover, the pawnbroker, the tramps and the tinker represent a society in which evil is uncontrolled; but in his aunt's home he finds refuge and rest.

The description of the storm at Yarmouth is deservedly famous. To David Copperfield the storm seems to be taking place in a dream. The noise of the wind, the pounding of the waves, the flying stones and sand, all throw his brain into a state of confusion. The storm comes to represent a turmoil and conflict in which all human beings are involved. Forces seem to be unleashed which are often forgotten, but which have the power to sweep men into oblivion. Among this fury

Ham's courage is the redemptive factor, and after his self-sacrifice, friend and enemy are reconciled.

This symbolic use of background scenery is very typical of Dickens, and has often been discussed. Oliver Twist is a poor dummy when he takes part in dramatic action, but when he accompanies Sikes on the nightmare journey out of London his experiences have a deeper significance. The rush through the streets in the early morning, the market with its filth and mire, the noise of the countrymen and the cattle, all confound Oliver's senses, leaving him stunned and bewildered. The journey ends as he walks towards the scene of the robbery through fog so damp that his hair and eyebrows become stiff with the half-frozen mixture that is floating about. The journey suggests that life itself is a passage through the shadows of a nightmare. As in the description of the storm at Yarmouth, Dickens evokes a sense of bewilderment, a feeling that all is chaos. Life exists, perhaps, in the midst of a thousand forms of evil, which man only partly understands and of which he is very much afraid. In *Hard Times*, Stephen Blackpool says of life "Tis a muddle', an experience of confusion that returns again and again in Dickens's novels, in the description of the marshes in *Great Expectations*, for example, and of the deserted workings in *Hard Times*.

In characters such as Fagin and Quilp, Dickens depicts Satanic malevolence, a delight in villainy which, one may suppose, is typical of the workings of the devil. When Oliver is recaptured, Fagin, taking off his nightcap, makes a great number of low bows to Oliver as a token of welcome. The mock politeness is a sign of that ebullience with which Fagin undertakes his exploits. On his first visit to Fagin's room, Oliver notices the walls and ceiling black with dirt, the candle stuck in a ginger-beer bottle, the frying-pan secured to the mantelshelf by a string. The room indicates the way of life of its inhabitants. Fagin himself is always dirty, and everything in his room shows his lack of self-discipline and physical laziness. There is no order, and when something is needed the easiest method is always chosen. Fagin is repeatedly associated with scenes of black mist, thick mud and sluggish rain, when everything feels cold and clammy to the touch. All these details build up a sense of what Fagin is like. We have received an impression of his personality even if we have not been given a detailed picture of the motives which turned him into a villain. Both Fagin and Quilp are monstrous figures, to whom evil is an irresistible temptation. As in the scenes in which evil seems a powerful and bewildering source of confusion, so in his treatment of these Satanic figures Dickens shows evil as a force which is unrestrained. The wrong-doing of Quilp is not directed to any simple purposes of self-interest; he has become a force of destruction which must crush all with which it comes into contact.

Dickens also understood the power of evil in its more insidious and subtle forms. Like Fielding, he considered affectation to be the source of all kinds of unhappiness. Examples of this occur in great number throughout his work. Pip's snubbing of Joe Gargery is a famous example, and shows how affectation can corrupt even the finest types of friendship. When Pip does not want Joe to meet the snob, Bentley Drummle, Dickens writes: 'So, throughout life, our worst weaknesses and meannesses are usually committed for the sake of the people whom we most despise' (ch. 27). The deep understanding of snobbishness revealed here is typical of Dickens.

Dickens's characters can choose to become instruments of confusion and evil, to allow their own anarchic passions free rein, or they can choose to obey their benevolent instincts, even though these do not at first seem to bring prosperity. There are characters such as Nancy in *Oliver Twist*, and Abel Magwitch in *Great Expectations*, whose evil doings are mitigated by a partial repentance, but usually Dickens saw life as made up of two clear divisions of people, the good and the evil. Dickens did not believe that moral issues are complicated. He was aware that circumstances can help to make villains, as with Magwitch, but at the same time he believed that every person, whatever his background, is given a clear choice between good and evil. His novels express a faith very different from that of many modern novelists, who see moral issues as usually confused, and whose characters are faced with problems in which the rights and wrongs are difficult to disentangle. Dickens believed that the choice between good and evil is usually clear and simple, and that we are fully responsible for our actions.

The episodes in which evil seems uncontrollable contrast with those which demonstrate a simple faith in human virtue. Dickens's conception of the good life has often been criticized. Humphry House analyses in detail the ideal of benevolence exemplified by characters such as Pickwick, Mr Brownlow, Mr Garland, Mr Cheeryble and Mr Boffin, and shows that Dickens has a not very clearly worked out belief that

only an increase of good-will in individuals can bring lasting reform
to society. More important than Dickens's ideal of benevolence is his
faith in the domestic affections. George Orwell said that the vagueness
of Dickens's discontent is a mark of its permanence, and the same might
be said of his conception of goodness. His conventional pictures of the
Victorian family have often been adversely criticized. In story after
story, the devoted husband, the hardworking wife, the thankful
children, the peaceful graveyard, and the dignified simplicity of the
poor are recurrent symbols. As in Tennyson's *The Two Voices*, these
idealized pictures are seen as of redemptive value. After long years the
convict returns to the Churchyard through which he gambolled as a
child, and the memory of his mother's devotion completes his conversion. It is easy to sneer at this ideal, and to refer to Dickens's own
family problems, but the ideal does represent an important saving
element in human life. Although in the set descriptions of cosy interiors
Dickens fails to present this ideal convincingly, there are certain
episodes in which he dramatizes domestic affection with a compelling
originality. A good example of this is provided by the scenes in
Gargery's house in *Great Expectations*. After Pip has been ordered by
Magwitch to steal food for him, he hides his bread and butter down
his leg. Pip relates:

> . . . it was our evening habit to compare the way we bit through our
> slices, by silently holding them up to each other's admiration now and
> then – which stimulated us to new exertions. To-night, Joe several times
> invited me, by the display of his fast-diminishing slice, to enter upon our
> usual friendly competition . . . (ch. 2)

Later on the secret communications between Joe and Pip are continued
when Joe crosses his two forefingers as a sign that Mrs Joe is in a cross
temper, and when he spoons extra soup to Pip to console him for the
harsh treatment meted out to him by Mrs Joe's guests. Although these
scenes offer little to analytic criticism, they are richly significant. Later
on in the novel Joe is treated with sentimental reverence, but here these
comic details represent convincingly the depth of his love for Pip.

Dickens's sanity and sense of proportion are also seen in his treatment
of Mrs Gargery on the Rampage. On one occasion when she is angry
because Miss Havisham has invited Joe alone to visit her, Mrs Joe goes
on the Rampage 'in a more alarming degree than at any previous
period'. When her flow of invective is exhausted, she expresses her

irritation by getting out the dust-pan and cleaning up with great vigour, even though it is night-time. Eventually she takes up a pail and scrubbing brush, and cleans Joe and Pip out of house and home, until they stand shivering in the backyard. This is slightly reminiscent of a very different scene in D. H. Lawrence's *Sons and Lovers*, when, after Mrs Morel has been turned out of doors by her husband, she stands in the moonlight smelling the perfume of the white lilies in the garden. The scene is deeply moving, but the relationship between Mrs Morel and her husband has not that representative quality which characterizes the comedy of Dickens. Similarly in *Aaron's Rod*, Aaron's lack of feeling for his wife and children points to Lawrence's failure to understand that friendship between man and wife which often lies deeper than all occasional disagreements, however passionate these may seem at the moment, and which depends very little on any form of sexual attraction. After the attempt to murder her, Mrs Gargery's repentance is not just a sentimental trick. It is a sign that she and Joe felt a sense of belonging to each other even in the midst of her Rampages, that they had that understanding and compassion for each other which people of conflicting temperaments who live together for a long period often achieve. Lawrence's characters are the exception, and Dickens's the norm. Pip very rightly looks back on his childish days as happy, for, in spite of repeated contacts with his sister's wedding-ring, he had a home to belong to, and Joe as a companion. He remembers Mrs Gargery with sympathy rather than with anger.

There are many other finely depicted family scenes, the Peggottys at Yarmouth and the Trotwoods at Dover, where Dickens shows his understanding of ordinary human goodness. Critics have often disparaged Dickens because he presents the servant as a sort of feudal retainer, but the idea of service expressed by Peggotty or Sam Weller is typical of something seen in ordinary people again and again. That Dickens's eyes often turn misty with emotion when he talks of self-sacrifice is true enough, and there are many examples of this in *The Old Curiosity Shop*, but Peggotty with the buttons bursting off her back and Sam Weller with his witticisms provide original and convincing examples of a true ideal of service.

At his best Dickens is dealing not with contemporary problems of the Poor Law, but with those human weaknesses and virtues which exist in any state of society. Kindness, good-humour and affection are vague, imprecise words for something which Dickens describes with great insight. Towards the end of *David Copperfield*, Betsy Trotwood reflects upon her marriage, and the husband who has abused her confidence: ' "Six-and-thirty years ago, this day, my dear," said my aunt, as we walked back to the chariot, "I was married. God forgive us all!" ' (ch. 54). In its simplicity this speech is comparable to some of Shakespeare's greatest lines. The commonplace words suggest how often men and women undergo this type of suffering, and the reference to time reminds us how long such unhappiness can last. In the concluding words 'God forgive us all!' she includes all men and women in her compassion, and her own experience is once more linked with the common lot.

In recent years the importance of intelligence and sensitivity has been emphasized not only by critics such as Dr Richards and Dr Leavis, but also by novelists such as Henry James, E. M. Forster and Virginia Woolf. In his essay, 'Is There a Life after Death?' Henry James suggests that the soul may be immortal, but that an after-life is possible only for those people who have been highly sensitive and richly conscious in this world. Dickens had not such a limited view of human life. He knew that love can be expressed just as deeply by Joe Gargery in his forge as by Lambert Strether in Paris. Any critic who believes that the most important types of love are confined to people of high sensitivity and intelligence understands little of life and is not competent to write about Dickens. Chesterton writes that 'in everybody there is a certain thing that loves babies, that fears death, that likes sunlight; that thing enjoys Dickens'. It is significant that in Henry James's *The Golden Bowl*, when Maggie is fighting to keep her husband from deserting her, she never justifies herself by referring to her baby. It is possible to argue that this is taken for granted, but the failure to dramatize the common affections in Maggie and her husband makes her struggle much less convincing. James did not understand the importance of the everyday feelings of ordinary people, their love for their children, and that deep affection between man and wife which can exist in all levels of society. When describing the hands who work in Bounderby's factory in Coketown, Dickens writes that 'there is an unfathomable mystery in the meanest of them, for ever'. He satirizes Steerforth, who tells Miss Dartle that the lower classes have not very fine natures, and that 'they may be thankful that, like their coarse skins, they are not easily wounded'. Dickens understood the greatness of people such as Peggotty and her brother, and although he does not analyse their psychology in detail, he expresses through comedy the dignity and wonder of their lives.

At the end of his book, Chesterton suggests that Dickens's works exemplify one of the paradoxes of reform:

> If we are to save the oppressed, we must have two apparently antagonistic emotions in us at the same time. We must think the oppressed man intensely miserable, and at the same time intensely attractive and important. We must insist with violence upon his degradation; we must insist with the same violence upon his dignity.[1]

The aim of this essay has been to show that in Dickens's novels an even more important paradox is expressed. The adventures of a character such as Pickwick show the absurdity of the whole of human life, and this absurdity has a comparable effect with that sense of bewilderment and confusion which Dickens so often describes. In the comic scenes man seems lost in an enigmatic universe where even his most significant experiences partake of the ludicrous. At other times Dickens's depiction of evil achieves tragic intensity. The power of evil seems a chaotic force which can never be controlled. This sense of absurdity and confusion, achieved in so many different ways, conflicts with the strongly emphasized faith in the value of life. This is seen not only in the treatment of the fool and of ordinary human affections, but also in Dickens's own delight in the variety of his experiences. The very gusto with which he enjoys the follies of his characters stands as a positive value, an energetic expression of a joy in life which acts as a counterbalance to the absurd. To this is linked a sense of the wonder of even the smallest impressions of day-to-day experience, a delight in the myriad impressions given to us through the senses. The happy endings of his stories were demanded by Victorian conventions, but they remain appropriate symbols of Dickens's faith in the vitality of his good people and of life itself. The world is not justified by Dickens as it is by the mechanical optimists; it is not justified as the best of all possible worlds. Its merit is not that it is orderly or explicable. Its merit is that it overflows with varieties of joy, and that ordinary men and women are redeemed from futility and pettiness by their capacity for love.

NOTE

1. *Charles Dickens* (1906) ch. 11.

GRAHAM GREENE

The Young Dickens (1950)

A CRITIC must try to avoid being a prisoner of his time, and if we are to appreciate *Oliver Twist* at its full value we must forget that long shelf-load of books, all the stifling importance of a great author, the scandals and the controversies of the private life; it would be well too if we could forget the Phiz and the Cruikshank illustrations that have frozen the excited, excitable world of Dickens into a hall of waxworks, where Mr Mantalini's whiskers have always the same trim, where Mr Pickwick perpetually turns up the tails of his coat, and in the Chamber of Horrors Fagin crouches over an undying fire. His illustrators, brilliant craftsmen though they were, did Dickens a disservice, for no character any more will walk for the first time into our memory as we ourselves imagine him, and *our* imagination after all has just as much claim to truth as Cruikshank's.

Nevertheless the effort to go back is well worth while. The journey is only a little more than a hundred years long, and at the other end of the road is a young author whose sole claim to renown in 1837 had been the publication of some journalistic sketches and a number of comic operas: *The Strange Gentleman, The Village Coquette, Is She His Wife?* I doubt whether any literary Cortez at that date would have yet stood them upon his shelves. Then suddenly with *The Pickwick Papers* came popularity and fame. Fame falls like a dead hand on an author's shoulder, and it is well for him when it falls only in later life. How many in Dickens's place would have withstood what James called 'the great corrupting contact of the public', the popularity founded, as it almost always is, on the weakness and not the strength of an author?

The young Dickens, at the age of twenty-five, had hit on a mine that paid him a tremendous dividend. Fielding and Smollett, tidied and refined for the new industrial bourgeoisie, had both salted it; Goldsmith had contributed sentimentality and Monk Lewis horror. The book was enormous, shapeless, familiar (that important recipe for popularity). What Henry James wrote of a long-forgotten French critic applies well to the young Dickens: 'He is homely, familiar and colloquial; he leans his elbows on his desk and does up his weekly budget into a parcel the reverse of compact. You can fancy him a grocer retailing tapioca and hominy full weight for the price; his style seems a sort of integument of brown paper.'

This is, of course, unfair to *The Pickwick Papers*. The driest critic could not have quite blinkered his eyes to those sudden wide illuminations of comic genius that flap across the waste of words like sheet lightning, but could he have foreseen the second novel, not a repetition of this great loose popular holdall, but a short melodrama, tight in construction, almost entirely lacking in broad comedy, and possessing only the sad twisted humour of the orphans' asylum? ' "You'll make your fortune, Mr Sowerby," said the beadle, as he thrust his thumb and forefinger into the proffered snuff-box of the undertaker: which was an ingenious little model of a patent coffin.'

Such a development was as inconceivable as the gradual transformation of that thick boggy prose into the delicate and exact poetic cadences, the music of memory, that so influenced Proust.

We are too inclined to take Dickens as a whole and to treat his juvenilia with the same kindness or harshness as his later work. *Oliver Twist* is still juvenilia – magnificent juvenilia: it is the first step on the road that led from *Pickwick* to *Great Expectations*, and we can condone the faults of taste in the early book the more readily if we recognize the distance Dickens had to travel. These two typical didactic passages can act as the first two milestones at the opening of the journey, the first from *Pickwick*, the second from *Oliver Twist*.

> And numerous indeed are the hearts to which Christmas brings a brief season of happiness and enjoyment. How many families, whose members have been dispersed and scattered far and wide, in the restless struggles of life, are then reunited, and meet once again in that happy state of companionship and mutual goodwill, which is a source of such pure and unalloyed delight, and one so incompatible with the cares and sorrows of the world, that the religious belief of the most civilised nations, and the rude traditions of the roughest savages, alike number it among the first joys of a future condition of existence, provided for the blest and happy!

> The boy stirred, and smiled in his sleep, as though these marks of pity and compassion had awakened some pleasant dream of a love and affection he had never known. Thus, a strain of gentle music, or the rippling of

water in a silent place, or the odour of a flower, or the mention of a familiar
word, will sometimes call up sudden dim remembrances of scenes that
never were, in this life; which vanish like a breath; which some brief
memory of a happier existence, long gone by, would seem to have
awakened; which no voluntary exertion of the mind can ever recall.

The first is certainly brown paper: what it wraps has been chosen
by the grocer to suit his clients' tastes, but cannot we detect already
in the second passage the tone of Dickens's secret prose, that sense of
a mind speaking to itself with no one there to listen, as we find it in
Great Expectations?

> It was fine summer weather again, and, as I walked along, the times
> when I was a little helpless creature, and my sister did not spare me, vividly
> returned. But they returned with a gentle tone upon them, that softened
> even the edge of Tickler. For now, the very breath of the beans and clover
> whispered to my heart that the day must come when it would be well for
> my memory that others walking in the sunshine should be softened as
> they thought of me.

It is a mistake to think of *Oliver Twist* as a realistic story: only late
in his career did Dickens learn to write realistically of human beings;
at the beginning he invented life and we no more believe in the
temporal existence of Fagin or Bill Sikes than we believe in the existence of that Giant whom Jack slew as he bellowed his Fee Fi Fo Fum.
There were real Fagins and Bill Sikeses and real Bumbles in the England
of his day, but he had not drawn them, as he was later to draw the
convict Magwitch; these characters in *Oliver Twist* are simply parts
of one huge invented scene, what Dickens in his own preface called
'the cold wet shelterless midnight streets of London'. How the phrase
goes echoing on through the books of Dickens until we meet it again
so many years later in 'the weary western streets of London on a cold
dusty spring night' which were so melancholy to Pip. But Pip was to
be as real as the weary streets, while Oliver was as unrealistic as the
cold wet midnight of which he formed a part.

This is not to criticize the book so much as to describe it. For what
an imagination this youth of twenty-six had that he could invent so
monstrous and complete a legend! We are not lost with Oliver Twist
round Saffron Hill: we are lost in the interstices of one young, angry,
gloomy brain, and the oppressive images stand out along the track like
the lit figures in a Ghost Train tunnel. 'Against the wall were ranged,

in regular array, a long row of elm boards cut into the same shape: looking in the dim light, like high-shouldered ghosts with their hands in their breeches-pockets.'

We have most of us seen those nineteenth-century prints where the bodies of naked women form the face of a character, the Diplomat, the Miser and the like. So the crouching figure of Fagin seems to form the mouth, Sikes with his bludgeon the jutting features and the sad lost Oliver the eyes of one man, as lost as Oliver.

Chesterton, in a fine imaginative passage, has described the mystery behind Dickens's plots, the sense that even the author was unaware of what was really going on, so that when the explanations come and we reach, huddled into the last pages of *Oliver Twist*, a naked complex narrative of illegitimacy and burnt wills and destroyed evidence, we simply do not believe.

> The secrecy is sensational; the secret is tame. The surface of the thing seems more awful than the core of it. It seems almost as if these grisly figures, Mrs Chadband and Mrs Clennam, Miss Havisham and Miss Flite, Nemo and Sally Brass, were keeping something back from the author as well as from the reader. When the book closes we do not know their real secret. They soothed the optimistic Dickens with something less terrible than the truth.

What strikes the attention most in this closed Fagin universe are the different levels of unreality. If, as one is inclined to believe, the creative writer perceives his world once and for all in childhood and adolescence, and his whole career is an effort to illustrate his private world in terms of the great public world we all share, we can understand why Fagin and Sikes in their most extreme exaggerations move us more than the benevolence of Mr Brownlow or the sweetness of Mrs Maylie – they touch with fear as the others never really touch with love. It was not that the unhappy child, with his hurt pride and his sense of hopeless insecurity, had not encountered human goodness – he had simply failed to recognize it in those streets between Gadshill and Hungerford Market which had been as narrowly enclosed as Oliver Twist's. When Dickens at this early period tried to describe goodness he seems to have remembered the small stationers' shops on the way to the blacking factory with their coloured paper scraps of angels and virgins, or perhaps the face of some old gentleman who had spoken kindly to him outside Warren's factory. He has swum up towards goodness from the deepest world of his experience, and on this shallow level the conscious brain has taken a hand, trying to construct characters to represent virtue and, because his age demanded it, triumphant virtue, but all he can produce are powdered wigs and gleaming spectacles and a lot of bustle with bowls of broth and a pale angelic face. Compare the way in which we first meet evil with his introduction of goodness.

> The walls and ceiling of the room were perfectly black with age and dirt. There was a deal table before the fire: upon which were a candle, stuck in a ginger-beer bottle, two or three pewter pots, a loaf and butter, and a plate. In a frying-pan, which was on the fire, and which was secured to the mantelshelf by a string, some sausages were cooking; and standing over them, with a toasting-fork in his hand, was a very old shrivelled Jew, whose villainous-looking and repulsive face was obscured by a quantity of matted red hair. He was dressed in a greasy flannel gown, with his throat bare. . . . 'This is him, Fagin,' said Jack Dawkins: 'my friend Oliver Twist.' The Jew grinned; and, making a low obeisance to Oliver, took him by the hand, and hoped he should have the honour of his intimate acquaintance.

Fagin has always about him this quality of darkness and nightmare. He never appears on the daylight streets. Even when we see him last in the condemned cell, it is in the hours before the dawn. In the Fagin darkness Dickens's hand seldom fumbles. Hear him turning the screw of horror when Nancy speaks of the thoughts of death that have haunted her:

> 'Imagination,' said the gentleman, soothing her.
> 'No imagination,' replied the girl in a hoarse voice. 'I'll swear I saw "coffin" written in every page of the book in large black letters, – aye, and they carried one close to me, in the streets tonight.'
> 'There is nothing unusual in that,' said the gentleman. 'They have passed me often.'
> '*Real* ones,' rejoined the girl. 'This was not.'

Now turn to the daylight world and our first sight of Rose:

> The younger lady was in the lovely bloom and springtime of womanhood; at that age, when, if ever angels be for God's good purposes enthroned in mortal forms, they may be, without impiety, supposed to abide in such as hers.

She was not past seventeen. Cast in so slight and exquisite a mould; so mild and gentle; so pure and beautiful; that earth seemed not her element, nor its rough creatures her fit companions.

Or Mr Brownlow as he first appeared to Oliver:

Now, the old gentleman came in as brisk as need be; but he had no sooner raised his spectacles on his forehead, and thrust his hands behind the skirts of his dressing-gown to take a good long look at Oliver, than his countenance underwent a very great variety of odd contortions. . . . The fact is, if the truth must be told, that Mr Brownlow's heart, being large enough for any six ordinary old gentlemen of humane disposition, forced a supply of tears into his eyes, by some hydraulic process which we are not sufficiently philosophical to be in a condition to explain.

How can we really believe that these inadequate ghosts of goodness can triumph over Fagin, Monks and Sikes? And the answer, of course, is that they never could have triumphed without the elaborate machinery of the plot disclosed in the last pages. This world of Dickens is a world without God; and as a substitute for the power and the glory of the omnipotent and omniscient are a few sentimental references to heaven, angels, the sweet faces of the dead, and Oliver saying, 'Heaven is a long way off, and they are too happy there to come down to the bedside of a poor boy.' In this Manichean world we can believe in evil-doing, but goodness wilts into philanthropy, kindness, and those strange vague sicknesses into which Dickens's young women so frequently fall and which seem in his eyes a kind of badge of virtue, as though there were a merit in death.

But how instinctively Dickens's genius recognized the flaw and made a virtue out of it. We cannot believe in the power of Mr Brownlow, but nor did Dickens, and from his inability to believe in his own good characters springs the real tension of his novel. The boy Oliver may not lodge in our brain like David Copperfield, and though many of Mr Bumble's phrases have become and deserve to have become familiar quotations we can feel he was manufactured: he never breathes like Mr Dorrit; yet Oliver's predicament, the nightmare fight between the darkness where the demons walk and the sunlight where ineffective goodness makes its last stand in a condemned world, will remain part of our imaginations forever. We read of the defeat of Monks, and of Fagin screaming in the condemned cell, and of Sikes dangling from his self-made noose, but we don't believe. We have witnessed Oliver's temporary escapes too often and his inevitable recapture: *there* is the truth and the creative experience. We know that when Oliver leaves Mr Brownlow's house to walk a few hundred yards to the bookseller, his friends will wait in vain for his return. All London outside the quiet, shady street in Pentonville belongs to his pursuers; and when he escapes again into the house of Mrs Maylie in the fields beyond Shepperton, we know his security is false. The seasons may pass, but safety depends not on time but on daylight. As children we all knew that: how all day we could forget the dark and the journey to bed. It is with a sense of relief that at last in twilight we see the faces of the Jew and Monks peer into the cottage window between the sprays of jessamine. At that moment we realize how the whole world, and not London only, belongs to these two after dark. Dickens, dealing out his happy endings and his unreal retributions, can never ruin the validity and dignity of that moment. 'They had recognized him, and he them; and their look was as firmly impressed upon his memory, as if it had been deeply carved in stone, and set before him from his birth.'

'From his birth' – Dickens may have intended that phrase to refer to the complicated imbroglios of the plot that lie outside the novel, 'something less terrible than the truth'. As for the truth, is it too fantastic to imagine that in this novel, as in many of his later books, creeps in, unrecognized by the author, the eternal and alluring taint of the Manichee, with its simple and terrible explanation of our plight, how the world was made by Satan and not by God, lulling us with the music of despair?

A. E. DYSON

The Old Curiosity Shop
Innocence and the Grotesque
(1966)

> And lastly, there was the girl;
> Beauty under some spell of the beast.
> (from R. S. Thomas's 'On the Farm')

I

The Old Curiosity Shop opens with the never-ending feet of London as a sick man might hear them, imagining the people, the faces, the destinies, 'the stream of life that will not stop, pouring on, on, on, through all his restless dreams, as if he were condemned to lie, dead but conscious, in a noisy churchyard, and had no hope of rest for centuries to come'. This vision of London is the narrator's, the old man (bequeathed to the novel by *Master Humphrey's Clock*) who sets the tale in motion and then withdraws. The opening chapter sets a tone which is to pervade the novel. As Dickens said later in his Preface, the story came from a deep region of his mind:

> I had it always in my fancy to surround the lonely figure of the child with grotesque and wild, but not impossible companions, and to gather about her innocent face and pure intentions, associates as strange and uncongenial as the grim objects that are about her bed when her history is first fore-shadowed.

The grotesque is always strong in Dickens, but here in *The Old Curiosity Shop*, it is the organising principle of his art. The characters are grotesque: Quilp and Kit, Dick Swiveller and Sally Brass, old Mr Trent and the Marchioness – and so is the setting: the curiosity shop, the Brass ménage, Quilp's riverside hideout, the picaresque world of giants and dwarfs, freaks and travelling showmen, bargees and outcasts through which little Nell and her grandfather flee. The morality is grotesque: good and evil, tragedy and comedy exist as in a distorting glass. Even the humour is grotesque. 'I don't eat babies,' says Quilp, 'I don't like 'em' (a wisecrack midway between Swift and sick comedy) – and there are discussions like this, in the Jolly Sandboys:

> 'How's the Giant?' said Short, when they all sat smoking round the fire.
> 'Rather weak upon his legs,' returned Mr Vuffin. 'I begin to be afraid he's going at the knees.'
> 'That's a bad look-out,' said Short.
> 'Ay! Bad indeed,' replied Mr Vuffin, contemplating the fire with a sigh. 'Once get a giant shaky on his legs and the public care no more about him than they do for a dead cabbage-stalk.'
> 'What becomes of old giants?' said Short, turning to him again after a little reflection.
> 'They're usually kept in caravans to wait upon the dwarfs,' said Mr Vuffin . . .
> . . . 'What about the dwarfs when *they* get old?' inquired the landlord.
> 'The older a dwarf is, the better worth he is,' returned Mr Vuffin; 'a grey-headed dwarf, well-wrinkled, is beyond all suspicion. But a giant weak in the legs, and not standing upright! – keep him in the carawan, but never show him, never show him, for any persuasion that can be offered.'

The worlds of Lewis Carroll and Franz Kafka both seem near, as a sense of strangeness spreads back from this mingling of homely atmosphere and ruthless logic into our more normal world. What race produces such a wisdom, so familiar and alien? Caricature is fundamentally serious, as in Hogarth; Mr Vuffin's freaks exist for public mirth and private profit, but in *The Old Curiosity Shop* most of the characters are freaks. Yet there is some resilience in the humour, a reminder of Kit and his strange, misshapen family, as well as of Quilp. Dickens, said Chesterton, 'could only get to the most solemn emotions adequately if he got to them through the grotesque'. Perhaps: but equally, only through the grotesque could certain of his artistic effects be achieved. When Dickens holds up his distorting mirror we see, surprisingly elongated or shrunken, ourselves – behaving much as we normally do. There is satire here, but much more than satire; the figures are caught in the mirror as in a spell. It is in a spell, too, that we meet the heroine, as the narrator first creates her for us, in an image haunt-ingly present long after he himself has bowed out:

> But all that night, waking or in my sleep, the same thoughts recurred, and the same images regained possession of my brain. I had, ever before me, the old dark murky rooms – the gaunt suits of mail with their ghostly silent air – the faces all awry, grinning from wood and stone – the dust, and rust, and worm that lives in wood – and alone in the midst of all this lumber and decay and ugly age, the beautiful child in her gentle slumber, smiling through her light and sunny dreams.

But this is the narrator, not the author; the 'light and sunny dreams' turn to waking nightmare, and there is no fairy-tale prince but Kit. In many respects *The Old Curiosity Shop* is the least sentimental of novels; little Nell's innocence is shadowed with ironies from the first.

    The Old Curiosity Shop (1841) belongs, in my view, with two other early Dickens novels, all of which stand among his greatest achieve-ments, although only one of them has had its proper due. These are *Oliver Twist* (1837–8) and *Barnaby Rudge* (1841), two other virtuoso exercises in the grotesque. It is hard to fit them into the conventional view of Dickens's development and this may be one reason why *The Old Curiosity Shop* and *Barnaby Rudge* have suffered comparative neglect. The conventional view assumes that there are two, or possibly three, phases in Dickens's career, with *Dombey and Son* (1846–8) (or *David Copperfield*, 1849–50) as the watershed, and an authorial progress from simplicity to complexity, optimism to pessimism, inspired slap-dash to Art. Naturally there is some truth in this, but the novels I am now grouping together do not easily fit. All three are remarkably unified in mood and tone, and their artistry is nearer to *Great Expecta-tions* (1860–1) than to *Nicholas Nickleby* (1838–9) and *Martin Chuzzlewit* (1843–4) on either side. The notion that *The Old Curiosity Shop* is 'sentimental', and *Barnaby Rudge* dull and badly organised except for the Riots, can have developed only through a remarkable tradition of critical neglect. At the risk of paradox, therefore, I want to by-pass the ending of *The Old Curiosity Shop*, which has hogged so much attention, and to look at the work as a whole. Only two critics seem to me to have written well on this novel: Edgar Johnson in his admirable biography *Charles Dickens: His Tragedy and Triumph*, and Steven Marcus in *Dickens: From Pickwick to Dombey*. Like all good critics, they give the impression of opening a debate, not of closing it;

certainly they make the high opinion of this novel held by many of Dickens's distinguished contemporaries, including Tolstoy, seem far more understandable than it normally does.

My own method will be to examine three characters, one evil, one good, one morally unclassifiable, and then to proceed to some central themes. But first, a few facts about the composition of the novel may be helpful. From the germ of Dickens's idea, first announced to Landor in February 1840, progress was extremely rapid. Rapidity was forced upon Dickens by circumstances. The newly founded weekly *Master Humphrey's Clock* made a splendid start, but sales slumped badly within a month. Clearly, the public wanted another full-length novel, and would let Dickens off with nothing less. Dickens, with his unerring mixture of business acumen and actor's clairvoyance, decided to oblige. The much-deferred *Barnaby Rudge* was once more shelved, and the new tale started before any detailed plans for it were complete. At first, Dickens still envisaged something much shorter, scarcely more than a moral fable or a sketch. But his own imagination took fire along with his public's; from the very first chapter, a truly organic growth seemed to flower. The author's chief delight in the early stages was with Dick Swiveller, whose 'behaviour in the matter of Miss Wackles', he wrote to Forster, 'will, I hope, give you satisfaction'. Up to half-way through, little Nell's fate seems to have hung in the balance. Forster claimed this, anyway, and gave himself the credit for her death. But the creative logic was ruthlessly pointing in one direction; as soon as Dickens became conscious of this, Nell was instinctively identified with Mary Hogarth, and he looked forward to writing the ending with intense dread. 'All night', he wrote, 'I have been pursued by the child; and this morning I am unrefreshed and miserable.' And again, 'I am breaking my heart over this story.' The death of little Nell required as much courage of him as anything in his writing career, and the general verdict in his lifetime confirmed his own feeling of success. The sales, by now, were enormous; when the crowds waited to learn Nell's fate on the quayside of New York, one hundred thousand copies were being sold. This was the largest number on first publication that any of his major novels ever achieved, though the Christmas books and stories later set up records of their own.

This was the first of the novels that Dickens wrote for weekly instead of monthly instalments, and he groaned endlessly about the restrictions thereby imposed. It was the same with *Barnaby Rudge* (the other *Master Humphrey's Clock* novel), and with *Hard Times* later in *Household Words*. The weekly space, he complained, gave him too little elbow-room; how could he develop the numerous characters and plots in such a space? Nonetheless, his art seemed in many ways more compressed and telling for the discipline; *Great Expectations* was also published later in weekly parts. *The Old Curiosity Shop* is characterised, too, by all of Dickens's early gusto; one senses here, as in *Pickwick*, the sheer delight which he took, in these early days, in his work.

II

To turn, then, to the characters. First, evil: and in addition to the Brasses, Dickens gives us the unforgettable figure of Quilp:

> The creature appeared quite horrible, with his monstrous head and little body, as he rubbed his hands slowly round and round, and round again – with something fantastic even in the manner of performing this slight action – and, dropping his shaggy brows and cocking his chin in the air, glanced upwards with a steady look of exultation, that an imp might have copied and appropriated to himself.

Quilp, says Chesterton, 'is precisely the devil of the Middle Ages; he belongs to that amazingly healthy period when even lost spirits were hilarious'. But hilarious for whom, one wants to ask: for Mrs Quilp? – for little Nell and her grandfather? – for the normal readers of the book? For the latter, certainly, in that we, at least, are protected by the normal barriers of art. Yet Chesterton's comment, despite its element of truth, can hardly satisfy. Isn't the 'hilarity' of Quilp largely the exuberance generated by all great art? And hasn't *this* great art a distinctive exuberance, more obviously peculiar to Dickens himself? It is in part an aesthetic quality, an Hogarthian energy of disorder and breakdown transcending the satiric impulse from which it starts. But it is also demonic exuberance straight from experience – from that area of experience where Dickens's artistry seems always to thrive. Quilp's vitality, and our own vitality drawn out in answer to it, is nearer to fear than to joy. If we laugh, this is partly to tame the demonic with incredulity; isn't Quilp, after all, a game with the reader, an example

of that Dickensian talent for exaggeration which we are only too eager
to admire? Doubtless Dickens realised this, and took pains to circum-
vent it, for Quilp creeps back in the uneasy silence following laughter,
or joins all too horribly in the laughter himself. His relish for evil is
almost creative, as though he were a Manichean devil, with a whole
world to be made out of malice and spite. His very ugliness is attuned
to inventiveness: we see him tormenting his wife with false endear-
ments, ugly grimaces, threats to bite her, and making from this an
evening of pure boredom transmuted, for him, by her fear. His eating
and drinking are prodigiously horrible, an outrage on nature. His one
relationship of mutual 'liking' – the motives of which, Dickens says,
are 'to no purpose' – is the strange give-and-take of blows and defiance
with Tom Scott.

Quilp's humour and malice cannot be distinguished or separated,
as he stage-manages his various horrific appearances throughout the
novel – grimacing in mirrors, hanging upside down from the roofs of
stage-coaches, standing on windowsills, or carefully arranged as a
crowning detail of the grotesque:

> . . . he soon cast his eyes upon a chair, into which he skipped with un-
> common agility, and perching himself on the back with his feet upon the
> seat, was thus enabled to look on and listen with greater comfort to him-
> self, besides gratifying at the same time that taste for doing something
> fantastic and monkey-like, which on all occasions had strong possession
> of him.

So he lurks, a gothic voyeur of secrets and suffering; and so in due
season he dies, his body swollen with water, and buried at a cross-roads,
with a stake through the heart. As, of course, he would have wished;
Dickens extends his own relish in melodrama to crown Quilp's end.
It is, indeed, the creative relish in mischief and destruction for which
we remember Quilp – that source in him of the mingled fear and
laughter which is the tribute of little Nell's innocence to his life. We
remember the moment when Quilp talks to Brass about his plan to
make little Nell – at this time fourteen – his second wife, and dwells
with revolting sensual relish on her charms. It is the scene where he is
forcing Brass to smoke tobacco frenziedly 'against infection from
fever', and Brass's comment, gasped out in the midst of this torture,
'What a remarkably pleasant way he has with children!' is quintessen-
tial – funny and horrible at once. There is also the splendid scene when

Quilp has made Dick Swiveller drunk and Dick, forgetting Quilp's presence, drops into maudlin soliloquy:

> 'Here's a miserable orphan for you. Here,' said Mr Swiveller, raising his voice to a high pitch, and looking sleepily round, 'is a miserable orphan!'
> 'Then,' said somebody hard by, 'let me be a father to you.'

Quilp still there, laconic and malicious – and the serious glance at father-and-son relationships enhances the well-judged cynicism of his remark. The timing is perfect, both Quilp's and Dickens's; the reader knows that Quilp has been making Dick drunk for a purpose, but he shares Dick's surprise that Quilp is still there. The pure humour is helped by our knowledge that Dick is a fair match for Quilp in all matters, including resilience; Mr Swiveller's tipsy self-pity is as zestfully creative as Quilp's relished false friendship and sinister charm. More genuinely sinister, because the victim is so much more vulnerable, is Quilp's taunting of poor Mrs Quilp with inventories of torments, when she makes her last pathetic attempt to approach him as his wife:

> I'll keep watch-dogs in the yard that'll growl and bite – I'll have man-traps, cunningly altered and improved for catching women – I'll have spring guns that shall explode when you tread upon the wires, and blow you into little pieces.

Like Shakespeare, Dickens endows some of his most evil characters with humour, energy and inventiveness; the paradox of Iago is interestingly parallel to Quilp. Like Shakespeare, too, he is more concerned to present evil than to explain it. 'How could you be so cruel?' sobs Mrs Quilp, and 'How could I be so cruel!' mocks the dwarf. 'Because I was in the humour. I'm in the humour now. I shall be cruel when I like.' This reminder of the irrationality of pure evil, its terror, goes beyond analysis. Its force is wholly in its truth.

It is no new observation to point to similarities between Quilp and his creator, but Quilp could indeed be a partial self-portrait, Quilpishly drawn. His ogrish geniality is close to Dickens's: is it Dickens or Quilp who writes of Sally Brass like this?

> . . . In face she bore a striking resemblance to her brother Sampson – so exact, indeed, was the likeness between them, that had it consorted with Miss Brass's maiden modesty and gentle womanhood to have assumed her brother's clothes in a frolic and sat down beside him, it would have been difficult for the oldest friend of the family to determine which was

Sampson and which Sally, especially as the lady carried upon her upper lip certain reddish demonstrations, which, if the imagination had been assisted by her attire, might have been mistaken for a beard. These were, however, in all probability, nothing more than eyelashes in the wrong place, as the eyes of Miss Brass were quite free from any such natural impertinences. In complexion Miss Brass was sallow – rather a dirty sallow, so to speak—but this hue was agreeably relieved by the healthy glow which mantled in the extreme tip of her laughing nose. Her voice was exceedingly impressive – deep and rich in quality, and, once heard, not easily forgotten . . .

And so on . . . The mingling of cruelty, playfulness and deadly accuracy is decidedly Quilpish, and while it is true that Dickens himself always looked for women who were fair game before tormenting them, when he found one – the mannish and shrewish Miss Brass, Cleopatra in *Dombey and Son*, almost any woman over twenty who tried to look young or who wore make-up – he had about as much mercy as Quilp. It is even possible that Kate Dickens had cause to remember poor Mrs Quilp in the years ahead, as Dickens dragged her over the ocean and across America one year, through hair-raising exploits in Europe the next. Dickens's account of his daily life was a saga of restless energy. From the obsessive walks at night in the streets of London, through endless amateur theatricals, to the fatal readings of his later years, he sought violent excitement as a daily food. All this side of him is mirrored in Quilp – which is perhaps why the dwarf's macabre imagination is so Dickensian. There is the morning when Quilp wakes up in a hammock in his riverside hideout, and ponders a possible metamorphosis in the night:

The first sound that met his ears in the morning – as he half opened his eyes, and, finding himself so unusually near the ceiling, entertained a drowsy idea that he must have been transformed into a fly or bluebottle in the course of the night – was that of a stifled sobbing and weeping in the room.

This pressure towards symbolism is as prophetic of Dickens's later techniques as it is of Kafka; it is a further reminder of how completely Quilp eludes 'explanations' of a normal kind.

Not, of course, that there are *no* explanations; Quilp's psychology is partly understandable in Freudian terms. The driving power of his life is hatred, and hatred is one classic response – perhaps the most spirited, certainly the most spontaneous – of the freak. Quilp is not content to be exploited like Mr Vuffin's dwarfs in a freakshow, and prized for his wrinkles; he is content only with punishing, and when possible destroying, the world where he must be a freak. Since revenge is the basic motive he uses his freakishness as the weapon most appropriately to hand. The torment is in the inescapable consciousness of a world alien to him; if the world solves the problem of coping with him by way of circuses, he will find an answering solution to the world. Where could his energy turn, if not to rage and destruction? The only completely full-blooded alternative is sanctity, but does the world take kindly to a sanctified dwarf? It is a triumph of Dickens's art that though he does not analyse, he creates understanding; Quilp's greatest hatred is reserved, surely incontrovertibly, for another grotesque, who responds to his predicament in the opposite way. One of the most powerful scenes occurs when Quilp destroys a ship's figure-head in a fit of uncontrollable malice, seeing in its ugliness not his own image (as Brass does), but Kit's. The intention, analysed, becomes a kind of sympathetic magic, but Quilp does not analyse; he acts, and enjoys a sense of release.

Our last view of Quilp in death is scarcely less effective; his appearance is a fitting crown to his life, and Dickens is left, now that Quilp himself is no longer able, to relish its flavour of irony and spite: 'The hair, stirred by the damp breeze, played in a kind of mockery of death – such a mockery as the dead man himself would have delighted in when alive – about its head.' Though Quilp's character is evil, he remains hilarious for the reader; in this, Chesterton was undoubtedly right. He belongs with a range of other characters – almost peculiar in English literature to Shakespeare and Dickens – in whom we meet the same striking paradox: that though they originate in satire, and are in varying degrees wicked, they establish themselves for very many readers as 'friends for life'. How does this come about? – certainly not by any perversity on the part of the readers, who are surely responding to an exuberance in the creation itself. Yet it is not wholly the alchemy of art that accounts for this paradox, though that must be part of it; for whereas Pecksniff, Mrs Gamp, Joe Bagstock, Mr Micawber, Podsnap, even Silas Wegg would be high on anyone's list of such characters, there are other evil characters in Dickens – Sir John Chester, Jonas Chuzzlewit, Carker, Uriah Heep for instance – for whom no such claim could be made. Tentatively, my own feeling is that this is to do with creativity. In various ways, no matter how twisted, Quilp, Pecksniff, Mrs Gamp, Joe Bagstock, Mr Micawber are among the great creative artists in Dickens's work. Their creations are often far from agreeable, yet they all take pleasure in creating; they convey the genuine energy and exuberance of the creator himself. In contrast, Chester, Carker, Jonas Chuzzlewit, Uriah Heep have only the cold simulacrum of artistic creation—a devious, purely intellectual resourcefulness, wholly dedicated to self: the Gorgon's bloodless alchemy against life. We remember these latter characters with all the pleasure created by Dickens's own artistry, but they do not light up with their own additional warmth from within.

The Old Curiosity Shop offers this kind of paradox in good measure, since it also contains another of Dickens's great creative characters, Dick Swiveller.

III

But before turning to Dick, let us look at the character who most nearly balances Quilp, and who bears the main burden of virtue in this novel (if we exclude the heroine): Kit Nubbles. Quilp evil, Kit good: but Kit scarcely less of a grotesque. His role is a fascinating cross of Knight and Fool; though his first appearance is as 'the comedy' of Little Nell's life, he is to carry Dickens's main perception of disinterested love. It is significant that he, like Quilp, makes use of his ugliness, but to produce laughter and happiness in the child:

> The lad had a remarkable manner of standing sideways as he spoke, and thrusting his head forward over his shoulder, as if he could not get at his voice without that accompanying action. I think he would have amused one anywhere, but the child's exquisite enjoyment of his oddity, and the relief it was to find that there was something she associated with merriment, in a place that appeared so unsuited to her, were quite irresistible. It was a great point, too, that Kit himself was flattered by the sensation he created, and after several efforts to preserve his gravity, burst into a loud roar, and stood with his mouth wide open and his eyes nearly shut, laughing violently.

This is not without its cost; Kit is one 'whose laugh had been all the time one of that sort which very little would change into a cry', and his destiny is far removed from the lady he serves. His family lives in an 'extremely poor and homely place', with an 'air of comfort about it'; it is 'rather a queer-looking family: Kit, his mother, and the children, being all strongly alike'. Kit's 'good-humour' is more a virtue than a mood; it is closer to eighteenth-century 'cheerfulness' than to romantic *élan*. There is a delightful and healing moment when Kit comes home with little Nell's bird, which Quilp has made him fight for, and an infectious gaiety spreads back from the immediate situation to the family group:

> Kit laughing so heartily, with his swollen and bruised face looking out of the towel, made little Joseph laugh, and then his mother laughed, and then the baby crowed and kicked with great glee, and then they all laughed in concert: partly because of Kit's triumph and partly because they were very fond of each other.

'Healing' this certainly is; its effect runs directly counter to the evil world of the Brasses and Quilp. Kit's is a good magic, which defines the limits of nightmare and keeps hope alive. It is as though Dickens were resolved to depict the reality of chivalry with none of its trappings – an undertaking profoundly subversive, in that Kit's class, appearance, social uncouthness seem at the opposite pole to chivalry, and clearly, he couldn't have married little Nell, even had she lived. He is a kind of polar opposite to Chester in *Barnaby Rudge*, whose perfect manners and frozen heart Dickens depicts with cold hatred. Kit, with none of the appearances of chivalry, has all the reality – which is why he is so central to a novel where the conflict of appearance and reality is a central theme. 'Codlin's the friend, not Short,' says Codlin – and his phrase links with similar professions of false friendship throughout the book – Quilp to Dick Swiveller, Sampson Brass to Kit. The theme is inverted in Kit's tribulations, first when he is represented to little Nell's grandfather as an enemy (by Quilp), and then when he is gaoled as a thief (at the instigation of Brass). In a world where the language of virtue is stolen by vice, what is virtue to say? This theme links the novel (it is one of several links) with *King Lear*: like a more agreeable Cordelia, little Nell becomes a touchstone of moral reality in a world of lies. For all the grotesquerie and deceitfulness, she knows the difference between friend and foe. In spirit, she is protected by her virtue, though in body she is subject to more tragic laws. She trusts Kit, despite all the appearances against him, and he is rewarded by her trust (it is, properly speaking, his only reward, since Barbara belongs well outside the ambience where Kit is a knight). The lower-class boy is not a disguised or incognito nobleman; his ugliness is not an irresistible romantic magnet, like Mr Rochester's; his devotion to little Nell points to none of the conventional romantic rewards. Dickens does not sentimentalise *here*, and he does not oversimplify; he offers, in defiance of conventions, the simple truth about virtue like Kit's. Kit imagines that his honesty will protect him against false accusations, but though little Nell understands him, the rest of the world is unimpressed. Kit is hauled trembling into court and found guilty; 'it's all one now', says the Turnkey, 'whether he did it or not'. Even Mrs Nubbles is not wholly sure of Kit, despite her loyalty, since her moral judgement is distorted by a puritanical and joyless religion which Kit, like his creator, hates. Yet Dickens achieves one of his most distinctive effects when Kit cries out in his innocence to know who doesn't trust him. While socially naive, this is morally challenging; trusting Kit is excellent insight in a wicked world.

Kit offers Nell his home, when she is homeless; his loyal protectiveness (unbeknown to her) when she is threatened; his cheerfulness when she is downcast. The effect is marvellously positive because it is so simply realistic; it stands up in a novel dominated by Quilp. Of course Kit's future bride must not be little Nell, but Barbara: poor Barbara! – so loyal and silly, so teased by Kit's obtuseness, so inferior to Kit in moral stature, so exposed by Dickens to avuncular winks, pinches and nods. What Barbara has to put up with! – not least, Kit's endless recitals of the virtues of Nell. But she puts up with it and wins through to marry Kit and cherish him; and she is exactly the kind of person that someone like Kit would, with luck, marry in actual life. It is this aspect of the novel which most jars today (except for the ending), yet Dickens's realism is scarcely at fault. The whole episode of Kit's courting – Mrs Nubbles' prompting, the visit to Astleys, the authorial gloatings – rings as true now as it ever did. The author simply steps into the shoes of a favourite uncle, and depicts courtship as if it were a supernumerary Christmas. Which, often enough, is what it is – even for an Arthur Seaton, one suspects, after the wild oats have been sown. The main thing in common is a blessed suspension of normal criticism; the underprivileged count their blessings, and aunt Jane hears that she is the grandest old lady in the world. The good things of life are enjoyed – food, shelter, drink, family and friends; and an evening out at Astleys is just as innocent as Dickens describes it, whatever Thackeray's worldlings, to take a contrary instance, would find.

There is something childlike in such times, the recapture of wonder; it is the good intoxication of the virtuous poor. The secret behind it Dickens knew as well as anyone; by his passionate crusade against poverty he had earned the right to celebrate it; by his refusal to use such terms as 'virtuous poor' in cold analysis, he could afford to let the reality be seen. And which of us can be called a social realist if we refuse this kind of reality? The human heart is not a sophisticated sport.

Kit marries Barbara, and it is right that he should, but I think that Dickens was uneasy about him, for somewhat different reasons, all the same. Did he realise that though Kit is so much more valuable than Quilp, he is also so much less interesting? Perhaps he wished a better destiny for Kit's virtue than life could possibly offer; perhaps he felt that allowances must too explicitly be made. By means of Barbara, he at least avoided the more serious embarrassments (serious aesthetic embarrassments) that confronted him later with Tom Pinch. Barbara is admirable for Kit, and Dickens is right to show this; but would Kit and Barbara have been among his own 'friends for life'?

IV

Quilp evil, Kit good, Dick Swiveller neither – simply one of the most splendid creations in the world. 'At length there sauntered up . . . a figure conspicuous for its dirty smartness' . . . and Dick saunters into the novel, 'merry, but not wise'. As he cheats, lies, drinks, charms, loves and looks after himself ('Love-making yes, Promising no,' said Dick. 'There can be no action for breach') he seems a perfect prototype for the anti-hero of today. His specious lies to creditors, his growing list of streets he can't risk being seen in, his plan to write a letter to his aunt covered with 'tears', his grandiloquent, half-rhyming soliloquies, his abortive wooing of Sophy Wackles – all these things exist in a world that Kingsley Amis has coarsened, brutalised and made his own. Like all good rogues, Dick Swiveller jests with himself. ' "Marchioness", said Mr Swiveller, rising, "the word of a gentleman is as good as his bond – sometimes better, as in the present case, where his bond might prove but a doubtful sort of security." ' He is lured into evil by Quilp, for reasons of vanity, poverty, self-interest and thoughtlessness, all of which the dwarf very fully understands and exploits.

But we never feel that he is essentially evil. He toys with evil only when he doesn't bother to imagine it: or rather, when his particular exuberance of imagination converts it into the innocence of farce. Given a real situation, and someone in need, he will always ring true. He is a hero as exempt from normal moral criteria as the third son of a fairy-tale, who is fated to make errors, get into scrapes, suffer for his sins, win our hearts, come out right in the end. It is no surprise to find Dick brooding on his destiny; we see ahead of him what his destiny is to be. So he decides to shield the Marchioness from the fairly serious crime of which he suspects her; and the Marchioness saves his life, and marries him.

Dick Swiveller is miles removed from little Nell, and the novel rightly insulates them; but he is well placed to make on Quilp, in comic vein, the comment that little Nell could also make:

> 'I not a choice spirit!' cried Quilp.
> 'Devil a bit, sir,' returned Dick. 'A man of your appearance couldn't be. If you're any spirit at all, sir, you're an evil spirit. Choice spirits,' added Dick, smiting himself on the breast, 'are quite a different-looking sort of people, you may take your oath of that, sir!'

Predictably, Dick fits admirably into Brass's ménage, when Quilp's malevolence has delivered him up to it; bemused by Sally Brass, and by her 'intolerable headdress', he nonetheless strikes up a manly bonhomie with her fairly soon. His initial temptation to knock the headdress off with a ruler he *just* suppresses; but only by gazing fixedly at her until almost hypnotised by the sight. When she leaves the room, his fullness of joy expresses itself in a 'manic hornpipe' – and, later, in characteristic verbal embroideries of his predicament, where everything is comedy – his unspoken rejoinders to Sally, cocky and irreverent; his taunting of his personal destiny 'as heroes do', says Dickens, 'when in a mess'. The whole Brass household becomes tinged with the comic-sinister; the arrival of the eccentric 'single gentleman' as lodger is like a projection of Dick's mind. 'She-dragons in the business, conducting themselves like professional gentlemen,' Dick reflects to himself, 'plain cooks three feet high, strangers walking in and going to bed without leave or licence in mid-day' . . . it is a fitting *milieu* for his humour to transform. Dick is a headling force in this world, as Kit is in Nell's – neither can alter evil, but each alleviates it in a distinctive way. Sally Brass, as mediated by Dick, is at her most grotesque but her least unpleasant; it is possible to see her, suddenly, simply as a mannish and bossy old maid. Certainly Dick brings out the best in her, not necessarily for sexual reasons; she finds him attractive for his vigour and health. He presides for a time as a Lord of Misrule, and his flamboyant misrule almost transforms the deeper evil of the house. This may be one reason why Dickens's very bitter and unusually badly written dismissal of the Brasses in his final chapter comes as a shock: it is obviously justified, yet Dick's imagination has very nearly converted the Brasses into a lighter frame.

Dick's function in the novel is purely natural – a sunny interlude in stormy weather. He lights up in the warmth of Dickens's approval – a force for good, outside all social conventions and in defiance of most of them: as incontrovertibly good as the superficially similar Sim Tappertit in *Barnaby Rudge* is bad. To an even greater extent than Quilp, he may strike us as partial self-portrait, an embodiment of that side of Dickens's manifold nature which loved to drink in convivial company, visit the theatre, play pranks, and sport in the light. It was Longfellow who, seeing this side of Dickens in America, said that he had 'a slight dash of the Dick Swiveller about him'; the 'slight dash', in clothing and social manner as well as mood, was the reason, no doubt, why Dickens remained an outsider, for all his fame. There is an episode recorded in Edgar Johnson's biography which catches Dickens in his Dick Swiveller mood:

> Once, when the Hogarths were all quietly sitting in the family drawing room, 'a young man dressed as a sailor jumped in at the window, danced a hornpipe, whistling the tune, jumped out again, and a few minutes later Charles Dickens walked gravely in at the door, as if nothing had happened, shook hands all round, and then, at the sight of their puzzled faces, burst into a roar of laughter.'

Dick is full of vitality and zest, of creative ingenuity as spontaneous as Quilp's, and harnessed to spontaneous goodwill. No wonder he is closer to his author than Kit – Kit who doesn't create, doesn't aspire, can't transform Sally Brass into a she-dragon and a kitchen-maid into a Marchioness, can't rise totally out of his background and class. Dickens loved Kit, admired him, fought his battles, extolled his virtues, but he spent his life escaping from Kit – from everything for which Kit ultimately stood. Kit might have irradiated a blacking factory with virtue, and almost redeemed it; it is Dick Swiveller who would have whistled himself up and away.

V

The various grotesques in *The Old Curiosity Shop* are interestingly contrasted, but one thing they have in common; they are not so much explained by their author as exhibited. Explanations appear and disappear, but our main impression of them deepens all the time.

It is sometimes assumed, even by Dickens's admirers, that there is something inferior in this method; George Eliot's novels, in particular, caused later Victorian critics to see psychological analysis as a *sine qua non*. Yet the triumphant exhibition of characters and events is one of the many things which Dickens has in common with Shakespeare, and in the very greatest art perhaps it must always come first. We have only to think of real life and its interesting people to realise that explanations take a very second place. Naturally, complex acts have many sources, but the sources hardly exhaust the acts, while 'explanations' can degenerate into the merely polemical exercise of friend or foe. If we ponder on Gladstone or Disraeli, Lloyd George or Winston Churchill, is there not first a memorable image, clear-cut and ineffaceable, with strong intimations of richness beneath? So it is in fiction, with Dickens's great characters – who have also, again like Shakespeare's, a distinct tinge of heaven or hell. 'Will you, I pray, demand that demi-devil' cries Othello 'Why he has thus ensnared my soul and body?' But Iago is silent and the critics are baffled; there are too many explanations, all plausible, all conflicting, none adequate to explain the horror we see. But the horror is real, and we cannot doubt it; in Iago, Goneril, Regan, Shakespeare enacts the mystery of iniquity, just as in certain other characters he enacts the mystery of good. In Coleridge's terms, such art moves on the plane of Reason rather than of Understanding; certain supreme realities are imaginatively realised to the full. To try to recapture such art for 'Understanding' can be deeply misleading; it has led certain critics of Dickens to mistake his central greatness for some kind of peripheral defect. We have heard of his 'Calvinism', his fatalism, his caprice, his use of 'coincidence', his propensity to 'caricature' or 'melodrama', all offered as excuses for quite non-existent faults. His characters have been quite particularly maltreated – to hear certain critics talking of extravagant humours, or repetitive verbal rhetoric, you would think they had never seen Mrs Gamp passing down the street.

My own view is that Quilp, Kit, the Brasses, Dick Swiveller exist because Dickens has created them; they radiate reality, lighting up the world and the people we know. In their prime reality, they are incontrovertible; who can say that Quilp wouldn't have treated his wife as he does, or that Dick Swiveller would have been less thoughtful about Kit? The world is full of Dickens's people because he created people; he looked at the world in its strangeness, and made what he saw.

This is not to assert that there are no rational explanations of his people; but simply, that rational explanations are as little complete for them as they are for ourselves. We are reminded in the greatest art that only by dulling our perceptions, hardening our morality, donning blinkers and muzzles, can we ever persuade ourselves that we 'fully understand'. This, again, accords with Coleridge's theory, which allowed the importance of rational understanding, but subordinated it to intuitive perception of the wonder of life. I suppose this is why, looking round us at friends and acquaintances, we so often feel: yes! – there to the life is Hamlet or Falstaff, Quilp or Dick Swiveller, in a way that we never quite feel: yes! – there is Elizabeth Bennet or Dorothea Brooke. The latter characters are deeply revealing to sensitive reflection, they are fine parables and *exempla*, but it is the former who have the unique unexpectedness of life. Indeed, it is because they remain unique that they seem universal; it is because we know, like Prufrock, that we are not Prince Hamlet nor were meant to be, that Prince Hamlet remains the mirror of us all. That, I take it, is why such figures are always highly idiosyncratic, in life as in literature; they are real with the full courage of their reality – the courage so easily whittled away by introspection and analytical thought. The universality of Jane Austen's characters is in their range of moral experience; the universality of Dickens's is in their unfailing illusion of life.

When critics maintain that Jane Austen's world is more 'real' than Dickens's, they usually seem to mean one of three things. The first is that the 'real' world consists only of middle-class, respectable people, and that any other kinds of people do not really exist. Surprisingly often this turns out to be the underlying assumption, if Jonas Chuzzlewit, or Miss Mowcher, or Jenny Wren is declared less 'real' than Fanny Price. The second is that such people do exist, but ought not to be depicted; that only a small range of humanity, suitably reduced by explanation, belongs to the province of art. The third, which I take to be the most sophisticated (if one leaves aside formal literary theory) is that literature exists as a kind of superior social reporting, in which ideas can be complex, but people have to be morally analysed, generalised and judged.

Jane Austen is much greater than people holding any of these assumptions usually realise, but she does not offend their assumptions in any too flagrant way. Dickens, on the other hand, does offend them; he offends the instinct for complacent and comfortable recognition which all these assumptions to some degree serve. His world is one which intelligence and sensitivity cannot plumb, cannot very radically heal or alter; it is a world where openness to experience, however sophisticated or unsophisticated, is a prerequisite to any other virtues there may be. The world of Quilp and Kit, Dennis the Hangman and Gabriel Varden, Captain Cuttle and Joey Bagstock, the Murdstones and Betsy Trotwood, Miss Havisham and Joe Gargery, Jenny Wren and Silas Wegg may be far removed from rational explanations and panaceas; it is not, however, removed either from real experiences that we might at some time encounter if we have eyes for them, or from the two or three apocalyptic explorations of human destiny that have shaped our lives. It accords very well with the grand melodrama of heaven and hell depicted by the Christian tradition, and with the grand inner melodrama depicted by Freud and Jung. It accords very much less well, as its author was the first to proclaim and realise, with the sober speculations of Jeremy Bentham, the *laissez faire* utilitarians, and the earlier Mill.

VI

In *The Old Curiosity Shop* such dramatic contrasts of character are heightened by the alternation of scenes of good and evil; the reader is frankly amazed by a world where such contrasts can be. How can Quilp's treatment of Mrs Quilp exist in the same universe as Nell's treatment of her grandfather, or Sampson Brass's spirit co-exist with Dick's? Dickens did not invent this world, but he did transform it. His creative energies both reflect the world, and make it anew.

We notice how characters and their backgrounds interact and interrelate with each other, in this grand exhibition of the grotesque. Mr Trent is so assimilated to the old curiosity shop that he seems like an extension of it. He carries it with him, until the whole world becomes the shop, and the novel's title remains true to the end. He emerges from the shop at the very start of the novel on his mysterious mission, and is swallowed up in the labyrinth of London streets. Is he a miser, a criminal, an extreme eccentric? -- we see him driven by restlessness like an ancient mariner, his compulsions reflected in the night-long anxieties of the child. He merges, in the night watches, into the child's reveries; she fancies ugly faces peering from the crooked chimney stacks, and would have to assure herself 'that everything was in its place and hadn't moved'. When men pass with a coffin, she thinks of someone lying dead; after the normal goodnight kiss, she lies awake in her bed, fearing suicide as the old man's end.

As in *Oliver Twist*, a child's consciousness seems merged in its destiny; unlike the other main characters in this novel, but like Oliver, she is mainly passive in her role. Though she sets out on her wanderings, and guides the old man through peril, it is surprising how little active impression we have. Our sense of her grows through our response to her predicament, not through a direct view of her thoughts, or her motives for choice. There is a curious trap here for the hostile reader – a trap which also exists, and for the same reason, in *Oliver Twist*. In all Dickens's later novels, children are presented differently. Florence Dombey, David Copperfield, Pip, Lizzie Hexam mature through suffering; Paul Dombey is a unique study of the mind of a sensitive and doomed child. But in *Oliver Twist* and *The Old Curiosity Shop*, the child's role is passive. Men and circumstances act upon the child, and are in turn judged by their effects. We are asked to imagine the plight of a human being in a particular setting; the setting itself is richly presented and the child is a normal, vulnerable human like ourselves. The trap for the reader, therefore, is to find Nell and Oliver 'wooden' – which amounts to an imaginative failure to enter into the experience of the book.

In *The Old Curiosity Shop* the setting has the intensity of myth, as well as its realism. '. . . let us wander barefoot through the world', says little Nell, as they set off on their wanderings; 'we will be happy'. They will be 'as free and happy as birds', agrees her grandfather, and the words resonate like symbols from a different world. Quilp likes *his* birds in cages, and Kit barely rescues little Nell's bird from death. The surrounding omens are all unpropitious. Little Nell is deliberately romanticising, to rally her grandfather; like a more humane Cordelia, she adapts strict truthfulness to the weakness of a grandfather-child. The old man's reply is tinged with senility. His vision of new happiness waiting for them is no more sanctioned than Lear's image of two birds in a cage. Yet this exchange is no more simply ironic than it is simply sentimental. The vision of idyllic wanderings through nature, far from cities, far from enemies, recalls old dreams of nature's love for a favourite child. The effect, in this darkened world, is close to the Epistle to the Hebrews: here we have no abiding city, but we seek one that is to come. The wanderers are indeed exiles, in search of a kingdom; though Dickens is seldom explicitly Christian in his earlier works, the myth of pilgrims and strangers had an early hold on his mind. (This is one reason why the ending of *The Old Curiosity Shop* ought not to be dismissed as 'religiose' until its claims to be religious have been understood first.) The setting out of the travellers is surrounded with enigma. As they pass out of sight, we return to Quilp, presiding over the destruction of their former home.

On the journey the old man's senility emerges in the feverishness with which he seeks to escape from his enemies, in his childlike pleasure in Punch and Judy and the travelling showmen, in the increasing complacency with which he accepts their reversal of roles. ('It is true', he admits long before this, 'that in many respects I am the child, and she is the grown person.') Nell is not a grown person, and he knows it; but this knowledge is altogether too painful to bear. The psychology of his gambling is wonderfully attuned to this moral escapism; Dickens's analytical insight receives a larger setting, as usual, than itself. Mr Trent knows that he gambles solely for Nell's sake, so is not Providence bound to favour his cause? This half-superstitious, wholly home-spun reasoning makes 'luck' respectable; and places the onus of bad luck squarely on Providence itself. So Providence can both be blamed, and freshly invoked, through each catastrophe; and meanwhile the fever in the blood, the compulsion, thrives on this hope beyond hope. With its simulacrum of reasoning and its irresistible compulsiveness, the old man's vice resembles delirium, or the borderline between sleep and waking in a troubled dream. Quilp's malice is a hard, external spotlight upon it, but Nell's suffering lights up the horror from within.

So gambling becomes part of the novel's prevailing grotesquerie, and seems more a symptom of evil than its ultimate cause. It is part of the web in which Nell finds her destiny, a Cordelia accompanying old-age on its path of ruin and death. There is the harrowing progress of the old man's failure under his sufferings; his intermittent bouts of gambling, with their erosion of dignity; and the final descent into plaintive despair. 'Nothing to fear', lies Nell, in her role of more humane Cordelia – and 'No-one is true to me', whines the old man, 'not even Nell.' The old man's physical and moral weakness are sadly familiar, but his words latch on to the novel's central theme of 'true' *versus* 'false'. As in *King Lear*, the reality of 'true' becomes increasingly real to its audience, but in no obvious manner does it operate healingly inside the tale. The child's heroism and love are refracted by the context; if they have a meaning, it must lie beyond tragic suffering in the human world.

VII

Some of the greatest writing in the novel is to be found in Chapters 43 to 45, when the first clear signs of Nell's illness appear. She has rescued her grandfather from his most terrible temptation – again by lying – and they are once more on their way.

> In the pale moonlight, which lent a wanness of its own to the delicate face where thoughtful care already mingled with the winning grace and loveliness of youth, the too bright eye, the spiritual head, the lips that pressed each other with such high resolve and courage of the heart, the slight figure firm in its bearing, and yet so very weak, told their silent tale . . .

It is now that the travellers strike the Industrial Midlands, and Dickens describes for the first time in his work (*Hard Times* was the next) a scene that had very powerfully affected him on the Birmingham to Wolverhampton road. In this novel the scene is depicted through the consciousness of the senile man and the tubercular girl; the feverishness of their vision turns it to nightmare as they stagger on, desperately tired and frightened, the girl fulfilling her parental responsibility to the last. The phantasmagoric quality seems distinctly 'modern'; perhaps their fevered vision mirrors a social reality, but no simple equation is allowed. It is a clear literary progenitor of the Circe episode in *Ulysses*, of the scene in Orwell's *A Clergyman's Daughter* when the heroine, down and out, spends a night among the derelicts in Trafalgar

Square. It is artistically more honest (if not necessarily more powerful) than Eliot's vision of London in *The Waste Land*, where a sick vision of the city is too simply translated into cultural myth.

Whether Dickens fully understood his own technique is, however, doubtful. The relevant passages are too long to quote in full, and selective quotation is bound to diminish the effect. They are reminiscent of certain other passages in Dickens when some nightmare vision of evil is imposed upon – or discovered in – scenes of squalor or violence: the riots in *Barnaby Rudge*, Jonas Chuzzlewit's night walk with murder, the railway passages leading up to Carker's death, the Terror in *A Tale of Two Cities* – at least one example springs to mind from every book. There are reasons to believe that Dickens aimed fairly directly at social and psychological realism in such scenes, and that he was more preoccupied with simple, powerful moral effects, than with the process of art. In a letter to Forster, who had been with him on his journey through the Black Country, Dickens expressed some slight dissatisfaction with what he had achieved. He had sworn to strike 'the heaviest blow in my power' on behalf of the industrial victims, and this experience was already set aside for a novel at some later date. He seems to have felt that his depiction in *The Old Curiosity Shop* fell short of the whole truth. This can hardly be because the pages fail in horror and misery; it must be that Dickens intended some more penetrating analysis of the social forces and philosophies which had brought such horror about. It was not until *Hard Times* that he expressed this 'truth' as he fully understood it – and there the didactic intention, the determination to confront utilitarian impoverishments of the spirit starkly and challengingly, produced a novel rich and powerful, but oddly removed from the normal resources of his strength. In *The Old Curiosity Shop* he moves in his more usual ambience; the description resonates more subjectively and suggestively than it does in the later book. Perhaps Nell's vision *is* that of a girl feverish and slowly dying; but if her images ring true to experience, is this not more disturbing, even, than a social tract? The social point is made glancingly; it is as little underlined as the relevance of Mr Trent's vice to the stock-jobbing and fraudulent financial empires in the City of London. But symbolic echoes are set up in the grotesque world – which seems poised, aesthetically, between Hogarth's Gin Lane, and Dantes' Hell.

It is in the middle of these fevered visions that Dickens produces one of his most memorable images of good. Little Nell and her grandfather are succoured by a coarse, poor, simple-minded workman, who offers them his god: the great blast-furnace fire where his life is passed. Nell is carried, saturated and ill, to the fire he has always worshipped, and lying beside it, she hears the strange tale of his life, and the pictures he sees in the flames. She falls, finally, into a deep and easy sleep, and the next day passes out of his life. The workman, anonymous, halting in communication, shut in his anxious melancholy, has made his offering to one less fortunate than himself. He is an astonishing, profoundly moving creation; he belongs to the creative region where Dickens is set wholly apart. Though the ending is slightly spoiled for sophisticated readers by some explicit moralising, the real power of the episode is beyond formulation at all. This, too, is the mark of Dickens's greatness; for all his fantastic creative insight, he does not forget the majority of simple readers who also hung on his words.

The novel ends with little Nell's death, and her grandfather's sorrow. The great crux of sentimentality I am avoiding here, though I think that an examination of the squeamishness of our own century about such real and life-giving emotions as sentimentality and heroism is long overdue. The ending of the novel is not as good as most of the rest of it, but it is far from failure. My purpose has been with the underlying unity of the rest.

STEVEN MARCUS

Barnaby Rudge: Sons and Fathers (1965)

O F all Dickens's novels, *Barnaby Rudge* has attracted least critical attention. Generally judged a failure, notwithstanding a number of excellent if bizarre passages about the Gordon riots, it is customarily dismissed as a work preparatory to *A Tale of Two Cities*.[1] And it is true that the prose of *Barnaby Rudge* is relatively undistinguished; except for the descriptions of the riots, it tends to be of a curiously uniform flatness. Moreover, the novel seems laboriously slow in getting up steam – more than a third of its length is apparently given over to preparation for the central action.[2] Edgar Johnson contends in this regard that Dickens's 'long delay in starting reinforces the suspicion that, by now, he didn't *feel* like writing *Barnaby* and was laboring against the grain'.[3] Another ground of complaint among readers is the apparent bifurcation of interest reflected in the novel's design; few critics have taken issue with Forster's assertion that 'the interest with which the tale begins, has ceased to be its interest before the close; and what has chiefly taken the reader's fancy at the outset, almost wholly disappears in the power and passion with which, in the later chapters, the great riots are described'.[4]

None of these judgments and explanations seems to me either accurate or adequate: *Barnaby Rudge* is a vastly better novel than its reputation in any way suggests. Dickens had held it in mind since 1836, had made a false start on it in the autumn of 1839 (which did not go beyond the writing of two chapters) and in January 1841 turned to it again, revising what he had already written and readjusting his conception of the novel to meet the exigencies of weekly publication in *Master Humphrey's Clock*.[5] This conception was nevertheless executed with a greater mastery, deliberateness and coherence than Dickens had ever revealed before. 'I didn't stir out yesterday,' he wrote to Forster in January, 'but sat and *thought* all day; not writing a line; not so much as the cross of a t or dot of an i. I imaged forth a good deal of Barnaby by keeping my mind steadily upon him.'[6] And a month later, after the birth of his son Walter Landor Dickens, he wrote from Brighton: 'I have (it's four o'clock) done a very fair morning's work, at which I have sat very close, and been blessed besides with a clear view of the end of the volume. As the contents of one number usually require a day's thought at the very least, and often more, this puts me in great spirits.'[7] He also now began to speak of his writing in terms of its strength – its strong effects[8] – anticipating his later notion of art as a form of power.

Nevertheless, he experienced consistent difficulties in the writing of the novel, most of them having to do with the contracted space into which he had to fit each number. 'I am getting on very slowly, I want to stick to the story; and the fear of committing myself, because of the impossibility of trying back or altering a syllable, makes it much harder than it looks.'[9] In the course of events, he decided to discontinue *Master Humphrey's Clock*, along with its scheme of publication, and in October 1841, addressed his readers with the reasons behind this conclusion.

> Many passages in a tale of any length, depend materially for their interest on the intimate relation they bear to what has gone before, or to what is to follow. I sometimes found it difficult when I issued thirty-two closely-printed pages once a month, to sustain in your mind this needful con-nexion; in the present form of publication it is often, especially in the first half of the story, quite impossible to preserve it sufficiently through the current numbers. And although in my progress I am gradually able to set you right, and to show you what my meaning has been, and to work it out, I see no reason why you should ever be wrong when I have it in my power, by resorting to a better means of communication between us, to prevent it.[10]

By 'meaning' in the novel Dickens clearly has in mind not some abstract moral or maxim, but a complex, enlarging state of con-sciousness which the novelist dramatizes or 'works out' in the course of the writing, a vision and interpretation of experience. Contrary to Forster's judgment (which, as I have indicated, has been the generally received one), the 'interest' of the novel's two parts is sustained, the parts are related with exceptional cogency, subtlety and maturity. *Barnaby Rudge* is the last work of Dickens's apprenticeship to his art

– though only our knowledge of what is to come makes it possible to describe the achievement of those first five novels as an apprenticeship.

From the mass of critical comment, one gets the impression that *Barnaby Rudge* is a novel which has been read out of the side of the eye. Few readers ever seem at ease with it. One source of this discomfort lies, I think, in its subject. *Barnaby Rudge* has an essential interest in politics, an interest that at once establishes its difference from *A Tale of Two Cities*, in which politics is ancillary to other matters. *Barnaby Rudge*, moreover, is concerned with authority in political and social relations, as well as in personal and private ones. Among its most notable qualities are the intelligence and skill with which it connects these two kinds of relations, and the steadiness with which it elucidates the 'intimate relation' between them. This insistence upon the reciprocal dependence of politics and character, upon the correspondence between political and personal motives, in effect denies to politics the autonomy – the claim to 'objectivity' – that those involved in politics regularly need to assert. This denial is perhaps one condition behind the uneasy response to the novel; another is that Dickens apparently came out for the wrong side. Although everyone knows now that unconsciously he identified himself with the rioters who burned into Newgate, he was at the same time deliberately suggesting a likeness between the rabble of the Gordon riots and the members of the Chartist agitation in the late 1830s.[11] And so, we conclude, Dickens was reading history inaccurately and unfairly, and the neglect and obscurity in which *Barnaby Rudge* remains has, I think, something to do with this conclusion. *Barnaby Rudge*, by coming out on the side of established power or authority, violates certain assumptions which many readers tend to believe it is the office of the novel to fortify.

The question of *Barnaby Rudge*, then, involves questions of historical fact and even conflicting interpretations of history; and they are matters by no means irrelevant to one's final sense of the novel. What is at issue here, however, is the character of Dickens's representation of the riots, the nature of the historical analogy he understood to exist and how these figure in the large interpretation of experience which the novel undertakes to realize.

The 'No Popery' campaign of 1780 was founded in the fanatical puritanism of Gordon and his close associates, a circumstance Dickens renders in Gordon's dress and speech, revealing through them Gordon's confused intellect and troubled character – his 'air of undefinable uneasiness, which inflicted those who looked upon him, and filled them with a kind of pity' and 'the rapidity of his utterance . . . the violence of his tone and gesture in which, struggling through his Puritan's demeanour, was something wild and ungovernable which broke through all restraint' (ch. 35). Dickens never doubts Gordon's sincerity or his concern for the poor, 'the mass of people out of doors' (ch. 35)[12]; and Dickens's final comment describes the decency of Gordon's behavior in Newgate: 'In bestowing alms among them he considered the necessities of all alike, and knew no distinction of sect or creed' (ch. 32).[13] But the generosity Dickens extended to Gordon apparently did not extend to his lieutenants or to the mob that wore the blue cockade.

Many of those who were banded together to support the religion of their country, even unto death, had never heard a hymn or a psalm in all their lives. But these fellows having for the most part strong lungs, and being naturally fond of singing, chanted any ribaldry or nonsense that occurred to them, feeling pretty certain that it would not be detected in the general chorus, and not caring much if it were. (ch. 48)

The few honest men in the movement abandoned it after the first attempt at intimidating Parliament, 'never, after the morning's experience, to return, or to hold any communication with their late companions' (ch. 50), leaving the work of organizing the mob and terrorizing the city to the opportunistic, the crazed, and the criminal.[14]

These details, among many others, make plain the analogy Dickens was drawing with Chartism. The center of the most exacerbated and violent wing of the movement (the party of 'physical-force') was in the North; Gordon was a Scot, and his campaign made its way south in the wake of his itinerant agitating. The apparent character of the Gordon riots – an alliance between extreme Puritanism and the most feared (because most prohibited) impulses towards insurrection, criminality, and savagery – seemed also, in the minds of many liberals in 1840, to resemble the character of the Chartists. The organization of local Chartist branches into 'classes', the payment of weekly dues, the mass outdoor meetings, the 'conferences', were practices directly taken over from the Methodists.[15] The Chartist movement had also taken to itself the organized campaign against the Poor Law amendment which had proceeded with increasing turbulence in the North since 1834. Its two leaders, Stephens and Oastler, both Tories, were extremely gifted speakers, and for both of them the religious appeal was absolute. For them the Bible was the source of all political and religious truth, and under their joint influence the factory and anti-Poor Law movements came to resemble a religious revival.[16]

Only the fact that theology was never of determining importance in the lives of many working-class Dissenters permitted the numerous sects to unite in political protest.[17] Indeed, with that sudden and unaccountable power which such movements frequently possess, Chartism attracted to itself a large number of the radical societies founded during the years after Waterloo (some of which had lapsed before Chartism revived them), assimilating Lovett's sophisticated London Working Man's Association as well as scores of provincial societies for 'the promotion of human happiness'.[18] The titles of some of the associations contributing to Gordon's campaign, in *Barnaby Rudge*, do not in themselves exaggerate the facts of either 1780 or 1839. 'The Friends of Reason, half-a-guinea. The Friends of Liberty, half-a-guinea. The Friends of Peace. . . . The Friends of Charity. . . . The Friends of Mercy. . . . The Associated Rememberers of Bloody Mary. . . . The United Bull-dogs, half-a-guinea' (ch. 36). In representing the Gordon riots as an amalgam of extreme religious zeal and primitive protest and radicalism (along with a substantial charge of predatory violence), Dickens accentuated the similarities between the disturbance of 1780 and what he conceived to be the dangerous circumstances of his own time. In doing so, Dickens raises the question of the spiritual and material circumstances in society out of which violence erupts. And in *Barnaby Rudge* he regards such eruptions as the inevitable result of contradictions which, continuing without resolution, make existence intolerable. Almost every personal and social relation in this novel reveals the presence of such contradictions.

In *The Old Curiosity Shop* Nell's pursuit of the past became a futile, infinite recession; the past itself was so elusive that it could be recaptured only in death. In *Barnaby Rudge*, the past persists in the present, in society and in personal life, and the novel opens with its immediate evocation: the Maypole Inn is the lost idyllic vision brought back to life. It is an ancient building, but its age seems hale and hearty (ch. 1); its sign and the actual Maypole that stands in front of the inn suggest its vital continuity with the distant past. Its famous bar is an Eden in which man feels at home again, secure, warm, abundantly provided

for (ch. 19). It is a sanctuary against the elements, 'the bleak waste out of
doors' (ch. 33); its fire, which is reflected in every shining object and
every eye, represents the warmth and light of civilized life. Its abundance and order, its 'goodly grove of lemons', make reference to an
even earlier age. It is, Dickens says, a holy place – he calls it 'the
sanctuary, the mystery, the hallowed ground' (ch. 54). It is a place of
rest and quietude, of inviolable order and privacy.

Yet this vision of Old England includes a vision of its master and
owner John Willet – Old Nobodaddy himself. He embodies that very
stasis which in *The Old Curiosity Shop* seemed so desirable; in him,
however, imperturbability has become imbecility, and liberation from
the passage of time has become a means of exercising tyrannical power.
Old John cannot endure movement or energy: 'He looked upon
coaches as things that ought to be indicted . . . disturbers of the
peace of mankind' (ch. 25). Neither can he endure change, and so has
acquired the arts of sleeping with his eyes open and smoking in his
sleep (ch. 33). He has in fact decided to deny that there is such a thing
as time, and to him his grown son will never be anything but a 'young
boy'. Old John maintains his authority and his demi-Paradise only
through tyranny; his denials of time, of change, of death, have led him
to deny the manhood of his son, have led him in fact to deny life itself.
The idyllic past represented by the Maypole, then, contains the seeds
of its own destruction.

Side by side with this conception of the idyll, stands another embodiment of the past, the Warren.[19] The Warren too is an ancient
building, but, unlike the Maypole, it is 'mouldering to ruin'. It is a
grave in which the past is buried; it is also a 'ghost of a house, haunting
the old spot in its old outward form' (ch. 13). In this place, twenty-two
years before the novel begins, a double murder has been committed.
Barnaby's father, the steward of the Warren, has murdered both its
owner (the elder Haredale brother) and a gardener who accidentally
witnessed the deed; he has then changed clothes with the latter and
thrown the body into 'a piece of water in the grounds' (ch. 1). Since
that time no one but Rudge's wife has ever seen him, and he is believed
to be dead. The consequence of this murder has been to transfix several
persons in time, to bind them permanently to the past. The murderer's
son, born at the Warren on the day of the murder (apparently just
after his mother learned the truth of the matter), is an idiot, imprisoned
in the timeless past; he will never grow or change, and bears in his

countenance a shadow of that horrible deed which took place on the day of his birth. It is as if he were murdered then too, and in the eyes of his murderer-father he seems 'a creature who had sprung into existence from his victim's blood' (ch. 69). The surviving Haredale brother is also bound in the past; he has spent twenty-two years at the Warren doing nothing except wait for the murderer to return. He is a decent man, but altogether in the grip of a mania for revenge. 'Nothing but the evidence of his own senses could satisfy that gloomy thirst for retribution which had been gathering upon him for so many years' (ch. 76). When the revenge is accomplished and Haredale has seen Rudge hanged, he finds he is still not liberated from the past, and suddenly recognizes this as having to do with his obsessive and unbending character.

> I sometimes think, that if I had to live my life once more, I might amend this fault – not so much, I discover when I search my mind, for the love of what is right, as for my own sake. But even when I make these better resolutions, I instinctively recoil from the idea of suffering again what I have undergone; and in this circumstance I find the unwelcome assurance that I should still be the same man, though I could cancel the past, and begin anew, with its experience to guide me. (ch. 79)

Heyling has again had his revenge, but this time it has made very little difference. It has, however, brought home the bitter truth of how ineffaceable the past is. The possibly more bitter knowledge that this truth does not alleviate the desire to eradicate the past is demonstrated with incomparable force in the scenes in which the Warren and Newgate are burned down.

In Rudge, the murderer, this theme comes into new focus. For Barnaby and his mother, and for Haredale, he personifies the past: he is the shadow cast across their daily lives, and wherever they go he haunts them (ch. 6), a grisly version of Claudius as Hamlet's ghost.[20] Rudge too is immobilized by the past; during the twenty years since he murdered his master, the owner of the Warren, he has been reliving the act, returning frequently to the site of the murder, where he shows up at the exact moment that the Warren is being burned to the ground and the alarm bell his victim rang is ringing again. In that terrible scene he rehearses the deed once more, stabbing at the phantom that has never left him (ch. 55). Finally captured amid the ruins of the Warren, he is taken to prison.

With these two embodiments of the past – the Maypole Inn and the Warren – Dickens established the principle of opposition and analogy on which the novel turns. First, there is a vision of the idyllic past, which has come to be dominated by tyrannic and imbecile authority. Adjacent to this is the secret, mouldering past in which all order and authority have been overthrown by the ultimate act of rebellion, murder. Life in either situation is intolerable: to submit to old John's authority is to be stifled in infancy; to destroy all authority, as Rudge did, is to become accursed. (These representations constitute a reversal of their counterparts in *The Old Curiosity Shop.*) But Dickens did something else in *Barnaby Rudge* which he had never quite done so clearly before. He reproduced and reinterpreted these local personal conflicts in the general social ones which in the last half of the story become the novel's chief concern.

In the several motives of the chief conspirators, in their varying ideas of the purpose of Gordon's campaign, these contradictory attitudes toward the past and authority reappear.[21] Sim Tappertit, for example, seems altogether confused. Habitually, he speaks of 'an altered state of society' (ch. 39) and wants to be thought of as a wild-eyed radical. At the same time all his notions of Utopia are retrospective:

> the 'prentices had, in times gone by, had frequent holidays of right, broken people's heads by scores, defied their masters, nay, even achieved some glorious murders in the streets, which privileges had gradually been wrested from them . . . the degrading checks imposed upon them were unquestionably attributable to the innovating spirit of the times, and . . . they united to resist all change, except such change as would restore those good old English customs. . . . After illustrating the wisdom of going backward, by reference to that sagacious fish, the crab . . . he described their general objects; which were briefly vengeance on their Tyrant Masters . . . and the restoration, as aforesaid, of their ancient rights and holidays. (ch. 8)

In Dennis this disordered notion of politics is restated in another way. He is willing to hang anyone and everyone in order to preserve the constitution, to destroy society in order to preserve authority.

> Parliament says 'If any man, woman, or child, does anything again any one of them fifty acts, that man, woman, or child, shall be worked off by Dennis.' George the Third steps in when they number very strong at the

end of a sessions, and says 'These are too many for Dennis. I'll have half
for *myself* and Dennis shall have half for *himself*;' and sometimes he throws
me in one over that I don't expect. . . . Well! That being the law and
the practice of England, is the glory of England, ain't it. . . . If these
Papists gets into power, and begins to boil and roast instead of hang, what
becomes of my work; if they touch my work that's a part of so many
laws, what becomes of the laws in general, what becomes of the religion,
what becomes of the country! (ch. 37)

Dennis cannot conceive of himself apart from his occupation, his
'sound, Protestant, constitutional, English work' (ch. 37), and he is
certain that the existence of the nation is continuous with his work.
His energies, his very identity, are committed to 'the great main object
of preserving the Old Bailey in all its purity, and the gallows in all
its pristine usefulness and moral grandeur' (ch. 70). He resembles no
one else in the novel so much as he does old John Willet; both of
them entrench their lives in order, authority and the preservation of
the past.

In Gordon these attitudes take a still more abberrant course. Gordon
is also in search of certain authority and finds it in the only place it
ever existed, in the long-since cancelled past. He dreams that he has
become a Jew (ch. 37) and finally becomes one (ch. 82). The puritan,
seeking absolute sanction, returns to the original source. Yet in the
course of that return he forms an alliance with his apparent antithesis,
Hugh. When Dennis cries 'No Popery', Hugh responds with 'No
Property' (ch. 38). Dominated by the impulse to level and obliterate,
Hugh is a latter-day Jack Cade, and Dickens drew part of his original
idea of him directly out of *Henry VI*. Like Cade, Hugh is the unwitting
instrument of another man; both of them are illegitimate; Cade was
born 'under a hedge', and Hugh has lived in a ditch (ch. 23); both are
fearless and indifferent to pain; Stafford calls Cade a groom, and Hugh
is an hostler; Cade intends to break open the jails, burn the records of
the realm, and destroy property – 'Henceforward all things shall be in
common'; both are illiterate and detest literacy; and like the leading
rioters in *Barnaby Rudge*, Cade proclaims that he is engaged in the
recovery and restoration of ancient freedoms.[22] Although Hugh is the
companion in arms of Dennis and Sim and Gordon, he has no inclination to reinstate the constitution or any older social authority. His
hatred of everything established – rank, institutions, customs – consti-
tutes his violence and rebelliousness.

In representing the characters of these individuals as a combination of malice, reactionary impulse and general resentment of whatever is, Dickens, in a curious way, characterized a quality of English radical movements. From the Peasants' Revolt and the Pilgrimage of Grace to the Luddite Riots and the Chartists, popular radical protest tended habitually to base its objections to a current law or condition on the ground that it was an infringement of some previously established one, and to demand that antecedent justice be restored.[23] Cobbett, for example, rested all his arguments against the Poor Law amendment on the assumption that the original act of 1601 was immutably valid;[24] and the widespread and obdurate resistance to that amendment was generally supported by the argument that the suspended form of relief was a right which had to be restored. This style of thinking was also common among the Chartists. The manifesto of the Chartist Convention of 1839 declared: 'The principles of our Charter were the laws and customs of our ancestors, under which property was secure and the working people happy and contented.' And they further stated that one of their objects was the defense of 'the laws and constitutional privileges' descended to them from their ancestors.[25]

It is fairly evident that Dickens had it in mind to distinguish between these outbursts and the French Revolution. *Barnaby Rudge* entertains no question of natural rights, nor does it contemplate a change in the structure of politics or the character of society. It is charged, nonetheless, with confusion and oppression, with a sense that communication with authority has become almost impossible, that social authority is insanely self-contradictory, and that the convulsive violence of the riots somehow expresses the true nature of the institutions against which they are turned. The squire (and justice of the peace) who would like to flog Barnaby into sanity is called by some

'a country gentleman of the true school', by some 'a fine old country gentleman', by some 'a sporting gentleman', by some 'a thorough-bred Englishman', by some 'a genuine John Bull'; but they all agreed in one respect, and that was, that it was a pity there were not more like him, and that because there were not, the country was going to rack and ruin every day. . . . He had no seat in Parliament himself, but he was extremely patriotic, and usually drove his voters up to the poll with his own hands. He was warmly attached to church and state, and never appointed to the living in his gift any but a three-bottle man and a first-rate fox-hunter. (ch. 47)

This moral imbecile (he later testifies to Barnaby's competence) represents the 'majesty' of institutions (ch. 51). It is this man who has, so
to speak, the power of calling out the Guards and whom, as much as
anyone else, the Guards defend.[26] At the same time his ideas are identical with both John Willet's and Dennis's. And were Sim in his place,
had Sim his institutional authority, he too would behave in quite
the same way. Parliament, the embodiment of institutional sovereignty,
does not seem much better. It extends its protection to Chester, relieves
him of pecuniary distress, and safeguards his career of knavery. It also
protects itself, Chester, and others, from the mob, the creature for
whose existence Parliament is finally responsible: 'the very scum and
refuse of London, whose growth was fostered by bad criminal laws,
bad prison regulations, and the worst conceivable police' (ch. 49).

The prospect which such considerations call up, the depths of
contradiction they uncover, without suggesting any solution, are
enough to make the most tough-minded recoil. Dickens did recoil,
into indecision and equivocation, and felt obliged to represent the
Happy Warrior, General Conway, holding the mob at bay outside
of Parliament and declaring 'I am a soldier, you may tell them, and I
will protect the freedom of this place with my sword' (ch. 49). A
similar unresolved contradiction in the novel is to be found in its
handling of the law. By nature the mob is both lawless and destructive
of law; one of its first undertakings is the sack of Lord Mansfield's
house, whence follows this passage: 'Worse than all, because nothing
could replace this loss [was the destruction of] the great Law Library,
on almost every page of which were notes in the Judge's own hand,
of inestimable value – being the results of the study and experience of
his whole life' (ch. 66). It is as if Buzfuz, Nupkins, Fang, Dodson and
Fogg, and the whole scurvy crew had pitched their wigs out the
window, turned in their gowns for gaiters, taken subscriptions to the
Westminster Review, and founded a society for legal aid to the poor.
But of course as soon as the riots are finally suppressed the law sets
out to apply some of the results of that lifetime's experience: 'When
the dignity of the law had been so flagrantly outraged, its dignity must
be asserted. The symbol of its dignity – stamped upon every page of
the criminal statute-book – was the gallows; and Barnaby was to die'
(ch. 76). And with decisive irony Dickens represents the huge crowd
that gathers before Newgate to witness the hangings as, again, the mob.
Here it is orderly and under control, but the emotions that shudder

through it, the desires for violence and annihilation, are the emotions of the rioting mob. On this occasion, however, these are being manipulated by authority and institutions.

There are some critics who seem to think that the problem that lies at the center of *Barnaby Rudge* is so easily understood that Dickens had no moral right to his equivocation and confusion. But they disregard the fact that the nineteenth century was presided over by the most important revolt against authority in human history. No part of civilized European life was unshaken by it and in a sense the history of the century is the record of an interminable series of efforts to deal with the new conceptions of authority that issued from the experience of the French Revolution. In Dickens's particular instance, what seems to have happened is that by 1841 his original imagination of authority and his original relation to it have undergone disruption. To be sure, he started out with a divided vision: Pickwick, Brownlow and the Cheerybles were representations of authority who could exercise their power benevolently only because they were generally detached from society and opposed to certain of its essential values and authorities. Institutional authority, on the other hand, was something to be avoided and resisted, to have the smallest possible stake in, and finally to flee. As I have argued, *The Old Curiosity Shop* was in part a final, violent attempt simultaneously to escape from society and to sustain the notion of an authority independent of it. In *Barnaby Rudge* escape is impossible, and the conflicts which the riots represent are unmistakably recreated in the novel's personal relations.

II

Essentially, *Barnaby Rudge* contemplates only one kind of personal relation – that of father and son. The novel presents five filial pairs. Each of them suffers from a profound disorder, and in each a father and a son confront one another in a dispute over power and authority. The experience of each filial pair illuminates and modifies the others, rendering with surprising subtlety and complexity Dickens's idea of the relation as a nexus of irreconcilable conflict. Taken together these relations depict in an unusually relevant and concrete way Dickens's heightened consciousness that something has gone wrong with the values by which men live.

Let us begin with the simplest of these relations – though it is simple
only in the sense that direct insight into the truth of experience is
sometimes simple. Sim Tappertit is to Gabriel Varden what Sam
Weller was to Pickwick. Yet Sim cannot acquiesce in the authority
of his master's station. He cannot because nature has deprived him of
the possibility of ever achieving true manhood. Though he is not
actually deformed, Sim is 'thin-faced, sleek-haired, sharp-nosed, small-
eyed', stands just above five feet, and is the leanest and least attractive
of figures. Nevertheless, within his humiliated body there is 'locked
up an ambitious and aspiring soul' (ch. 4). What Sim aspires to is
power, primarily sexual power. We recognize this aspiration in the
marvelous and pitiful play he makes of admiring, in his cracked
fragment of looking-glass, the size and shapeliness of his little legs:
'If they're a dream . . . let sculptures have such wisions, and chisel
'em out when they wake. This is reality. Sleep has no such limbs as
them' (ch. 31). We recognize it in the fantasy of the power to subdue
beautiful women and dumb animals that Sim imagines his eyes to
possess. But we recognize as well that Sim's legs are sticks, that his eye
is dull, and that he knows this too and suffers from the knowledge.
Without putting any fine construction on it – since Dickens did not
– Sim feels that he has been castrated, and by Varden, his 'master',
whose easy-going robustness does nothing but aggravate Sim's sense
of general grievance, and whose buxom daughter Dolly hopelessly
inflames Sim's lust. The revolutionary society of apprentices is Sim's
invention, having taken 'origin in his own teeming brain, stimulated
by a swelling sense of wrong and outrage' (ch. 8). Sim's object in this
regard, and the immediate connection Dickens establishes between
Sim's sense of having been cheated of manhood and his political
activity, appear in his first overt act of rebellion, his forgery of Varden's
master-key. Altogether aware of what he was about, Dickens conceives
this with what one can only call shameless brilliance; the 'clumsy
large-sized key', which Sims draws from 'the right hand, or rather
right leg pocket of his smalls' (ch. 18) represents the power he wants
to take and such power as he has already taken from his master. The
key gives him a secret power of entry and exit to Varden's house,
emancipating the apprentice every night to become the captain of his
band of 'Prentice Knights.[27]

Yet Sim is destined to be brought back to his humiliation. He has
been observed by the admiring Miggs, who expresses her yearning

for him by calling him a boy – 'she invariably affected to regard all male bipeds under thirty as mere chits and infants' (ch. 9) – and who responds to Sim's desire for masculinity by filling the keyhole with coal-dust. Thus, it is Sim's remorseless fate to attract to himself a woman whose instinctive response to men is to deny their manhood, to be confronted in the most painful way with the image of himself he dreads most. He shivers in 'her chaste, but spider-like embrace' (ch. 51), and when she is seized by excitement or passion and begins panting for breath, and laying her hand against her heart, he notices with distaste what 'was most apparent under such circumstances . . . her deficiency of outline' (ch. 22). But Sim's classic chastisement is completed and his destiny of perpetual humiliation fulfilled when, toward the end of the riots, he suffers a catastrophe that might almost have been predicted: his legs, 'the pride and glory of his life, the comfort of his existence . . . [are] crushed into shapeless ugliness' (ch. 71); and after his legs have been amputated and he has been supplied with wooden ones, he finds he must 'stump back to his old master, and beg for some relief'. The relief is in fact no relief at all: 'By the locksmith's advice and aid, he was established as a shoe-black' (ch. 82). Subsequently, he marries a woman who treats him – as one might expect.

In another instance of personal rebellion, Joe Willett turns against his father, but the conditions which induce Joe's insubordination are in every way more justifiable than Sim's. Joe's situation reproduces in objective fact Sim's subjective imagination of his own. Joe is a 'strapping young fellow of twenty, whom it pleased his father still to consider a little boy, and to treat accordingly' (ch. 1). At the same time, old John is convinced that the world has run downhill since his own youth: 'The world's undergone a nice alteration since my time, certainly. My belief is that there an't any boys left . . . that there's nothing now between a male baby and a man – and that all the boys went out with his blessed Majesty King George the Second' (ch. 1). He harrasses and constrains his son in the name of the authority of tradition, the same rationale, we recall, by which Dennis justifies his desire to destroy society. And it is exactly this kind of ambiguity – enlisting identical arguments in the service of opposite, or ostensibly opposite, purposes – which gives *Barnaby Rudge* its peculiar, though abstract, density.

Varden, recognizing that the dissension between Joe Willett and his father is serious, offers 'coherent and sensible advice to both parties, urging John Willett to remember that Joe was nearly arrived at man's estate, and should not be ruled with too tight a hand, and exhorting Joe himself to bear with his father's caprices, and rather endeavour to turn them aside by temperate remonstrance than by ill-timed rebellion' (ch. 3). But they cannot compose their difference:

> Old John having long encroached . . . on the liberty of Joe . . . grew so despotic and so great, that his thirst for conquest knew no bounds. The more young Joe submitted, the more absolute old John became . . . and on went old John in the pleasantest manner possible, trimming off an exuberance in this place, shearing away some liberty of speech or action in that, and conducting himself in his small way with as much high mightiness and majesty, as the most glorious tyrant that ever had his statue reared in the public ways . . . his Maypole cronies . . . would shake their heads and say that Mr Willet was a father of the good old English sort; that there were no new-fangled notions or modern ways in him; that he put them in mind of what their fathers were when they were boys . . . that it would be well for the country if there were more like him. . . . (ch. 30)

Their relation, Dickens seems to imply throughout the novel, is perhaps innately discordant, founded on antipathy. Indeed, in many ways *Barnaby Rudge* seems to pose the question of whether there may not exist in personal life and in society certain relations of conflict, injustice and suffering which are not susceptible to reconciliation. The energies that are opposed to one another and the issues they encompass are those we recognize as pertaining to the conduct of power – personal and sexual power, social and political power. In *Barnaby Rudge*, Dickens regards these energies as being at every point thwarted, diverted from their proper objects, and turned aside into violent and self-destroying courses.

Under such conditions, Varden's counsel is empty wisdom indeed. Persistently followed it would be a counsel of despair. Joe cannot go on living without asserting his personal will and independence; but old John's principal satisfaction in life consists in degrading and humiliating his son. Moreover, old John's presumptions of omnipotence are not the simple by-products of his preternatural slowness of wit; somewhere amid his unregenerate perceptions is an instinct of fear – that his son's manhood will someday bring about the loss of his own. Were old John to recognize the validity of Joe's claim to maturity he would also have to recognize that his authority as a father is neither unconditional nor eternal. His apprehensions in this regard are also behind his desire to exist outside of time, in a literal Eden.

As in Eden, it is in connection with sexuality that the crisis between the Willets finally breaks out. Old John has characteristically dealt with it by exclusion and denial: 'He looked with no favourable eye upon young girls, but rather considered that they and the whole female sex were a kind of nonsensical mistake on the part of Nature' (ch. 21). When Chester informs him that Joe has been acting as an intermediary between Edward, Chester's son, and Emma Haredale, old John takes up his cue. 'I know my duty. We want no love-making here, sir, unbeknown to parents', which is to say we want no love-making, and old John combines his 'strong desire to run counter to the unfortunate Joe' with 'his opposition as a general principle to all matters of love and matrimony' (ch. 29). And when he subsequently arraigns Joe in public, he commits a final violation of his son's masculine dignity. ' "You're the boy, sir," added John, collaring with one hand, and aiding the effect of a farewell bow to the visitor with the other, "that wants to sneak into houses, and stir up differences between noble gentlemen and their sons. . . . Hold your tongue, sir." ' This is 'the crowning circumstance of his degradation' (ch. 30), and Joe, goaded beyond endurance, explodes, knocks one of his father's cronies into a heap of spitoons and runs away to join the army, that brutal proving-ground of masculinity.

The crisis of old Willet's relation to his son is consummated in the spectacle of the Gordon riots. Driven by pandemic, ruthless fury against all authority, the rioters break into the Maypole and wreck it, destroying all those precious objects which old John has thought of as proof of his unassailable power, and, as a final outrage, they saw down the Maypole itself and thrust it through the shattered windows of the bar.[28] Old John's authority is thus violently wrested from him, and he is rendered not merely impotent but inanimate. While the bar is being sacked 'he said nothing, and thought nothing', observes 'the destruction of his property, as if it were some queer play or entertainment, of an astonishing and stupefying nature, but having no reference to himself – that he could make out – at all' (ch. 54). The irony of this retribution lies in its becoming a fulfillment. It gives old John what he has always wanted: to be delivered from time and change. 'John saw this desolation, and yet saw it not. He was perfectly contented to sit there, staring at it, and felt no more indignation or discomfort in his bonds than if they had been robes of honour. So far as he was personally concerned, old Time lay snoring, and the world stood still' (ch. 55). For those rare moments in which John does recognize what has happened, Dickens maintains a perfect balance of pathos and rigor. For example, John looks about the bar, seeking dimly to understand: 'And then a great, round, leaden-looking, and not at all transparent tear, came rolling out of each eye, and he said, as he shook his head: "If they'd only had the goodness to murder me, I'd have thanked 'em kindly" ' (ch. 56). One cannot conceive of a finer touch than that opaque, congealed tear.

As for Joe, he returns from the American War without his left arm, but it is a loss which does not merely represent a punishment for having presumed to rebel against his father. Dickens has made it quite clear in the course of the Willets's conflict that Joe's rebellion was inevitable and necessary, and that the conditions which made it so bring about his disfigurement. Yet old John, in his mist of stupefaction, seems to believe that Joe's mutilation is somehow self-imposed, and makes no connection between himself and what his son has undergone until just before he dies. Dickens thus withholds what would in this instance have been a cheap rectitude, the satisfaction of confronting a parent with the ugly proof of his guilt. The sins of the fathers in *Barnaby Rudge* are brought to retribution, but none of the sons enjoys the luxury of revenge. Joe returns to nurse his idiot father, who can only stare at his son's stump of an arm and like a cracked record repeat: 'It was took off in the defence of the Salwanners in America where the war is' (ch. 72), and whose dying words falter in a poignant, reflexive irony: 'I'm a-going, Joseph . . . to the Salwanners' (ch. 82).

We find a third maimed son in Barnaby, whose life has been blighted by his father even before he was born. Barnaby's 'blindness of intellect' destines him to remain forever a child, forever dependent on parental or adult authority. Like Nell, like Abel Garland, he will never grow up or grow old (ch. 17). But Barnaby's grace of affliction is more affliction than it is grace. He bears on his countenance a look of convulsed fear, and in his manner there is a constant restlessness, both of which he has inherited from his father. His dress is equally expressive of 'the disorder of his mind'.

> His dress was of green, clumsily trimmed here and there – apparently by his own hands – with gaudy lace. . . . A pair of tawdry ruffles dangled

at his wrists, while his throat was nearly bare. He had ornamented his hat
with a cluster of peacock's feathers, but they were limp and broken, and
now trailed negligently down his back. Girt to his side was the steel hilt
of an old sword without blade or scabbard; and some parti-coloured ends
of ribands and poor glass toys completed the ornamental portion of his
attire. (ch. 3)

In Dickens's conception of Barnaby we recognize something of the
Holy Fool, and something more of Tom o' Bedlam – the influence of
King Lear on this novel is, in fact, of considerable interest. We sense
also, and very markedly, the presence of Wordsworth – the Idiot Boy
and his pony, the child of the mad mother in 'Her Eyes are Wild',
poor, slighted Ruth and her wild lover from the 'green savannahs',
and Margaret, who dreads 'the rustling of the grass' and senses in 'the
very shadows of the clouds' a power that shakes and frightens her.[29]

Like Smike, Barnaby is pursued by his father. He dreams of being
followed by 'something – it was in the shape of a man . . . came
softly after me – wouldn't let me be – but was always hiding and
crouching, like a cat in dark corners, waiting till I should pass' (ch. 6).
And like Smike he is haunted by a dream of a certain room in which
some terrible violence has been done (ch. 17). But Barnaby is not
simply the innocent, helpless victim of his father; and the mark of
Cain which he bears suggests that at this moment Dickens's feelings
about the violated child and the avenging son have been brought
closer together. Indeed, Barnaby, who has never seen his father, first
encounters him in an accidental and violent collision on the road
(ch. 17) – as Oedipus encountered Laius. They grapple with each other,
and after the murderer has escaped, Barnaby begins in turn to hunt
him down, seeking to capture him and have him hanged at Tyburn.
Imitating the robber for his mother, Barnaby, who resembles his
father, appears 'so like the original he counterfeited, that the dark
figure peering out behind him might have passed for his own shadow'
(ch. 17). He is in fact his father's double, just as Oliver was, but though
he is an innocent victim, he has inherited something of the nature of
his violator.

In Barnaby's nature, innocence alternates with generalized emotions
of anger, vindictiveness and violence, and his innocence is of course
qualified by them. He is capable of behavior whose consequences are
indistinguishable from those which proceed from calculated wickedness. This notion is suggested with poetic economy in Dickens's

description of Barnaby walking guard with his flag-staff outside the
stable in which Hugh and Dennis lie:

> the careful arrangement of his poor dress, and his erect and lofty bearing,
> showed how high a sense he had of the great importance of his trust, and
> how happy and how proud it made him. To Hugh and his companion who
> lay in a dark corner of the gloomy shed, he, and the sunlight, and the
> peaceful Sabbath sound to which he made response, seemed like a bright
> picture framed by the door, and set off by the stable's blackness. The whole
> formed such a contrast to themselves, as they lay wallowing, like some
> obscene animals, in their squalor and wickedness on the two heaps of
> straw, that for a few moments they looked on without speaking, and felt
> almost ashamed. (ch. 52)

For Barnaby is the unwitting ally of those creatures in the stable,
having no way of knowing they are wicked, and he is as much at
home with them and the mob as he is with his mother and Varden.
Indeed, when the soldiers come to arrest him, he retreats out of the
sunlight into the darkness of the stable and strikes at them furiously
until he is subdued (ch. 57).

The other side of this ambivalence is brought to its most dramatic
expression in the scene in Newgate when father and son meet yet once
more. As soon as Barnaby recognizes the murderer, he springs at him
and tries to bear him to the ground; when the murderer finds himself
overpowered, he tells Barnaby who he is, and Barnaby, at the point
of extreme violence, falls back and then springs at him once more to
embrace him in spontaneous affection (ch. 62). But no reconciliation
is possible. Though Barnaby reaches out with a poignant impulse of
love toward the person who has injured him most, Rudge remains
'an unyielding, obdurate man . . . in the savage terror of his condition
he had hardened, rather than relented' (ch. 76), and goes to his death
execrating his wife and son as his enemies. There are, Dickens is clearly
saying, some ravages of experience which cannot be patched up, which
neither love nor good-will nor submissiveness repair. In this relation,
as in those of Sim and the Willets, the contradictions are essentially
intransigent and immutable.

Nor is there, in *Barnaby Rudge*, any relief in the idyllic vision of life.
Barnaby is capable of this vision and of achieving the state it comprehends only by virtue of his defects. He is able to feel regenerated
by the unity of being he finds in nature only because he exists outside
of time, and has no memory, and all experience comes to him afresh

(ch. 45). Psychically, he already inhabits an idyllic world, like old John, but in this novel Dickens connects that world with Barnaby's kind of incompleteness, and with his incapacity for ever developing. Dickens makes it perfectly clear that Barnaby can envision these happy scenes only because his senses are unable to encompass actuality. 'The sun went down, and night came on, and he was still quite tranquil; busied with these thoughts, as if there were no other people in the world, and the dull cloud of smoke hanging on the immense city in the distance, hid no vices, no crimes, no life or death, or cause of disquiet – nothing but clear air' (ch. 68). When Barnaby and his mother are discovered in their rural retreat by Rudge's agent Stagg, the blind man, and Mrs Rudge despairingly cries that now they are finally lost, Stagg calmly replies 'Not lost, widow . . . only found' (ch. 45).

Barnaby, moreover, is not isolated from the daily world as Nell was, but is placed at the center of it; and Barnaby's innocence is exposed to that order of experience least susceptible to it – politics. In politics, innocence often counts for less than nothing. For innocence has the power of grace only in a society informed by the moral authority of love, and politics is neither inspired nor informed by that moral authority. Moreover, in *Barnaby Rudge* that microcosm of politics, the family, has also become estranged from that authority. In this novel Dickens sees rebellion and irresponsibility in the political life of a people as concomitant with rebellion and irresponsibility in its filial relationships.

This irresponsibility and its consequences, the major theme of *Barnaby Rudge*, are most fully elaborated in the relation between Mr Chester and his two sons, Edward and Hugh. Chester deliberately manipulates his sons in the service of his personal interests and justifies his behavior by referring it to the 'natural' morality of the filial relationship: 'If there is anything real in this world, it is those amazingly fine feelings and those natural obligations which must subsist between father and son . . . on every ground of moral and religious feeling. . . . The relationship between father and son, you know, is positively quite a holy kind of bond' (ch. 12). Chester is another of Dickens's prodigal parents. He has squandered his fortune and has determined in consequence that Edward will redeem the family's straitened circumstances by marrying an heiress – a marriage which will of course enable Edward to secure his father 'a genteel provision in the autumn of life' (ch. 12). Chester regards the primary natural obligation of his son to be 'the preservation of that gentility and becoming pride' (ch. 32) which Edward has inherited from him. And were Edward, like Nicholas Nickleby, a dutiful son, he would doubtless consider his father's improvidence as a small matter when put beside the value of this inheritance. Since apparently he does not, Chester demands absolute authority over his son, and when he learns of Edward's secret courtship of Emma he contrives to thwart it and expose his son to humiliation in her presence.

Dickens must almost certainly have had in mind Gloucester and his two sons – the 'legitimate Edgar' and nature's servant, Edmund – when he conceived Chester and his. Edward's first appearance in the novel, involving an incident which recalls a similar one in *King Lear*, reveals him to be a victimized and defenseless young man: having gone out at night without a weapon to protect himself he has been attacked in the street and stabbed. And in his relation with his father Edward manifests a similar state of vulnerability and defeat. Like Sim and Joe, Edward feels humiliated by his father, but, unlike them, he is quite conscious of his impotence. Having been bred to expectations of fortune and leisure, he cannot easily accommodate himself to his father's revelation about his future. 'I have been, as the phrase is, liberally educated, and am fit for nothing. I find myself at last wholly dependent upon you, with no resource but in your favour' (ch. 15). Although he 'cannot bear this absolute dependence', he is at the same time reluctant to resist, or even to protest his father's commands: 'If I seem to speak too plainly now, it is, believe me father, in the hope that there may be a franker spirit, a worthier reliance, and a kinder confidence between us in time to come' (ch. 15). Even a parent less determined upon coercion than Chester might be justified in turning a deaf ear on so limp an utterance. Edward's weakness merely provokes Chester into pressing harder against him, and again he insists on the supreme value of what he has given to his son – his station in society and an education to prepare him for it – and concludes: 'Having done that, my dear fellow, I consider that I have provided for you in life, and rely upon your doing something to provide for me in return' (ch. 15). The son finds himself absolutely dependent on a father who is tyrannically bent on foisting his own dependence on his son. By demanding that Edward provide for him – that his son become the father, so to speak, and himself the child – Chester is preventing his son from becoming a man. The relation of Sam and Tony Weller is now standing on its head.

At one point, Edward's response to his father's canny wickedness is to sit in a corner, 'with his head resting on his hands, in what appeared to be a kind of stupor' (ch. 15), much like the stupefaction of Smike. But when his father presses on, bidding him remember 'your interest, your duty, your moral obligations, your filial affections, and all that sort of thing which it is so very delightful and charming to reflect upon', the crisis is reached and Edward rises to the occasion just enough to answer that 'it is sad when a son, proferring . . . his love and duty in their best and truest sense, finds himself repelled at every turn, and forced to disobey' (ch. 32). Chester then curses and disowns his son, and Edward wanders vaguely off into exile for five years – to the West Indies, where, we are asked to believe, he makes his fortune (ch. 78). His disobedience has come as close to non-resistance as such things can. Nevertheless, Edward finally gets what he deserves – Emma Haredale, who is just about as alive as he. Because in his extreme situation he continues to behave out of regard for the copybook maxims and Varden's advice, Edward, of all the sons in the novel, seems the most depressed, violated, and hopelessly unmanned.[30]

Once again Dickens associates this static and depressed condition with an undercurrent of fear about age and loss of masculinity, as Chester's desire to be supported by his son implies. When Edward opens a conversation by addressing him as 'father', he quickly replies: 'don't call me by that obsolete and ancient name. Have some regard for delicacy. Am I grey, or wrinkled, do I go on crutches, have I lost my teeth, that you adopt such a mode of address' (ch. 32). And when after five years the novel picks up with Chester again, Dickens remarks that he has not changed at all: 'the complexion, quite juvenile in its bloom and clearness; the same smile . . . everything as it used to be: no mark of age or passion, envy, hate, or discontent: all unruffled and serene, and quite delightful to behold' (ch. 40). Like John Willet, he remains untouched by time, unmarked by either its sheer physical erosions or by his own flagrant conspiracy to deny manhood to both his sons, pit them against each other, and use them for his own purposes. Edward and Hugh, like Oliver and Monks, like Edgar and Edmund, are (one expects this from Dickens by now) each other's counterparts; and in undertaking to turn them against each other and to ruin them both, Chester is enacting the disorder and corruption in the conduct of authority which is enacted on every other level of the novel.

More than anyone else in *Barnaby Rudge*, Chester's bastard son Hugh seems justified in his hatred of authority, for he is a victim of its meanest and most arbitrary inequities. All he knows of his father is that he was a gentleman. His mother, a handsome gypsy deserted and left destitute by her lover, was lured into passing forged notes and promptly apprehended (ch. 75). 'I was a boy of six – that's not very old – when they hung my mother up at Tyburn for a couple of thousand men to stare at' (ch. 23). The boy's mongrel dog 'was the only living thing except me that howled that day. . . . Out of the two thousand odd – there was a larger crowd for its being a woman – the dog and I alone had any pity. If he'd have been a man, he'd have been glad to be quit of her, for she had been forced to keep him lean and half-starved; but being a dog, and not having a man's sense, he was sorry' (ch. 23). Hugh was then 'turned loose', and managed somehow to survive, at first by minding cows and frightening birds, later by tending horses, and then becoming hostler at the Maypole.

More than a Jack Cade or even an Edmund, there is a side of Hugh that resembles Barnardine in *Measure for Measure* – 'a dreadful idle vagrant fellow . . . always sleeping in the sun in summer, and in the straw in winter time' (ch. 10). He is, like Shakespeare's character, ultimately indifferent to his own existence:

> it will soon be all over with you and me; and I'd as soon die as live, or live as die. Why should I trouble myself to have revenge on you? To eat, and drink, and go to sleep, as long as I stay here, is all I care for. If there was but a little more sun to bask in, than can find its way into this cursed place, I'd lie in it all day, and not trouble myself to sit or stand up once. That's all the care I have for myself. Why should I care for *you*? (ch. 74)[31]

John Willet sums up the character in which Hugh is held by society: ' "that chap that can't read or write, and has never lived in any way but like the animals he has lived among, *is* a animal. And," said Mr Willet, arriving at his logical conclusion, "is to be treated accordingly" ' (ch. 11). And so he is, by everyone except Barnaby. Old John personifies the general belief when he remarks, 'If he has any soul at all . . . it must be such a very small one that it don't signify what he does' (ch. 12).

The single loyalty and identification in Hugh's life is to be found in his feeling for his mother. From the beginning he has an apprehension that her fate awaits him, and when it finally does come he greets it as his inheritance (ch. 74). Cast out of society, abandoned, relegated to the stable, denied a claim to humanity and a place in human life, he is a very different kind of Oliver Twist. Civilization itself rejects Hugh, and he of course remains uncivilized; society outlaws him, and he remains lawless; humanity rejects him, and he becomes inhuman. He is a creature of the forest, and appears plunging through the bushes (ch. 20); he is a centaur and a 'handsome satyr' (ch. 21); he is 'Maypole Hugh', who in the scene during which Willet and Chester agree that there will be no love-making, climbs nimbly to the top of the maypole, spins John's wig about on the weather-cock, and slides down again with 'inconceivable rapidity' (ch. 29). Hugh is Dionysus, whom society has denied, whose existence it tries to negate, and his exclusion from any place in it is one of the principal symptoms of its disorder. He is Dionysian in his love of physical intoxication, and in the brutal ecstasy of release that drunkenness brings to him (chs. 23, 59). He represents that primitive energy which if it is denied sooner or later breaks out in a rage of rebellion and cruelty which threatens to destroy the persons and institutions that deny it. It is Hugh who leads the sacking of the Maypole Inn, who burns down the Warren, and whose idea it is to destroy 'every jail in London. They shall have no place to put their prisoners in. We'll burn them all down; make bonfires of them everyone' (ch. 60). And like Quilp, he is an embodiment of feral, uncivilized sexual energy, though Hugh's sexuality is neither infantile nor generalized. It is direct, impetuous and peremptory, and the violence always latent in it terrifies Dolly, a girl not easily frightened (ch. 21). When he appears during the riots, as a figure 'who wielded an axe in his right hand, and bestrode a brewer's horse of great size and strength, caparisoned with fetters taken out of Newgate', leading the mob and 'dashing on as though he bore a charmed life . . . proof against ball and powder' (ch. 67), he might be Dionysus in his aspect of brutish destroyer, or a strikingly deformed version of the hero, of Perseus or St George.[32]

It is perfectly clear that behind the kind of representation Dickens achieves in Hugh are not only Shakespeare and romanticism, but an ageless popular tradition of tales of wild and savage men. But it is also evident that Dickens is very much on his own, that he commands his own unique medium and mode of presentation, and that with *Barnaby*

Rudge he had begun to move in regions of feeling and awareness where, in his own age, he was virtually alone. In Dickens's time there was no current vocabulary, there were no accessible terms – which is to say there were no adequate conceptions – for articulating the new experiences that were coming in upon him with such impact. Dickens invented them, and altered the nature of expression in English literature.

It was this power Dickens had of suddenly wresting out of the language a new way of apprehending experience to which Henry James testified. In *A Small Boy and Others*, James recalled his childhood acquaintance with Dickens's novels. He describes 'the force of the Dickens imprint . . . in the soft clay of our generation' as ineffaceable. Dickens entered 'into the blood and bone of our intelligence', and James felt that in reading him he 'had been born, born to a rich awareness, under the very meridian'. Dickens was, he goes on to say, 'the great actuality of the current imagination', an actuality so compelling and pervasive as to lay his audience under a kind of bondage: 'He did too much for us surely ever to leave us free – free of judgment, free of reaction, even should we care to be, which heaven forbid: he laid his hand on us in a way to undermine as in no other case the power of detached appraisement.'[33] Dickens's use of poetic and mythical images, his inclination toward parable and the elaborate, symbolic plot, are inseparable from the intensity and immediacy of registration, the energy of perception, the vivid grasp upon actuality which blaze out almost every moment in his prose.

The quasi-mythical, quasi-heroic vengeance of Hugh, however, ends in bitter irony and failure: he never finds his father, but his father finds and destroys him. That failure leads us to consider another aspect of this remarkable character. Beneath Hugh's destructive impulses exist other impulses and capacities of response which reveal themselves in his behavior toward Sim and Barnaby, the least masculine, most crippled characters in the novel. When Sim puts himself forward as Hugh's superior and leader, Hugh, conscious of the absurdity, responds with a robust and instinctive tact which has nothing to do with the sentiments of pity or condescension.

The bare fact of being patronised by a great man whom he could have crushed with one hand, appeared in his eyes so eccentric and humorous, that a kind of ferocious merriment gained the mastery over him, and quite subdued his brutal nature. He roared and roared again; toasted Mr

Tappertit a hundred times; declared himself a Bull-dog to the core; and vowed to be faithful to him to the last drop of blood in his veins.

All these compliments Mr Tappertit received as matters of course – flattering enough in their way, but entirely attributable to his vast superiority. His dignified self-possession only delighted Hugh the more; and in a word, this giant and the dwarf struck up a friendship which bade fair to be of long continuance, as the one held it to be his right to command, and the other considered it an exquisite pleasantry to obey. (ch. 39)

All Hugh's coarseness and ferocity notwithstanding, no one else in the novel achieves this spontaneity and propriety of response. It is, moreover, no accident that Barnaby and Hugh are close friends; Barnaby's blinded intellect permits him to perceive in Hugh a fellow-creature and friend, 'as if instead of being the rough companion he was, he had been one of the most prepossessing of men'. But if Barnaby only sees Hugh through a glass darkly, Hugh accepts this vision, despite its eccentricity, for what it is. Somehow it is an act of faith. ' "I'm a Turk if he don't give me a warmer welcome than any man of sense," said Hugh, shaking hands with him with a kind of ferocious friendship, strange enough to see' (ch. 53). Of course this affection does not prevent Hugh from snatching Barnaby out of his mother's custody and involving him in the riots, which leads to Barnaby's almost being hanged. But neither does it prevent him from genuine regret for having done so, and it is with perfect justice that Dickens places in Hugh's mouth the reproval of the canting Newgate Ordinary, and that it is Hugh in the guise of a 'savage prophet' who condemns the criminal insensibility – more reprehensible, as he remarks, than his own brutality – which sentences Barnaby to be hanged (ch. 77).

This small but authentic capacity for affection renders Hugh's experiences with his father increasingly poignant and disturbing. In the presence of Chester all Hugh's rampant masculinity, all his outraged energy of self, are neutralized and turned aside. Confronted with Chester's unruffled elegance – his 'cool, complacent, contemptuous, self-possessed reception' of this centaur, 'tainted with the cart and ladder' – Hugh's manhood dissolves. He becomes 'humbled and abashed . . . irresolute and uncertain'. For the first time he feels that his rough speech and negligent manner of dress reveal in him an inferior humanity, that the elegance and comfort of Chester's rooms expose his naked coarseness. 'All these influences,' Dickens goes on to say, 'which have too often some effect on tutored minds and become of almost resistless power when brought to bear on such a mind as his, quelled Hugh completely' (ch. 23). And having told Chester about the incident in which he accosted Dolly, and about the bracelet he took from her, Hugh at once falls into his power. 'The ascendancy which it was the purpose of the man of the world to establish over this savage instrument was gained from that time. Hugh's submission was complete. He dreaded him beyond description; and felt that accident and artifice had spun a web about him, which at a touch from such a masterhand as his, would bind him to the gallows' (ch. 23).

Thus Hugh, like his brother Edward, has become utterly dependent upon his father, and Chester again uses that authority to serve his own interests, which happen to involve his son's destruction. In so far as Chester embodies the values of civilized society and its institutions, he also embodies the full corruption of those values. In so far as the legal authority of society is justified in creating and perpetuating the essential circumstances in Hugh's life, and in so far as its moral authority is concerned to justify the denial and outlawing of what he represents, then Chester's treatment of him follows from that justification. And when, as in *Barnaby Rudge*, society does incline to justify that behavior, and the similar behavior of other fathers and personages in authority, then, Dickens implies, something has gone wrong in the nature of society. The equilibrium of antagonistic needs and desires which it is society's function to maintain – since it cannot reconcile them – is shattered. Civilized authority then tends ineluctably to devolve into privileged oppression. Those energies of life which can never be civilized or fully controlled, which trouble even the best civilizations, which try to divert them, now cease to be even recognized, much less accommodated. The deep discordance of impulses which in *The Old Curiosity Shop* were so distressing to Dickens has become reactivated again in *Barnaby Rudge*, affecting all society now as well as personal life. And, as these impulses are pulled further apart, Dickens saw, they tend to represent themselves as autonomous and self-justifying entities. And so there begins the dreadful, familiar declension: power into will, will into appetite, and appetite, the universal wolf, seconded by will and power, becomes the universal prey that at last eats up itself. The moral becomes the immoral; the amoral becomes the bestial and criminal; fathers emasculate their sons, and rude sons try to strike their fathers dead. The plague of nature, which it was civilization's original purpose to allay, returns as the holocaust of society.

In *Barnaby Rudge* there is no avoiding this bitter irony. It does not matter how many Newgates or Warrens Hugh pillages and burns; he is still being controlled and exploited by the person he most despises yet can never find. Hugh dies unenlightened, the instrument of the man whose victim he has always been. And the malediction he delivers against his father as he is about to be hanged is turned, by its irrelevance to Chester's death, into one more twist of the knife. For Chester dies at the hands of Haredale, who has always treated Hugh with brutal contempt and whom Hugh has always hated. Hugh's revolt brings an intolerable situation to an intolerable fulfillment.

III

Nowhere in *Barnaby Rudge* do we find anything that genuinely suggests reconciliation; nowhere is an understanding arrived at; nowhere are reciprocal concessions brought about. Contradictions in authority are neither resolved nor appeased; they terminate only in exhaustion, defeat, or death. And in this respect the guiding influence of *King Lear* in Dickens's conception of the novel seems especially distinct. Both that supreme work and *Barnaby Rudge* regard as complex and morbid and unnatural certain disturbances in the relations to authority of the family and the state.[34] In both, the questions of paternal authority and rebellion against it are connected with a certain sinister kind of sexuality. And, as I have indicated, certain characters and relations in *Barnaby Rudge* seem to be inspired directly by Shakespeare. Dickens even assimilates a bit of the storm, and each of the novel's two parts begins with a symbolic storm, in which Dickens may be seen to acknowledge his indebtedness.[35] But a more generalized relation makes itself felt in the language of the novel. I do not mean that *Barnaby Rudge* simply echoes *King Lear*, though it frequently does. I mean rather that Dickens's larger attitudes and intentions are registered everywhere in the local life of the prose. For example, certain recurring images and combinations of images, through which the central relations in the novel are built up, appear in *Barnaby Rudge* with a pervasiveness, consistency and sureness of touch different in degree, and in the degree of awareness they imply, from Dickens's earlier novels.

Though it is not within the scope of this study to conduct a detailed examination of these images, a few of the most important ones should be noticed. A good many of them express ideas of breaking out, breaking in, and another state which is a curious fusion of the two. Often these images have to do with a notion of the individual person as a vessel threatened by too great internal pressure, or of his being a vessel withstanding pressures both from within and without.[36] For example, while Joe Willet is complaining that because he submits to his father's arbitrary demands no one believes he has 'a grain of spirit', and that if he doesn't relent 'I shall be driven to break such bounds', old John stares glassily at the boiler in his bar as if, like that vessel, his son had sides of metal and could endure indefinite pounds of compression (ch. 3). Again, in Sim's little body is 'locked up an ambitious and aspiring soul. As certain liquors, confined in casks too cramped in their dimensions, will ferment, and fret, and chafe in their imprisonment, so the spiritual essence or soul of Mr Tappertit would sometimes fume within that precious cask, his body, until, with great foam and froth and splutter, it would force a vent, and carry all before it' (ch. 4). And Sim himself speaks of bursting out personally (ch. 8) and breaking out politically (ch. 11). Dennis is similarly described: 'A dingy handkerchief twisted like a cord about his neck, left its great veins exposed to view, and they were swollen and starting, as though with gulping down strong passions, malice, and ill-will' (ch. 37).

Closely connected with this kind of image is the idea of 'restlessness' – Dickens's characteristic expression for an undefined neurotic disturbance, which in later years he frequently used to describe himself. Barnaby's 'terrible restlessness' (ch. 5) has to do with his 'terror of certain senseless things – familiar objects he endowed with life; the slow and gradual breaking out of that one horror, in which, before his birth, his darkened intellect began', and with the periodic emergence in him of a 'ghastly and unchild-like . . . cunning' (ch. 25), the other side of his mindless gaiety and innocence. Gordon's 'restlessness of thought and purpose' and 'undefinable uneasiness' are revealed through the incoherence of his speech 'in which, struggling through his Puritan's demeanour, was something wild and ungovernable which broke through all restraint' (ch. 35). Even these few scattered examples suggest that the essential conception of the novel took shape in Dickens's mind in various ideas and images of compression and repression, of fermentation and intoxication, of swellings and explosions and of corrosive anxiety and tenseness stretched to the breaking point. These images, developed in the course of the novel's action, are brought to their consummate expression in the eruption of the riots: in the breaking down of restraints, in drunkenness, fire and general explosive violence.[37]

The images of breaking in are more varied, and certain of them indicate a shifting point of view. On a number of occasions, for example, people lock themselves inside houses. Mrs Rudge 'chained and double-locked the door, fastened every bolt and bar with the heat and fury of a maniac' (ch. 5), in her fear that Rudge, who incessantly shadows her, will break in – as in fact he later does, invading her rural refuge, a spirit irrupted from the past (ch. 45). When Miggs locks Sim out she indulges a hysterical little fantasy about his intentions by exclaiming to herself. 'Oh! what a Providence it is, as I am bolted in!' And when Sim, frustrated at not getting in, kicks at the door, she shoves her head out the window and faintly cries: 'Is it thieves?' Sim calls out that it isn't, and Miggs replies 'Then . . . it's fire', bringing together in a moment of comic absurdity two of the novel's central representations of violent invasion (ch. 9).

The most radical personal embodiment of this impulse to break into something – into whatever signifies belonging to the human community – is the murderer Rudge, 'a houseless, rejected creature', who walks the streets each night, able only to imagine the 'happy forgetfulness each house shuts in'. And Dickens describes the conditions of this extremity:

> to have nothing in common with the slumbering world around, not even sleep, Heaven's gift to all its creatures, and be akin to nothing but despair; to feel, by the wretched contrast with everything on every hand, more utterly . . . cast away than in a trackless desert; this is a kind of suffering, on which the rivers of great cities close full many a time, and which the solitude in crowds alone awakens. (ch. 18)

So severe is his alienation that he frequently returns to the prison to sit before it and gaze 'upon its rough and frowning walls as though even they became a refuge in his jaded eyes' (ch. 18). For the outcast Rudge, the impulse to break into prison is a paradox comparable to Oliver's breaking into the Maylies and finding that he has come home. Yet when Rudge is imprisoned he finds himself no less alone; his terror of isolation is equalled only by his terror of human contact. When the mob breaks into Newgate the contradiction is expressed, for he is afraid both of being left there and of being found: 'Thus fearful alike, of those within the prison and of those without; of noise and silence; light and darkness; of being released, and being left there to die; he was so tortured and tormented, that nothing man has ever done to man in the horrible caprice of power and cruelty, exceeds his self-inflicted punishment' (ch. 65).

In Dickens's representations of the mob, the ideas and images connected with breaking out and breaking in are raised to another degree of intensity. The mob, interested in breaking into everything, in exposing whatever is private, in liberating what is suppressed, is at the same time the quintessence of breaking out, of explosiveness. The private self breaks out of its own boundaries and is absorbed into the anonymous self of the mob, mass violence and personal identity being, as Dickens saw, incompatible. And as we see in the description of the burning of the Warren, the unleashing of that destructive impulse by means of mob violence inevitably culminates in self-destruction.

> If Bedlam gates had been flung open wide, there would not have issued forth such maniacs as the frenzy of that night had made. There were men there, who danced and trampled on the beds of flowers as though they trod down human enemies, and wrenched them from the stalks, like savages who twisted human necks. There were men who cast their lighted torches in the air, and suffered them to fall upon their heads and faces, blistering the skin with deep unseemly burns. There were men who rushed up to the fire, and paddled in it with their hands as if in water; and others who were restrained by force from plunging in, to gratify their deadly longing. On the skull of one drunken lad – not twenty, by his looks – who lay upon the ground with a bottle to his mouth, the lead from the roof came streaming down in a shower of liquid fire, white hot; melting his head like wax. (ch. 55)

The explosive rage of the mob betrays its secret self-hatred in the enactment of its hatred of all things that exist, of the world itself; its object is universal destruction, which is the mad nihilistic equivalent of the unification of all things, the primal paradise regained. At the burning into Newgate this paradox is complicated still further. Dickens refers to the fire as an 'infernal christening' (ch. 64), and it is indeed a baptism into Hell, a birth out of life and into death; for the paradox of fire lies in its being a process of life and energy so intense that it is pure destructiveness. In these scenes, the problem of authority and the impossibility of resolving it is brought before us once more: and the burning of Newgate is no more a resolution than the hanging of Hugh.

The final convulsion of the riots, represented in the burning of the houses in several quarters of the city, is described as an apocalypse, a vision of judgment.

> The tumbling down of nodding walls and heavy blocks of wood, the hooting and the execrations of the crowd, the distant firing of other military detachments, the distracted looks and cries of those whose habitations were in danger, the hurrying to and fro of frightened people with their goods; the reflections in every quarter of the sky, of deep, red, soaring flames, as though the last day had come and the whole universe were burning; the dust, and smoke, and drift of fiery particles, scorching and kindling all it fell upon; the hot unwholesome vapour, the blight on everything; the star, and moon, and very sky, obliterated; – made up such a sum of dreariness and ruin, that it seemed as if the face of Heaven were blotted out, and night, in its rest and quiet, and softened light, never could look upon the earth again. (ch. 68)

And Dickens goes on to describe something even more terrible than this: the spectacle at one of the burning and pillaged houses, which belonged to a vintner.

> The gutters of the street, and every crack and fissure in the stones, ran with scorching spirit, which being damned up by busy hands, overflowed the road and pavement, and formed a great pool, into which the people dropped down dead by dozens. They lay in heaps all round this fearful pond, husbands and wives, fathers and sons, mothers and daughters, women with children in their arms and babies at their breasts, and drank until they died. While some stooped with their lips to the brink and never raised their heads again, others sprang up from their fiery draught, and danced, half in a mad triumph, and half in the agony of suffocation, until they fell, and steeped their corpses in the liquor that killed them. . . . From the burning cellars, where they drank out of hats, pails, buckets, tubs, and shoes, some men were drawn, alive, but all alight from head to foot; who, in their unendurable anguish and suffering, making for anything that had the look of water, rolled, hissing, in this hideous lake, and splashed up liquid fire which lapped in all it met with as it ran along the surface, and neither spared the living nor the dead. On this last night of the great riots . . . the wretched victims of a senseless outcry, became themselves the dust and ashes of the flames they had kindled, and strewed the public streets of London. (ch. 68)

It is a spectacle of the drunken energy of life turning into a frenzied dance of death, a spectacle which alludes to the burning lake in *Paradise Lost*. In the riots and in the revolt of sons against fathers – both of which are desperate responses to real injustices – what society has forbidden is unleashed. And Dickens's recognition in *Barnaby Rudge* is that such a bursting out of what has been prohibited is not only inimical to society, but has become, through the very extremity of the repression it represents, destructive of what it has set out to fulfill: the self, and existence itself.

Dickens located the source of this suicidal passion not in some general intolerability in the conditions of the universe, but in a radical disorder in the individual's relation to authority, which comprehends his most intimate personal relations as well as his relation to society. Nowhere is Dickens's sense of this disorder more penetrating than in the final scenes in Newgate: in a mind of unbelievable pre-vision, Dennis, Hugh and Barnaby, the three prisoners, suggest the three institutions of the mind that Freud was to name and describe. As depicted in the novel, moreover, these faculties have been twisted and distorted out of all proper shape. Dennis the hangman is a kind of super-ego gone berserk: hanging, punishment, torture and retribution are the ideas he has lived by; he has been willing even to destroy society in order to preserve his warped notion of lawfulness and decency. Hugh, the centaur, the creature of the Maypole and the woods, is the id given over to brutal aggression; repressed, rejected, denied a rightful place in the civilized community, his instinctual energies are directed to the annihilation of all authority, society, community and self. Barnaby is a paradigm of the defective ego, an imbecile, who, though he manifests a simple enjoyment of himself and life, is without power to understand and deal with the world, and is in consequence manipulated and battered on every side both by society and the forces that undermine it – at the mercy, in other words, of both superego and id. In this collocation of the hangman, the centaur, and the 'idiot', in their difficult contradictory and finally impossible relation to authority and hence to anything or anyone, we find the novel's final vision of its theme. All the violence with which *Barnaby Rudge* is filled, and which in a sense is its real subject, does nothing to resolve the unendurable conditions in either personal life or society that the existences of these three men typify.

What Dickens saw foreshadowed in Chartism was not the fantasy produced by some 'middle-class scare'; he saw beyond it into what we have seen happen in the twentieth century – that politics and the life of society come more and more to resemble externalizations of the life of the unconscious mind, and that the disorders in society and personal life are confluent and interpenetrating and grow steadily more difficult to bear and control, and steadily more dangerous. Dickens saw the possibility of society's committing suicide, of its being driven by the deepening contradictions in its own unmistakable nature to self-annihilation. To have seen this in 1840 was to have gazed into the heart of the affliction that goes by the name of modern civilization. Ironically, it is only genius that is thus privileged to glimpse into the abyss, and to pay the price that is so often exacted for it, the necessity of living with an intense and personal awareness of humanity's life of pain. With *Barnaby Rudge* it was clear that Dickens, the supreme entertainer, the performer, the clown, had begun to pay that price.

NOTES

1. One exception is the chapter in John Butt and Kathleen Tillotson, *Dickens at Work* (1957) pp. 76–89, on the sources and composition of *BR*.

2. The end of this protracted introduction comes in ch. 36, which Dickens awkwardly ends with 'And the world went on turning round, as usual, for five years, concerning which this Narrative is silent.'

3. Edgar Johnson, *Charles Dickens: His Tragedy and Triumph* (New York, 1952; London, 1953) p. 249. Butt and Tillotson, pp. 76–7, argue against this idea.

4. John Forster, *The Life of Charles Dickens*, ed. J. W. T. Ley (New York and London, 1928) p. 170.

5. *The Letters of Charles Dickens* (in the Nonesuch Dickens, 1938), I 71–2, 231, 249, 296. See also Forster, pp. 164–5; Johnson, pp. 244–5, 248–9, 268, 306; Butt and Tillotson, pp. 76–89. At various times Dickens had agreed to write *BR* as a three-volume novel and in monthly numbers; consequently, the decision to publish it in miniscule weekly instalments involved considerable readjustment.

6. *Letters*, I 297.

7. *Letters*, I 302. Each number of *MHC* ran to about 7000 words.

8. *Letters*, I 297, 302, 335, 344–5.

9. *Letters*, I 317; see also 343–4, 353. The contracted space and Dickens's sense of being constrained by it very likely have something to do with the flatness of the novel's prose.

10. 'To the Readers of *Master Humphrey's Clock*', reprinted in Butt and Tillotson, pp. 88–9.

11. Edmund Wilson, *The Wound and the Bow* (1941) pp. 15–19; Johnson, pp. 311–17; Humphry House, *The Dickens World* (1941) pp. 179–80, 214; T. A. Jackson, *Charles Dickens: Progress of a Radical* (1937) p. 28.

12. The 'people out of doors' was a phrase much in currency during the era of the Poor Law amendment and the Chartist agitation, but almost surely little used in 1780.

13. Indeed, Dickens was far too generous with Gordon for Forster's taste. He wrote Forster: 'He always spoke on the people's side, and tried against his muddled brains to

expose the profligacy of both parties. He never got anything by his madness, and never sought it. The wildest and most raging attacks of the time, allow him these merits: and not to let him have 'em in their full extent, remembering in what a (politically) wicked time he lived, would lie upon my conscience heavily.' Forster's rejoinder to this effort of disinterestedness was the assertion that Dickens could not see 'the danger of taxing ingenuity to ascribe a reasonable motive to acts of sheer insanity'. Forster, p. 168.

14. Doubt has never been cast on the fidelity to fact of Dickens's account of the riots. Butt and Tillotson, pp. 84–7, summarize Dickens's research and his use of historical material in *BR*. See also J. Paul de Castro, *The Gordon Riots* (1926).

15. Robert F. Wearmouth, *Methodism and the Working-class Movements of England, 1800–1850* (1937) pp. 77, 100–28.

16. Mark Hovell, *The Chartist Movement* (Manchester, 1918), pp. 85, 89. See also E. Halévy, *Triumph of Reform* (1950) pp. 289–301.

17. Hovell, op. cit. p. 89. 'The methods rather than the theology of Methodism were turned directly to the purposes of political agitation.' See also House, pp. 107–8.

18. Wearmouth, op. cit. pp. 70–2.

19. Any interpretive comment on the biographical significance of Dickens's use, in this context, of the name Warren would, I think, be superfluous.

20. That Dickens had the ghost of Hamlet's father in mind is evident in the monologues he supplies to Rudge; e.g. see ch. 17.

21. Originally Dickens planned to have three madmen, escaped from Bedlam, leading the mob. Forster, p. 168.

22. The scenes of Cade's appearance are 2 *Henry VI* III i; IV ii, iv, vi–viii, x.

23. This argument was also found useful by John Locke. See *Two Treatises of Civil Government*, book II, ch. 13, par. 158. This line of argument is summarized in Leslie Stephen, *The English Utilitarians* (1950) I 17, 126 ff.

24. See *Cobbett's Legacy to Labourers* (1834) *passim*; also *A History of the Protestant Reformation in England and Ireland* (1896) pp. 270–5.

25. *The Life and Struggles of William Lovett* (1876) pp. 209 ff.

26. When the Horse Guards are called out to disperse the mob (ch. 49), Dickens remarks their unaggressiveness, making certain that no associations with Peterloo will creep in.

27. One notes in passing how sublimely free writers and artists were to deal with such matters before Freud. Nowadays it is only the vulgar and uninstructed writer who is free to resort to this kind of symbolism.

28. Dickens handles the Maypole here as he did Sim's key; the symbolic meaning emerges with spontaneous naturalness out of its function in the narrative. Cf. Hawthorne's story 'The Maypole of Merry Mount', in *Twice-Told Tales*.

29. The influence of Scott and popular drama on this conception has also been noted.

30. Edward is to the very end of the novel conciliatory to his father. See ch. 75.

31. In *Measure for Measure* IV ii, Barnardine is described as 'A man that apprehends death no more dreadfully but as a drunken sleep—careless, reckless, and fearless of what's past, present or to come: insensible of mortality and desperately mortal.'

32. In *Invisible Man* (New York, 1952; London, 1953), Ralph Ellison's portrait of Ras the Destroyer, a Negro African nationalist, who leads a race riot in Harlem, seems modelled partly on Hugh, and works toward a similar effect.

33. *Henry James: Autobiography*, ed. F. W. Dupee (New York and London, 1956) pp. 68, 69.

34. In *King Lear* disorder in the family is directly responsible for disorder in the state. In *Barnaby Rudge* disorder in the two regions of experience are connected first by analogy, and then through characters who move from a disordered family situation into a similar disorder in society.

35. In ch. 2 Dickens seems unquestionably to have *Lear* in mind, as he describes the frequent effects of 'unusual commotion' in the elements on men 'bent on daring enter- prises, or agitated by great thoughts'; 'In the midst of thunder, lightning, and storm, many tremendous deeds have been committed.'

36. These images also have a central function in Carlyle's *The French Revolution*, which Dickens had read and the influence of which he acknowledged.

37. The rumor that the rioters intended to 'throw the gates of Bedlam open, and let all the madmen loose' (ch. 67) remained a rumor only because Dickens allowed Forster's 'sound counsel' to prevail. Forster, p. 168.

J. HILLIS MILLER

Martin Chuzzlewit (1958)

I

Mr Mould was surrounded by his household gods. He was enjoying the sweets of domestic repose, and gazing on them with a calm delight. The day being sultry, and the window open, the legs of Mr Mould were on the window-seat, and his back reclined against the shutter. Over his shining head a handkerchief was drawn, to guard his baldness from the flies. The room was fragrant with the smell of punch, a tumbler of which grateful compound stood upon a small round table, convenient to the hand of Mr Mould; so deftly mixed, that as his eye looked down into the cool transparent drink, another eye, peering brightly from behind the crisp lemon-peel, looked up at him, and twinkled like a star. (ch. 25)

MR MOULD is enclosed within his own space. There is nothing around him which is not his world, which does not mirror back to him his own nature, minister to his own comfort of body and mind. Like a marine animal which secretes its own shell, Mr Mould lives in an environment which contains nothing out of harmony with his character and his way of life. He can enjoy completely a placid, calm repose because nothing whatsoever visible to him is a threat. His peaceful 'gaze' is met everywhere by a return look which is not the hostile stare of something alien but is as much his own, himself, as his own face in the mirror. At the center of the scene is Mr Mould's tumbler of punch in which 'another eye', which is yet his own eye, brightly returns his glance. In the room is his family, a further extension of himself. Between Mr Mould and his family pass reciprocal smiles in a closed circle of domestic affection: 'Mr Mould looked lovingly at Mrs Mould, who sat hard by, and was a helpmate to him in his punch as in all other things. Each seraph daughter, too, enjoyed her share of his regards, and smiled upon him in return' (ch. 25). But the spatial extension of his identity does not stop with the walls of his 'harem'. Beyond the window, beyond the 'rural screen of scarlet runners' through which Mr Mould's 'moist glance' wanders 'like a sunbeam', as if he were the light source of his own world, the 'wider prospect' reveals only more of the same, more of Mr Mould. What he sees is a small shady churchyard which he regards 'with an artist's eye' (ch. 25). It is something he himself has made. And if his glance out the window is like a sunbeam, it is met by a return of light which is like a human look, and for the third time, at the limit of his vision and the edge of his world, Mr Mould's look is reciprocated: 'The light came sparkling in among the scarlet runners, as if the churchyard winked at Mr Mould, and said, "We understand each other" ' (ch. 25).

The 'household gods' which 'surround' Mr Mould like a warm cocoon extend to the farthest limits of his view. This cocoon is made of a series of screens which enclose Mr Mould: the handkerchief over his head, the screen of flowers at the window, and finally the opposite end of the churchyard, beyond which nothing can be seen. And throughout all pervades the fragrant smell of punch, a sort of symbol of the homogeneity and self-centeredness of Mr Mould's milieu. What is beyond, the boisterous life of a great city, all the other people living within their own circumscribed worlds, can be detected only as a barely audible hum. The outside world is wholly unable to penetrate within the successive layers of protection with which Mr Mould has surrounded himself. He remains safe, 'deep in the City': 'The premises of Mr Mould were hard of hearing to the boisterous noises in the great main streets, and nestled in a quiet corner, where the City strife became a drowsy hum, that sometimes rose and sometimes fell and sometimes altogether ceased . . .' (ch. 25).

In these passages we are given only what can be seen and heard, the room, and its objects, the view from the window, the gestures and speech of Mr Mould, and the simplest notation of Mr Mould's subjective state, his 'calm delight'. This subjective state is described as belonging to him in the way a property, color or density, belongs to an object. But this does not mean that there is a hidden subjective life masked behind this appearance. Many of the characters in *Martin Chuzzlewit* have no secret interior lives whatever. They exist wholly spread out into their bodies and into their environments. Mr Mould lives in a world that is so completely himself, he is so completely at home, that he has no possible opportunity to make a withdrawal of his consciousness from what he is conscious of. And in the same way the objects have no separate existence. They exist only as humanized objects, as parts of Mr Mould. There is thus no distinction here between the realm of consciousness and that of objects. What exists instead is a single homogeneous continuum which stretches without differentiation from Mr Mould out to the periphery of his vision. The eye which looks at his eye from his punch, the churchyard which winks at him, are as much alive and as little self-conscious as Mr Mould himself.

The lack of a division into subjective and objective worlds is suggested by the recurrence of an unusual grammatical form. Instead of saying 'Mr Mould's legs', Dickens says 'the legs of Mr Mould'. Mr Mould's legs are not appendages possessed by him, and therefore in a way separate: they are *of* him, within the intimate circle of his existence. Dickens goes on to speak of 'the hand of Mr Mould', and finally uses the locution in a way which strikingly suggests that everything surrounding Mr Mould has equal status as an extension of himself: he speaks of 'the premises of Mr Mould'.

In Balzac's novels, as in *Martin Chuzzlewit*, characters surround themselves with a cocoon or ambience which is their world. But in Balzac we see this happening. It is a result of the subjectivity and imagination, and, above all, of the volition of the character, as he imposes himself on the world of objects. But in Dickens the character does not coerce objects by imagination or will to match his nature. Rather, the objects, like the gesture, appearance, and expression of the character, are from the first moment we see the character perfect clues, for the spectator, to his mentality, and it is impossible to imagine the process by which this situation came into existence.

From the total enclosure of such characters within their own lives it follows that they are so unable to imagine any other kind of life that they are wholly without perspective upon their own lives. It is impossible for them to see themselves or their profession as others see them, and they are thus able to endure what would shock or repel another person. As Pecksniff says, quoting the old proverb, 'Use is second nature' (ch. 19). Dickens was fascinated by the process of Mithridatean acclimatization whereby a person can become accustomed to an environment which would be intolerable to anyone else. His habit of visiting slums, prisons, and insane asylums was, in one of its aspects, evidence of this obsession. Thus Martin Chuzzlewit is at first disgusted and humiliated by his life of poverty in London, but he soon becomes used to it: 'And it was strange, very strange, even to himself, to find, how by quick though almost imperceptible degrees he lost his delicacy and self-respect, and gradually came to do that as a matter of course, without the least compunction, which but a few short days before had galled him to the quick' (ch. 13). And so, Mr Mould and his family have become so gradually 'subdued to what they work in' that no element of undertaking has any horror for them. What to another person would seem a sinister and disquieting place is to the Moulds as soothing as a pastoral landscape. There is a rural screen of scarlet runners outside the window, and the sound of coffin-making in the workshop reminds Mr Mould of 'the buzz of insects' and 'the woodpecker tapping': 'It puts one in mind of the sound of animated nature in the agricultural districts' (ch. 25).

So little self-conscious are many characters in *Martin Chuzzlewit* and consequently so little endowed with memory that unless a change within themselves or in the world outside takes place almost instantaneously it will not even be noticed. If such a change takes place 'steadily, imperceptibly, and surely' (ch. 43), 'by the easiest succession of degrees imaginable' (ch. 40), it will be to the character as if no change had taken place. Hence Dickens' need of asserting the swiftness of a metamorphosis in appearance if it is to be recognized as such: 'But the strangest incident in all this strange behaviour was, that of a sudden, in a moment, so swiftly that it was impossible to trace how, or to observe any process of change, his features fell into their old expression . . .' (ch. 18).

Since there is no possibility of perceiving progressive change in this world, it is not possible to enter it by slow transitory stages, but only by a sudden leap over the impenetrable barriers which separate it from all the other scenes of the novel. The description of the Moulds at home opens a chapter and follows directly after a chapter which involves wholly different characters. Dickens does not give us any means of connecting these two contiguous chapters. The connection can only be seen much later when the novel is complete and all the relationships between the hermetically sealed milieus of the novel can be seen in a single, retrospective, panoramic glance. In another passage, at the beginning of a chapter which, again, has nothing to do with the preceding one, Dickens makes explicit the essential discontinuity of the world of the novel: 'The knocking at Mr Pecksniff's door, though loud enough, bore no resemblance whatever to the noise of an American railway train at full speed. It may be well to begin the present chapter with this frank admission, lest the reader should imagine that the sounds now deafening this history's ears have any connexion with the knocker on Mr Pecksniff's door . . .' (ch. 21). As in the cinematic technique of montage, one visual or auditory sensation gives way to another which is like it, but which belongs to a different place or time. There may turn out to be a multitude of hidden relationships linking all of the apparently disconnected characters and events of the novel in a tight causal web. But these events are experienced, by the reader and by the characters, as if they were entirely isolated:

> As there are a vast number of people in the huge metropolis of England who rise up every morning, not knowing where their heads will rest at night, so there are a multitude who shooting arrows over houses as their daily business, never know on whom they fall. Mr Nadgett might have passed Tom Pinch ten thousand times; might even have been quite familiar with his face, his name, pursuits, and character; yet never once have dreamed that Tom had any interest in any act or mystery of his. Tom might have done the like by him, of course. But the same private man out of all the men alive, was in the mind of each at the same moment; was prominently connected, though in a different manner, with the day's adventures of both; and formed, when they passed each other in the street, the one absorbing topic of their thoughts. (ch. 38)

Two elements may be distinguished here: the actual interdependence of Tom Pinch and Nadgett, and their ignorance, at the time, of this fact. Each of the characters is entirely sealed within his own life, and all the other characters, except those within his own domestic milieu, are entirely a mystery to him.

In *Martin Chuzzlewit*, then, the isolation of Oliver Twist in his underground prison is rediscovered as the essential condition not of outcasts but among people in the free surface world who, unlike Oliver, are perfectly satisfied with their lot. But what is wholly missing in *Martin Chuzzlewit* is the possibility of a rediscovery of the lost past, a recovery of it which will liberate one from the enclosure of the present. The revelations at the end of *Martin Chuzzlewit* illuminate and integrate all that has gone before but this retrospective discovery of meaning does not extend prior to the beginning of the story. Nothing is discovered which is not part of the present time of the action. No meaning reaches out of the past to transform and redefine the present. The difference is radical. The problem which faces the characters of *Martin Chuzzlewit* is Oliver Twist's problem too: how to achieve an authentic self, a self which, while resting solidly on something outside of itself, does not simply submit to a definition imposed from without. But the manner in which this goal was reached in *Oliver Twist* is wholly denied to the characters of *Martin Chuzzlewit*. The arena of *Martin Chuzzlewit* is the present, a present which is irrevocably cut off from the past and in which society in the sense of an integrated community has been replaced by a fragmented collection of isolated self-seeking individuals.

II

The aim of *Martin Chuzzlewit*, as Dickens himself said, is to show 'how selfishness propagates itself; and to what a grim giant it may grow, from small beginnings' (Preface to the first cheap edition, *MC*, p. xi). But selfishness exists in the novel not only as the ethical bent of the characters, but also as the state of isolation in which they live. The novel is full of people who are wholly enclosed in themselves, wholly secret, wholly intent on reflexive ends which are altogether mysterious to those around them. As Sairey Gamp says, in what might serve as an epigraph for the entire novel: '. . . we never knows wot's hidden in each other's hearts: and if we had glass winders there, we'd need keep the shetters up, some on us, I do assure you!' (ch. 29). This self-enclosure is explicitly made the predominant trait of some of the characters of *Martin Chuzzlewit*: '. . . the whole object of [Nadgett's] life', says Dickens, 'appeared to be, to avoid notice, and preserve his own mystery' (ch. 38). The key term for Nadgett is 'secret'. He represents in a pure state what the characters of *Martin Chuzzlewit* look like not from within their own private worlds, as in the case of our vision of Mr Mould, but from the outside. Nadgett's behavior, his speech, his action and appearance can be seen and described, but they remain unintelligible, preserving untouched within the secret of what he is: '. . . he was born to be a secret. He was a short, dried-up, withered, old man, who seemed to have secreted his very blood; for nobody would have given him credit for the possession of six ounces of it in his whole body. How he lived was a secret; where he lived was a secret; and even what he was, was a secret' (ch. 27). Why does Nadgett remain an unfathomable secret? He is not hidden behind protective screens, like Mr Mould. He is out in the open where he can be inspected. Even the contents of his pocketbook are no secret. Nevertheless he cannot be known. *What* he is cannot be known, in spite of the evidence, because it is wholly impossible to find out *who* he is. There is no possible direct access to the inner life of Nadgett. What is missing here, and throughout *Martin Chuzzlewit* for the most part, is any inter-subjective world. There is no world of true language, gesture, or expression which would allow the characters entrance to one another's hearts. And Dickens does not permit himself, except on a very few occasions, to employ the convention of the omniscient narrator, able to enter at will the inner consciousness of his characters. The world of *Martin Chuzzlewit* is a public world, a world in which what exists is only what could be seen by any detached observer. It is in this sense that it is a fundamentally comic world. For the essential requirement of comedy is an unbridgeable gap between narrator (and reader) and the characters. Far from identifying himself with the subjective experiences of the characters, and realizing them from the inside, the reader of *Martin Chuzzlewit*, like the narrator and the characters themselves, in their relations to one another, remains separated from the personages. He may attribute to the characters the subjective states appropriate to the speech, expression, or gesture which he sees, but the characters actually exist as their appearance and their actions and only as these. They are simply visible, audible, tangible objects, animate, but apparently otherwise exactly like other objects in the world.

For some characters such as Mr Mould, this presents no problem. Mould exists only as undertaker and as pampered family man. He has no secret. But for certain people, like Nadgett, the manifest data do not hang together and one is forced to assume the existence of something hidden, something which is on principle utterly beyond the reach of mere detached observation. And yet Nadgett is not a special case. He is one example of a large group produced by the peculiar conditions of modern urban life: 'he belonged to a class; a race peculiar to the City; who are secrets as profound to one another, as they are to the rest of mankind' (ch. 27). The city has brought about this crisis in our knowledge of our neighbor by separating altogether public role and private self. Constant changes of employment, the lack of distinguishing outward characteristics to label members of each profession, the sheer size of the urban community, all these tend to make it more and more impossible to identify a person satisfactorily in terms of his occupation. There is no way to reach Nadgett's secret subjective self. But neither is there any way to define him certainly by his public roles, for he carries in his pocketbook 'contradictory cards', which label him as coal merchant, wine merchant, commission agent, collector, and accountant (ch. 27). Such are the conditions of city life that it is impossible to know which of these professions he actually practices, if any.

In the end Nadgett exists not as a coherent and intelligible self, either private or public, but as a collection of eccentric and baffling appearances, wholly external appearances which are known to be no true index to that large proportion of his life which remains secret: 'He was mildewed, threadbare, shabby; always had flue upon his legs and back; and kept his linen so secret by buttoning up and wrapping over, that he might have had none – perhaps he hadn't. He carried one stained beaver glove, which he dangled before him by the forefinger as he walked or sat; but even its fellow was a secret' (ch. 27).

Very many are the cases in *Martin Chuzzlewit* where the visible glove of gesture or expression does not permit us to discover its hidden and invisible fellow, its subjective meaning:

> She withdrew into the coach again, and he saw the hand waving towards him for a moment; but whether in reproachfulness or incredulity, or misery, or grief, or sad adieu, or what else, he could not, being so hurried, understand. (ch. 40)

> Now if Mr Pecksniff knew, from anything Martin Chuzzlewit had expressed in gestures, that he wanted to speak to him, he could only have found it out on some such principle as prevails in melodramas, and in virtue of which the elderly farmer with the comic son always knows what the dumb-girl means when she takes refuge in his garden, and relates her personal memoirs in incomprehensible pantomime. (ch. 3)

> Mr Jobling pulled out his shirt-frill of fine linen, as though he would have said, 'This is what I call nature in a medical man, sir.' (ch. 41)

> His very throat was moral. You saw a good deal of it. You looked over a very low fence of white cravat (whereof no man had ever beheld the tie, for he fastened it behind), and there it lay, a valley between two jutting heights of collar, serene and whiskerless before you. It seemed to say, on the part of Mr Pecksniff, 'There is no deception, ladies and gentlemen, all is peace, a holy calm pervades me.' (ch. 2)

'Seemed to say', 'as though he would have said' – the behavior and appearance of the personages seem to be a language, seem to have a meaning, but how is one to know which is the true meaning? There is no possible comparison of outer appearance and inner reality by which the detached spectator or the isolated characters can establish the validity of an interpretation.

The characters of *Martin Chuzzlewit* tend to exist, then, not through the visible expression of a coherent inner life, but as fixed and innate idiosyncrasies behind which one cannot go, because there is apparently nothing behind them. '. . . why does any man entertain his own whimsical taste? Why does Mr Fips wear shorts and powder, and Mr Fips's next-door neighbor boots and a wig?' (ch. 39). There is no answer. For Dickens the idiosyncrasy of character is an absurd and irreducible fact. Everyone in *Martin Chuzzlewit* resembles the boarders at Todgers', each of whom has a 'turn' for something or other, but no one of whom has an existence with any psychological depth or integration: 'There was . . . a gentleman of a smoking turn, and a gentleman of a convivial turn; some of the gentlemen had a turn for whist, and a large proportion of the gentlemen had a strong turn for billiards and betting' (ch. 9). When there is a party at Todgers', 'every man comes out freely in his own character' (ch. 9). There is nothing else he can do. The endless repetition by such a character of an eccentricity which is superficial and meaningless and yet is the only identity he possesses is as spontaneous and undeliberate, and as little human, as the putting forth of maple leaves by a maple tree.

But what happens if there is some failure in the mechanism of self-expression? What happens if his environment does not make it possible for such a character to indulge his 'turn'?

What can happen is shown in Chevy Slyme, one of the least savory members of the Chuzzlewit family. Slyme has failed utterly to be anyone, to play any recognized social role at all, and the result is, paradoxically, not a sense of his own nonentity, but a sense of his infinite value. Cut off entirely from reality, his self-esteem has swelled to hyperbolic proportions. '. . . he is,' says Tigg of Slyme, 'without an exception, the highest-minded, the most independent-spirited, most original, spiritual, classical, talented, the most thoroughly Shakspearian, if not Miltonic, and at the same time the most disgustingly-unappreciated dog I know' (ch. 4). Chevy Slyme, like Dostoevsky's 'underground man', is intensely self-conscious, intensely aware of his freedom and of his uniqueness. Tigg calls him 'the American aloe of the human race' (ch. 7); 'nobody but himself', he says, 'can in any way come up to him' (ch. 7). And Chevy himself says, 'I have an independent spirit. . . . I possess a haughty spirit, and a proud spirit, and have infernally finely-touched chords in my nature, which won't brook patronage. Do you hear? Tell 'em I hate 'em, and that's the way I preserve my self-respect; and tell 'em that no man ever respected himself more than I do!' (ch. 7). But Chevy is wholly incapable of bringing into actual existence his magnificent possibilities. Any particular fulfillment of himself in terms of a task undertaken and work done would mean the acceptance of limitation, and the destruction of all the other potentialities of his nature. Slyme feels that he is capable of anything, and this keeps him from being anything. What he wants and expects is that society should accept the possibility for actuality, that he should be recognized for what he is, as if he were a wholly intrinsic and self-sufficient being, like God, not limited by the disgusting necessity of bringing a being into existence through action. His nullity is not his fault, but society's: 'I am the wretchedest creature on record. Society is in a conspiracy against me. I'm the most literary man alive. I'm full of scholarship; I'm full of genius; I'm full of information; I'm full of novel views on every subject; yet look at my condition! I'm at this moment obliged to two strangers for a tavern bill! . . . And crowds of impostors, the while, becoming famous: men who are no more on a level with me than – Tigg, I take you to witness that I am the most persecuted hound on the face of the earth' (ch. 7).

Chevy had begun by 'putting forth his pretensions, boldly, as a man of infinite taste and most undoubted promise' (ch. 7). And yet he never does achieve any self at all because there is never anything outside of himself which recognizes and sustains his being. Or if there is anything at all it is only the insubstantial stuff of language, the language which his friend Tigg employs to give their only reality to his unfulfilled possibilities. Slyme, then, exists only in terms of his friend, and only so long as his friend is with him and talking about him. He seems 'to have no existence separate or apart from his friend Tigg' (ch. 7).

Slyme is proof that, for Dickens, no human being can be sufficient unto himself. A man attains an enduring identity, if at all, only through the establishment of a correspondence between something within and something without.

III

The characters of *Martin Chuzzlewit*, then, must leave their ambient milieus, the milieus that are so intimately fused with themselves, and seek in the outer world, the world that is alien and unfamiliar, some support for their own beings. Mr Mould must leave his own 'premises' and enter into the 'strife' of the city; Tom Pinch must lose his innocent faith in Pecksniff and go down to London; and Martin Chuzzlewit must leave England altogether and go to America.

This exit from himself plunges the individual immediately into a labyrinth. In a moment he loses the way:

> Todgers's was in a labyrinth, whereof the mystery was known but to a chosen few. (ch. 9)

> [Tom Pinch] lost his way. He very soon did that; and in trying to find it again, he lost it more and more. . . . So, on he went, looking up all the streets he came near, and going up half of them; and thus, by dint of not being true to Goswell Street, and filing off into Aldermanbury, and bewildering himself in Barbican, and being constant to the wrong point of the compass in London Wall, and then getting himself crosswise into Thames Street, by an instinct that would have been marvellous if he had had the least desire or reason to go there, he found himself, at last, hard by the Monument. (ch. 37)

> Mr Pecksniff, with one of the young ladies under each arm, dived across the street, and then across other streets, and so up the queerest courts, and down the strangest alleys and under the blindest archways, in a kind of frenzy: now skipping over a kennel, now running for his life from a coach and horses; now thinking he had lost his way, now thinking he had found it; now in a state of the highest confidence, now despondent to the last degree, but always in a great perspiration and flurry. . . . (ch. 8)

But in losing his way, the protagonist loses himself. In *Oliver Twist* the hero began lost, at the center of a labyrinth, seeking through a maze of hostile ways his absent identity. But in *Martin Chuzzlewit* the characters are initially 'found', or so they think, surrounded, like Mr Mould, with a friendly and reassuring world which mirrors back themselves. Their entrance into the labyrinth is the discovery of a world which is not consubstantial with themselves. It is thus the exact reverse of the labyrinth of *Oliver Twist*: a process of the unintentional losing of oneself rather than a frantic attempt to become 'found'.

The state of mind of the person who has thus inadvertently entered the maze is one of increasing bewilderment and anxiety. What had begun as a deliberate and rational attempt to find his way to a certain goal becomes 'frenzy', a perpetual state of 'great perspiration and flurry'. At last he realizes the truth, that he is irrevocably off the track, and an utter state of resignation and hopelessness ensues. He gives himself up for lost: 'You couldn't walk about in Todgers's neighborhood, as you could in any other neighborhood. You groped your way for an hour through lanes and bye-ways, and court-yards, and passages; and you never once emerged upon anything that might be reasonably called a street. A kind of resigned distraction came over the stranger as he trod those devious mazes, and, giving himself up for lost, went in and out and round about and quietly turned back again when he came to a dead wall or was stopped by an iron railing, and felt that the means of escape might possibly present themselves in their own good time, but that to anticipate them was hopeless' (ch. 9). This 'resigned distraction' is something like the catatonic trance of certain types of insanity. The 'stranger' is faced with a world which refuses altogether to yield a sense, to relate itself to his mind. He is both within and without at the same time, within the hostile maze from which he wishes desperately to escape, and outside the hidden meaning behind the 'dead walls'. In fact he is doubly shut out, estranged now from the comfortable home he has so recently left, and unable to understand the world he has so abruptly entered. Like Martin Chuzzlewit, cast out by his grandfather and alone in London, he has 'a pretty strong sense of being shut out, alone, upon the dreary world, without the key of it' (ch. 13).

• At this halfway point, en route, there are, it seems, two choices. The protagonist can go forward seeking a way out of the maze, or he can run back into the safety of home – like the 'people who, being asked to dine at Todgers's had travelled round and round for a weary time, with its very chimney-pots in view; and finding it, at last, impossible of attainment, had gone home again with a gentle melancholy on their spirits, tranquil and uncomplaining' (ch. 9). But it is in taking the latter alternative that a person may make an astonishing discovery. The milieu which had seemed so solid and enduring as long as he dwelled monotonously within it has suddenly, through his absence, itself entered the world of vertiginous change: 'Change begets change: nothing propagates so fast. If a man habituated to a narrow circle of cares and pleasures, out of which he seldom travels, step beyond it, though for never so brief a space, his departure from the monotonous scene on which he has been an actor of importance, would seem to be the signal for instant confusion. As if, in the gap he had left, the wedge of change were driven to the head, rending what was a solid mass to fragments, things cemented and held together by the usages of years, burst asunder in as many weeks. The mine which Time has slowly dug beneath familiar objects, is sprung in an instant; and what was rock before, becomes but sand and dust' (ch. 18). The discovery of sand and dust where there had been solid rock leads inevitably to a shocking deduction: the world which had seemed so perdurable while the individual was within it, such a substantial support for his selfhood, had actually not been constitutive of the self at all. Rather it was the self which, by dwelling permanently at the center of certain objects, had constituted them as an integrated whole. Home is not really a protective cocoon. It is only the presence of the inhabitant which makes it seem so and which makes it keep on seeming so. In actuality, each milieu is only a kind of insubstantial fabric, a psychic rather than an objective phenomenon. The human presence at the center is the creative idea which makes it and holds it together. When that is removed by the inhabitant's own removal the whole scene collapses into fragments and he discovers a world that is everywhere, from the center to the horizon, a mere agglomeration of disconnected things: 'Tiers upon tiers of vessels, scores of masts, labyrinths of tackle, idle sails, splashing oars, gliding row-boats, lumbering barges, sunken piles, with ugly lodgings for the water-rat within their mud-discoloured nooks; church steeples, warehouses, house-roofs, arches, bridges, men and women, children, casks, cranes, boxes, horses, coaches, idlers, and hard-labourers: there they were, all jumbled up together, any summer morning, far beyond Tom's power of separation' (ch. 40). At first this scene reveals itself as a group of independent objects, each one of which, like the boarders at Todgers', 'comes out strongly in [its] own nature'. Each noun is matched by an adjective, or rather, not by a mere adjective of static quality, but by a verbal adjective, a participle. Each such form defines its object as existing in a ceaseless and repetitive activity which is the very expression of its nature: 'splashing oars, gliding row-boats, lumbering barges, sunken piles'. But each of these activities, except for chance collisions, remains wholly isolated, unrelated to the others, like the particles in a Brownian movement. It is not possible to discover a hierarchy among these objects, or a causal chain, or a central principle of organization. In the end the world no longer even seems to be inhabited by active entities. It becomes merely an indefinite number of self-enclosed objects, 'all jumbled up together'. Men, horses, bridges, it is all the same: even the division into kingdoms of animal, vegetable, or mineral is lost. Finally, as the list is extended, the items even cease to be things and become mere names, names which, it is true, correspond to different parts of the visual field, but labels which now seem to be increasingly superficial. They identify only surface distinctions which cover without depth an undifferentiated mass underneath, a mass which is beyond anyone's 'power of separation', and is the sheer pulp or stuff of things.

We may find ourselves at last at the center of the world, at the center of the maze. But what we discover there is that the world has no center, but is an unimaginable number of plural and interchangeable objects, plural because each individual is only one among an unlimited supply of the type, and interchangeable because no individual entity has any distinct quality or value of its own: 'Then there were steeples, towers, belfries, shining vanes, and masts of ships: a very forest' (ch. 9). In the end we face simply a forest, a wilderness, wilderness upon wilderness, in which each separate entity is to be defined only by its hostility, by its implacable resistance to our attempts to comprehend it, to find ourselves in it: 'Gables, housetops, garret-windows, wilderness upon wilderness' (ch. 9).

In a world of this sort a person cannot pretend to have a precise object in view. To attend to a certain object or to attend to another, it is all the same, and in the end such a person reaches a complete state of indifference, of ennui, of passive despair, in which he returns over and over again to the same object because there is absolutely no difference now between one object and another: 'In his first wanderings up and down the weary streets, he counterfeited the walk of one who had an object in his view; but, soon there came upon him the sauntering, slipshod gait of listless idleness and the lounging at street-corners, and plucking and biting of stray bits of straw, and strolling up and down the same place, and looking into the same shop-windows, with a miserable indifference, fifty times a day' (ch. 13).

IV

There comes a time when this state of mind is radically changed by a qualitative alteration in the spectator's apprehension of things. The appearance of the world does not change. But suddenly he feels, he knows, that this spectacle, which refuses so absolutely to respond to the demand for fixity and intelligibility, is only the mask for something hidden within. He can sense now beyond any possibility of doubt that the external world has a significance, but this hidden meaning cannot be perceived except as a kind of atmosphere in the circumambient world, and as a spontaneous state of fascinated curiosity which this atmosphere produces in the spectator: 'There was a ghostly air about these uninhabited chambers in the Temple, and attending every circumstance of Tom's employment there, which had a strange charm in it. Every morning when he shut his door at Islington, he turned his face towards an atmosphere of unaccountable fascination, as surely as he turned it to the London smoke; and from that moment, it thickened round and round him all day long . . .' (ch. 40).

The word 'mystery' is Dickens' term for this sense that there is hidden in the world something alien and yet like oneself in that it would have a personal meaning if that meaning could be discovered. The self-enclosed inhabitants of the London of *Martin Chuzzlewit* live, like the boarders at Todgers', in close proximity to other human activities of which they are totally ignorant. On the other side of the wall of one's own cell in the beehive there is another cell, and who can tell what is going on there? '. . . the grand mystery of Todgers's was the cellarage, approachable only by a little back door and a rusty grating: which cellarage within the memory of man had had no connexion with the house, but had always been the freehold property of somebody else, and was reported to be full of wealth: though in what shape – whether in silver, brass, or gold, or butts of wine, or casks of gunpowder – was matter of profound uncertainty and supreme indifference to Todgers's, and all its inmates' (ch. 9).

The boarders at Todgers' have become accustomed to the proximity of danger and mystery, but not so Tom Pinch. He is haunted by the sense that there is something present behind each of the opaque appearances which meets his eye. But it is something of which he is totally ignorant. These appearances contain their mystery and even speak it in their own language, but he cannot understand this language. It is like being in a strange country in the midst of people whose speech one cannot comprehend: 'It seemed to Tom, every morning, that he approached this ghostly mist, and became enveloped in it, by the easiest succession of degrees imaginable. Passing from the roar and rattle of the streets into the quiet court-yards of the Temple, was the first preparation. Every echo of his footsteps sounded to him like a sound from the old walls and pavements, wanting language to relate the histories of the dim, dismal rooms; to tell him what lost documents were decaying in forgotten corners of the shut-up cellars, from whose lattices such mouldy sighs came breathing forth as he went past . . .' (ch. 40). This journey is the reverse of the movement from the center of Mould's room out to the noisy city. It is a transition from noise to calm, from the labyrinth to an enclosed home. But it is as if one were entering Mould's premises when Mould and his family were absent and had to infer from the inanimate objects what sort of man he must be. The information is there, but it is indecipherable. And it is impossible to be sure whether the data spring from the objects or from oneself, whether the noise one hears is the sound of one's own footsteps or comes from the old walls and pavements. And yet it is impossible not to deduce from these appearances the presence *somewhere* of another human being, even if such a presence defies common sense: 'The mystery and loneliness engendered fancies in Tom's mind, the folly of which his common sense could readily discover, but which his common sense was quite unable to keep away, notwithstanding. . . . Misgivings, undefined, absurd, inexplicable, that there was some one hiding in the inner room – walking softly over head, peeping in through the door-chink, doing something stealthy, anywhere where he was not – came over him a hundred times a day . . .' (ch. 40).

A character like Tom, at this stage of his exploration of the external world, has reached a strange impasse. He can no longer rest assured that he is in effect the only person in the world, the only spiritual presence around which things organize themselves. He knows now that someone else exists, and he knows that he cannot remain safely in his self-enclosure. The very continuation of his existence depends on establishing some kind of satisfactory relation to what is outside himself. But this alien world and the people hidden behind its walls remain mysteries. The people especially exist as an inexplicable menace, something behind the door, in the other room, spying on him, hiding

wherever he is not, never seen directly, and yet present and active
everywhere in the world. How can he come face to face with this
incomprehensible and ubiquitous threat, seize it, understand it, and
control it?

In *Martin Chuzzlewit*, the apogee of this relation to the world is a
striking passage describing the view from the roof of Todgers'
boardinghouse.[1] This is a text of capital importance for the entire work
of Dickens, since Dickens here most explicitly expresses the dangerous
end point to which his characters can be brought by the attitude of
passive and detached observation:

> After the first glance, there were slight features in the midst of this
> crowd of objects, which spring out from the mass without any reason,
> as it were, and took hold of the attention whether the spectator would or
> no. Thus, the revolving chimney-pots on one great stack of buildings,
> seemed to be turning gravely to each other every now and then, and
> whispering the result of their separate observation of what was going on
> below. Others, of a crook-backed shape, appeared to be maliciously
> holding themselves askew, that they might shut the prospect out and
> baffle Todgers's. The man who was mending a pen at an upper window
> over the way, became of paramount importance in the scene, and made a
> blank in it, ridiculously disproportionate in its extent, when he retired.
> The gambols of a piece of cloth upon the dyer's pole had far more interest
> for the moment than all the changing motion of the crowd. (ch. 9)

The observer of this scene knows that there is a spiritual life other
than his own present somewhere, but he does not know exactly where
it is, and is forced to attribute life indiscriminately to everything he
sees. As a result, the spectator perceives a nightmarish animation of
what ought to be inanimate objects, from the revolving chimney pots
which seem to whisper gravely to one another to the piece of cloth
which 'gambols' with an apparently intrinsic life of its own. And this
animation is deliberately and intensely inimical to man. The chimney
pots are gossipy spies, or are maliciously hiding the view from the
observer on Todgers' roof, or from Todgers' itself, which is here
conceived of as an animate being.

Before all this life the observer is absolutely passive. He is at the
mercy of these things and especially at the mercy of their motion.
There is no stability in the world he sees, but, more astonishingly, he
discovers that to this constant metamorphosis of things there corresponds a metamorphosis of himself. When something changes in the

scene outside himself, he too changes. The perpetual change in things imposes itself on the spectator until, in the end, he exists as the same person only in the infinitesimal moment of an enduring sensation.

But the spectator on Todgers' roof discovers something even more disquieting. He discovers that the withdrawal of something from the scene produces not simply a blank in his consciousness, a blank which he can easily replace with his own interior life, but an unfillable gap. The exterior and visible void is 'ridiculously disproportionate in its extent' because it proves to the observer his own interior nothingness. The removal of the man in the window is the removal of an irreplaceable part of himself, and the observer comes to make the discovery that he is, in one sense, nothing at all, since he is nothing in himself, and, in another sense, is everything, since he can become by turns everything he beholds.

The climax of this experience is a double disintegration of the self. On the one hand, the view from Todgers' brings the spectator a recognition of his aloneness and lack of a stable and substantial self. But, on the other hand, and in the same moment, this alien world, this collection of objects which has no relation to the observer, and no meaning for him, rushes into the inner emptiness, and swamps and obliterates his separate identity. Moreover, this movement of things into the self is matched by a corresponding plunge of the self into things. The ultimate danger is that the looker-on will fall headforemost into the hosts of things, and lose himself altogether:

> Yet even while the looker-on felt angry with himself for this, and wondered how it was, the tumult swelled into a roar; the hosts of objects seemed to thicken and expand a hundredfold; and after gazing round him, quite scared, he turned into Todgers's again, much more rapidly than he came out; and ten to one he told M. Todgers afterwards that if he hadn't done so, he would certainly have come into the street by the shortest cut: that is to say, head foremost. (ch. 9)

v

Mere passive observation, it seems, will not do. Active steps must be taken to escape from the situation of vacillation and nonentity. If the external world merely encountered will yield neither a sense nor a support, the individual must take matters in hand, either build an impregnable defense against the outside world, or cleverly manipulate it, force it to recognize and sustain him.

There are some characters in *Martin Chuzzlewit* who are perfectly aware that there is an alien world outside themselves, but who are able to live by a continual manipulation of that world and of other people. Through this manipulation they transform what is alien into an instrument ministering to their own selfish needs. Sairey Gamp is the magnificent dramatization of this way of inhering in the world. It is a way very different from that of Mr Mould. Mould is present and visible in all that surrounds him as milieu, but what surrounds him is like himself, and therefore is a direct expression of his nature. But Sairey is present in things which are unlike herself and separate from her. She thus is at once present in and absent from her milieu. Presented wholly from the outside, from the point of view of the detached observer, she is Dickens' fullest expression of the paradoxical inherence in a body and in the objective world of a consciousness which always transcends its body and can never be identified with any object.

This presence-absence is strikingly apparent in the animation of objects in the neighborhood of Sairey. Her maltreatment of Tom Pinch is not, apparently, intentional, but is caused by the independent malice of her umbrella: 'This tremendous instrument had a hooked handle; and its vicinity was first made known to him by a painful pressure on the windpipe, consequent upon its having caught him round the throat. Soon after disengaging himself with perfect good humour, he had a sensation of the ferule in his back; immediately afterwards, of the hook entangling his ankles; then of the umbrella generally, wandering about his hat, and flapping at it like a great bird; and, lastly, of a poke or thrust below the ribs, which gave him . . . exceeding anguish . . .' (ch. 40). Sairey's ignorance of the malign actions of her umbrella is akin to her complete insensitivity to her patients. '. . . may our next meetin',' she says to Mrs Prig, 'be at a large family's, where they all takes it reg'lar, one from another, turn and turn about, and has it businesslike' (ch. 29). All things, for Sairey Gamp, including her own body, and her clothes, are dissociated from her, and yet are related intimately to her. They are dissociated from her in so far as she takes no account of them as they are in themselves, the objects as mere objects, the people as other human beings with lives of their own. These 'realistic' and 'objective' elements in the world disappear altogether for Sairey. She is cut off from them, and has no idea, for example, of what her patients Lewsome and Chuffey are suffering or thinking. What does connect her intimately to the world both of objects and people, so intimately that her mark is apparent everywhere around her, is the fact that everything is used by her to satisfy her own selfish desires. This dissociation produces the immense comic tension of her appearances. Everything but her own mind with its selfish intents is objectified, and so complete is the cleavage between Sairey and her own body that even her own actions seem to be performed not by human volition, but by inanimate objects horribly endowed with life. So it is not Sairey herself who insists that her luggage must be treated in a certain way, but the luggage itself which has certain human requirements: 'every package belonging to that lady had the inconvenient property of requiring to be put in a boot by itself, and to have no other luggage near it, on pain of actions at law for heavy damages against the proprietors of the coach' (ch. 29). It is not Mrs Gamp's stipulation, but an 'inconvenient property' of the luggage itself, and the language of the rest of the sentence suggests that not Mrs Gamp, but the luggage itself, will sue the coach company. In the next sentence the personification is explicit: 'The umbrella with the circular patch was particularly hard to be got rid of, and several times thrust out its battered brass nozzle from improper crevices and chinks, to the great terror of the other passengers' (ch. 29). There is a hidden human malignity here acting blindly through insentient objects. It is not simply the fact that objects appear to be unnaturally human; this fact itself is the unmistakable evidence that somewhere a human intelligence exists, a human intelligence which has somehow got itself magically entangled with inanimate objects and acts through them, but without full cognizance of what it is doing. The umbrella is not conscious. It is the sign of consciousness, an object magically endowed with life by the presence of consciousness. The fact of Sairey's intensely self-centered consciousness makes everything in her neighbourhood orient itself around her like iron filings around a magnet. Thus everything in her proximity is evidence of her presence – the pattens, the umbrella, the rearrangement of her patients' rooms (and the patients) for her comfort, the famous bottle on the chimney piece – all testify to the existence of Sairey Gamp. But the fact that she transforms everything, including other people, into what they are not, does not give us direct access to her subjectivity. The evidence of her subjectivity is a masked evidence. We do not know it directly, but only through the transformation of things in her neighborhood, the animation of umbrella and luggage, and the change of people into something which approaches the status of pure instrumentality. Everywhere we see signs through which we can directly and intuitively understand Sairey, but we have no direct access to that toward which the signs point. Sairey herself remains alone, apart, above, and beyond all her evident inherence in the world, and it is this ambiguous presence-absence which is the real source of the brilliant comedy of the scenes in which she appears.

But in the end Sairey fails, fails because she has never ceased to be alone, selfish. Her way is very firmly rejected by Dickens when he includes her among the villains exposed in the denouement, and has old Martin Chuzzlewit give her advice 'hinting at the expediency of a little less liquor, and a little more humanity, and a little less regard for herself, and a little more regard for her patients, and perhaps a trifle of additional honesty' (ch. 52). But more essentially, perhaps, Sairey fails because she can never bring together the two halves of her contradictory presence-absence in the world. On the one hand, she remains wholly alone, isolated in a private world of self-seeking which is so narrow that it uses even her own body as the instrument of its gluttonous pleasure. But, on the other hand, whatever outside herself she becomes related to is immediately transformed into an extension of herself. She never succeeds any more than did the spectator on the roof of Todgers' in establishing a relation to something which, while remaining other than herself, is support for herself.

If Sairey dramatizes the cul-de-sac into which total selfishness leads, there are two characters who express the unexpected theme of the impasse to which total unselfishness leads. One of these, Tom Pinch, is hardly intended to have this meaning by Dickens. But it is difficult to see his story except as proof that the man who is wholly unselfish ends with nothing but the esteem of those around him, and the privilege of serving them. Tom's primary loss is Mary, but he actually lacks any real familial or social role. He exists as a sort of supernumerary bachelor uncle, affectionately patronized by all his friends and relatives, and their wives and children. His closest relation is to a member of his own family, his sister, familially the same, rather than other. This relation is the kind of thing that made it possible for George Orwell to talk about incestuous domestic relationships in Dickens' novels. But the key symbol for Tom is a striking expression of an even more narrow enclosure: he habitually plays the organ to himself alone in the twilight: 'And that mild figure seated at an organ, who is he? Ah Tom, dear Tom, old friend! . . . Thy life is tranquil, calm, and happy, Tom. In the soft strain which ever and again comes stealing back upon the ear, the memory of thine old love may find a voice perhaps; but it is a pleasant, softened, whispering memory, like that in which we sometimes hold the dead, and does not pain or grieve thee, God be thanked!' (ch. 54). The sentimentality of this passage is itself a sign of Dickens' uneasiness. He wants to present Tom as an attractive figure, but he cannot help betraying by his patronizing tone the fact that he would rather sympathize at some distance from such a character, than actually be such a person. Indeed, Tom is shown throughout the novel as something of a fool. His name recalls 'Poor Tom's a-cold', and 'Tom Fool'; it is the stock name for a harmless lunatic. Tom is more to be admired from the safe standpoint of worldliness, than actually to be imitated. He may, like the innocent good fool of Erasmus, be rewarded in heaven (though little is made of this), but from the point of view of life in this world, the real arena of Dickens' novels, his life is, after all, a negative affair.

The case of Mark Tapley is more explicit. Mark's selfishness is to want 'credit' for being 'jolly', that is, cheerful and unselfishly helpful in all situations. 'My constitution is', he says, 'to be jolly; and my weakness is, to wish to find a credit in it' (ch. 48). Mark can only get 'credit' for his jollity if he is jolly in a situation which is so hopelessly unpleasant that not one element of his jollity derives from anything outside himself. But over and over again he discovers that his mere presence transforms a scene and the people in it from being disagreeable to being themselves jolly, and thus a source of Mark's own jollity. We come to recognize that there is a lack of generosity in the desire to be wholly alone in one's unselfishness. It means being among people wholly selfish themselves, so that there is no 'income' of charity for one's own generosity and kindliness. Mark takes a perverse pleasure in finding himself among selfish people, and this is very close to taking pleasure in contemning human beings, not in loving them. The only healthy unselfishness, Mark discovers, takes pleasure in the return of the gift to the giver. Mark finds that unselfishness always must be a reciprocal relation, and wisely abandons his selfish attempt to get 'credit' for it: 'findin' that there ain't no credit for me nowhere; I abandons myself to despair, and says, "Let me do that as has the least credit in it, of all; marry a dear, sweet creetur, as is wery fond of me: me being, at the same time, wery fond of her: lead a happy life, and struggle no more again' the blight which settles on my prospects"' (ch. 48). Mark has to reconcile himself to getting pleasure (that is, being, paradoxically, selfish) in the very process of giving pleasure.

But most of the characters are unwilling to consider such reciprocity, and instinctively try every means they can find to do without other people. One of these instinctive evasions is the attempt to establish within the self a reflexive relation. This means dividing the self up into two parts, a self-division which may take several forms.

It is possible to divide the self into a self which serves and a self which is served, as, for example, does Martin Chuzzlewit, who 'is his own great coat and cloak, and is always a-wrapping himself up in himself' (ch. 33). Such a splitting will allow a person to perform selfish acts as though they were acts of public service and generosity. Thus, Pecksniff is shown 'drawing off his gloves and warming his hands before the fire, as benevolently as if they were somebody else's, not his' (ch. 3), and he is even able to divide himself from his digestion, and look upon that process as a wonderful piece of machinery of general utility to mankind: 'I really feel at such times as if I was doing a public service' (ch. 8). The subterfuge here is the simple one of treating oneself impersonally as if one were another person. It is not the self-seeking consciousness which is enjoying the meal or the warm fire, but an objective body which is separate from consciousness, and toward which one should feel the same sort of altruism one owes the human race in general.

But there can be an even more radical schism in the self, not simply a splitting up into what Dorothy Van Ghent calls 'a me-half and an it-half',[2] but a division into two subjectivities, a self which exists and a self which recognizes and justifies that existence. One sign of the complete isolation and secrecy of Nadgett's life is the fact that he sends letters to himself (ch. 27). His communication is entirely internal; the only I-thou dialogue he takes part in is within himself. The most fully developed form of such an internal dialogue, however, is the relation between Sairey Gamp and the nonexistent Mrs Harris. Like a child whose imaginary playmate will take the blame for her misdeeds, praise her for her good, and provide an escape from her new awareness of her separate identity, Sairey creates in Mrs Harris a justification for her existence: ' "Mrs Harris," I says . . . "leave the bottle on the chimley-piece, and don't ask me to take none, but let me put my lips to it when I am so dispoged, and then I will do what I'm engaged to do, according to the best of my ability." "Mrs Gamp," she says, in answer, "if ever there was a sober creetur to be got at eighteen pence a day for working people, and three and six for gentlefolks – night watching," ' said Mrs Gamp, with emphasis, ' "being a extra charge – you are that inwallable person" ' (ch. 19). Mrs Harris is justification for Sairey both in the sense of offering an apparently independent definition of her nature, and in the sense of upholding that definition against all those who doubt her honesty. And yet, being unreal, existing only in Sairey's mind, Mrs Harris is entirely within Sairey's control. She has remained true to her nature as selfish. She depends on nothing outside of herself. It is no wonder that Betsy Prig's doubting of the existence of Mrs Harris produces such a violent quarrel, and leaves the shattered Sairey 'murmuring the well remembered name which Mrs Prig had challenged – as if it were a talisman against all earthly sorrows . . .' (ch. 49). Mrs Harris is indeed Sairey's fundamental support and self-defense. Without Mrs Harris, Sairey Gamp would not exist as herself.

Another form of self-division reveals the secret bad faith which undermines all such attempts to find within the self a substitute for the outside world and for other people. A character may separate himself into a false self which is exposed to the public gaze and a real self which remains safely hidden within. The external self forms a hard opaque surface which other people cannot pierce. Such a person manipulates the self he is for others while keeping the authentic self beyond their reach, like Nadgett, who remains a secret by keeping himself 'wrapped up in himself' (ch. 38), and like Pecksniff, who tries 'to hide himself within himself' (ch. 30). This strategy is, like the invention of an imaginary friend, a technique of disguised self-creation, but there is something ominous in the fact that it is an external, public self which is created, a self which the character disengages from himself in the very motion of creating it. Nevertheless, it has the inestimable advantage of keeping his actual thoughts and intentions a secret, and very many are the characters in *Martin Chuzzlewit* who survive by delivering over to the public as hostage a false image of themselves. Sometimes both selves may have objective expression, one that is open to the public, and another that must be deliberately hidden. Such a person is Mrs Todgers, who has 'affection beaming in one eye, and calculation shining out of the other' (ch. 8). This self-division can even be manifested in a permanent dissociation of a person's face into two distinct and incongruous profiles: 'Two gray eyes lurked deep within this agent's head, but one of them had no sight in it, and stood stock still. With that side of his face he seemed to listen to what the other side was doing. Thus each profile had a distinct expression; and when the movable side was most in action, the rigid one was in its coldest state of watchfulness. It was like turning the man inside out, to pass to that view of his features in his liveliest mood, and see how calculating and intent they were' (ch. 21). The paradox here is that the sightless, expressionless profile accurately externalizes Scadder's inner nature. By a physical accident the hidden self is betrayed at a surface area which is not under the control of the will, and Scadder is, without being able to help it, 'turned inside out'.

At the limit, the two profiles separate altogether, become two people, and we have the motif of the *Doppelgänger*. Thus, Jonas Chuzzlewit disguises himself, and sneaks out of his bedroom by a back entrance to murder Tigg. Everyone in the house thinks he is still in his room. While acting out the evil intention of his inner self, he has left behind the appearances of the self other people thinks he is. But this other self takes on a life of its own, and haunts the murderer: 'He was so horribly afraid of that infernal room at home. This made him, in a gloomy, murderous, mad way, not only fearful *for* himself but *of* himself; for being, as it were, a part of the room: a something supposed to be there, yet missing from it: he invested himself with its mysterious terrors; and when he pictured in his mind the ugly chamber, false and quiet, false and quiet, through the dark hours of two nights; and the tumbled bed, and he not in it, though believed to be; he became in a manner his own ghost and phantom, and was at once the haunting spirit and the haunted man' (ch. 47). Jonas is, one may believe, afraid of the public self for two reasons. It is the avenue through which the hidden self may be discovered. Someone may break open the locked door of his bedroom and discover that he is not there. But, more subtly, the horror of his apprehension of himself as murderer, completely cut off now from all honest social relations, is expressed in a fear of the very solidity of his other self. In a way, the self other people think he is has no existence at all, but in another way it has a much more substantial existence than his interior self, since it is at least recognized and believed in by other people. So great is the distance between the two selves that they are wholly irreconcilable and cancel one another out. What had started as an attempt to create and sustain the self by an internal reciprocal relation ends as a process of self-destruction.

It is self-destructive in a very special way. All the attempts to form a reflexive relation have the strange result of testifying indubitably to the existence of other consciousnesses, and to each man's unwilling dependence on other people. Such strategies set at war the individual's private self and the self he is for others, and in the end prove that the very attempt to be self-sufficient has had as a hidden premise the existence of other minds. Gazing into a mirror, archetypal image of a reflexive relation, turns out to be gazing not at one's secret self, but at the way one looks to others. It turns out to be a confession that one *is* what one appears in the eyes of others. Thus Jonas, after the murder, 'looking in the glass, imagined that his deed was broadly written in his face' (ch. 47). Or there is Pecksniff, who, after Tom Pinch's belief in him has been shattered, 'look[s] at himself in the parson's little glass that hung within the door' (ch. 31), as if to reassure himself that he still exists! And finally there is Mr Mould at a funeral, 'glancing at himself in the little shaving-glass, that he might be sure his face had the right expression on it' (ch. 19). But all these characters, far from creating themselves in their own mirror image, are actually accepting as the essential definitions of themselves what they look like to other people, or are at least taking great trouble to manufacture a public self. They are all like the Honourable Elijah Pogram, who 'composed his hair and features after the Pogram statue, so that any one with half an eye might cry out, "There he is! as he delivered the Defiance!" ' (ch. 34).

The characters of *Martin Chuzzlewit* are doubly at the mercy of others: on the one hand, another person may at any time pierce the carefully constructed social shell, and, on the other, even if this does not happen, each person depends absolutely on the others, since it is only in their eyes that the public self exists at all.

And there is no longer any illusory belief in the existence of any area of safety. The portentous figure of the spy haunts *Martin Chuzzlewit* as he does Dickens' other novels. A man may think he is alone, but the spy is there all the time, in the most unlikely avatars, secretly looking on. Apparently Nadgett wants nothing but to protect himself from others and to avoid human contact altogether: 'The secret manner of the man disarmed suspicion . . . ; suggesting, not that he was watching any one, but that he thought some other man was watching him' (ch. 38). But, seemingly so secret, Nadgett is actually engaged in a very intense one-way human relationship, as Jonas discovers too late: 'This man, of all men in the world, a spy upon him; this man, changing his identity: casting off his shrinking, purblind, unobservant character, and springing up into a watchful enemy!' (ch. 51).

There is no help for it. Each man must seek some kind of direct relationship to other people, a relationship which recognizes the fact of their consciousness, and makes it an integral part of the structure of his own inherence in the world.

VI

Perhaps man's most primitive, instinctive reaction to other people is the attempt to coerce them by brute force to act toward him in the way he wishes. This is the temptation of sadism. There are many sadists in Dickens' novels, but no character in Dickens, except, perhaps, Quilp, is more purely and undilutedly a sadist than Jonas Chuzzlewit. Jonas marries Mercy Pecksniff entirely for revenge. He wishes to escape from the image of himself which Mercy has freely formed by destroying that freedom itself. Before their marriage Mercy treats Jonas as if he were no threat to her at all, as if she could safely call him anything she likes, as if she could safely 'hate and tease' (ch. 20) Jonas all her life. Jonas marries Mercy in order to destroy in her this power over him: 'You made me bear your pretty humours once', he says, 'and ecod I'll make you bear mine now. I always promised myself I would. I married you that I might. I'll know who's master, and who's slave!' (ch. 28). The only human relationship Jonas can imagine is the relationship of master and slave. If he is not master he is slave, and he has felt himself enslaved by Mercy's words and by her attitude toward him. His method of retaliation is to coerce Mercy by physical force into the attitude toward him he wants. Or rather, since he hardly reaches this sort of sophistication, he attempts to destroy in Mercy the power to form any image of him at all. He is 'determined to conquer his wife, break her spirit, bend her temper, crush all her humours like so many nut-shells – kill her, for aught I know' (ch. 28). But, as the sequence of planned acts in this passage reveals, Jonas can only destroy all 'spirit' in Mercy by destroying Mercy herself. As long as there is any consciousness in Mercy at all she will be able to reassert with a single look her power to form an opinion of him.

And Jonas is indeed led to murder by just such an attempt to remain independent, to escape the power of another over him. Tigg is, he thinks, the only man who knows he has murdered his father, the only man who sees beneath what he apparently is to what he really is. But paradoxically it is in the very attempt to keep his secret and remain on the surface what he has always been that Jonas inexorably becomes what Tigg thinks he is. He has not really killed his father at all, though he thinks he has, but he does kill Tigg in the attempt to keep his crime (which existed only in intention) and his real nature (which has remained until now only potential) hidden from public knowledge. He thus becomes in reality what he has heretofore been only in possibility. But, more startlingly and dramatically, Dickens describes a progressive change in Jonas' outward appearance which modulates him from what he is early in the story, a comic figure, a blustering braggart and coward, to a melodramatic personification of pure evil. This metamorphosis begins at the moment Tigg tells him he has found out his supposed secret (ch. 38), and crystallizes when he attempts to flee the country, is stopped by Tigg, and forms a settled intention to escape Tigg by murdering him: 'He had the aspect of a man found out, and held at bay; of being baffled, hunted, and beset; but there was now a dawning and increasing purpose in his face, which changed it very much. It was gloomy, distrustful, lowering; pale with anger, and defeat; it still was humbled, abject, cowardly, and mean; but, let the conflict go on as it would, there was one strong purpose wrestling with every emotion of his mind, and casting the whole series down as they arose' (ch. 41). The 'whole series' of other possible moods and accompanying selves is giving way here to a single dominant self, the self Jonas will permanently become when he actually kills Tigg. When the murder is discovered the transmutation is complete, and we see Jonas last, just before he poisons himself, writhing in anguish on the floor, like 'some obscene and filthy animal, repugnant to the sight' (ch. 51). Jonas has become altogether, inside and out, what Tigg took him for. The sadist, far from controlling his identity by controlling others, has ended entirely at the mercy of others and of their freedom to control him.

It is useless, then, to attempt to coerce another person overtly. He is not so easily or safely controlled. But perhaps it is possible to choose willingly to be a slave rather than master. Such a person will simply let other people make him whatever they wish, live in pure passivity. Forgetting altogether the possibility of a valid inner life, he will accept the public self as the real and only self and live as sheer appearance. A man who does this may not be certain what sort of self he will have, but such is the power of surface that by the mere passive activity of displaying himself a being of sorts will spring into existence. This is apparently the technique of the porter of the Anglo-Bengalee Disinterested Loan and Life Assurance Company. This man lives so completely on the surface that Dickens calls him simply 'the waistcoat': 'there was a porter on the premises – a wonderful creature, in a vast red waistcoat and a short-tailed pepper-and-salt coat – who carried more conviction to the minds of sceptics than the whole establishment without him. No confidences existed between him and the Directorship; nobody knew where he had served last; no character or explanation had been given or required. No questions had been asked on either side. This mysterious being, relying solely on his figure, had applied for the situation, and had been instantly engaged on his own terms' (ch. 27). Like the Anglo-Bengalee itself the porter exists entirely as appearance, an appearance behind which, it may be, there is nothing at all.

Dickens' America is an entire society which lives as pure surface, a surface which hides a profound void. Dickens acutely saw that America, the country where all conventions and traditions had been destroyed for the sake of the free development of the individual, could for that very reason become, and was indeed becoming, a country where authentic individuality was impossible. Dickens' Americans are already, in David Riesman's phrase, 'other-directed'. They have no inner life; they exist only in public. This means, in the end, that they exist only as language. Dickens' Americans are characterized by their inexhaustible flow of talk. But a person who exists only as language will depend absolutely on the presence of some other person in whose mind that language will have meaning. Alone he will be nothing. Moreover, the words he speaks and exists in may be arbitrary. They may have no integral relation to anything within himself. Such a person can by a mere act of will transform himself by transforming what he says. America is for Dickens primarily the place of double-talk and of double-think, the place where theft is called 'independence', a violent vagabond is called 'a splendid sample of our na-tive raw material, sir' (ch. 33), and the tarring and feathering of an opponent 'planting the standard of civilisation in the wilder gardens of My country' (ch. 33). The Americans are unable to carry on any dialogue or conversation. They can only make speeches, speeches in which reality is utterly buried beneath vaporous clouds of words. As is shown by authentic examples of the kind of language Dickens was parodying, metaphor or personification cut loose from any tradition of substantial analogy was the habitual trope of even the most distinguished American orators of the middle nineteenth century.[3] In Dickens' parodies of American parliamentary and journalistic language hyperbolic metaphor is the chief means of leaving reality behind:

> Verdant as the mountains of our country; bright and flowing as our mineral Licks; unspiled by withering conventionalities as air our broad and boundless Perearers! Rough he may be. So air our Barrs. Wild he may be. So air our Buffalers. But he is a child of Natur', and a child of Freedom; and his boastful answer to the Despot and the Tyrant is, that his bright home is in the Settin' Sun. (ch. 34)

> . . . may the British Lion have his talons eradicated by the noble bill of the American Eagle, and be taught to play upon the Irish Harp and the Scotch Fiddle that music which is breathed in every empty shell that lies upon the shores of green Co-lumbia! (ch. 21)

But America is not the only institution which exists entirely in a hyperbolic language having no foundation whatsoever in reality. The Anglo-Bengalee exists chiefly as words, as the name of the company 'repeated at every turn until the eyes are dazzled with it, and the head is giddy' (ch. 27). Nor are Scadder, Pogram, and Chollop the only characters who use a language which is mere modulated air, referring to nothing real. 'We shall go forth to-night by the heavy coach – ,' says Mr Pecksniff, 'like the dove of old, my dear Martin – and it will be a week before we again deposit our olive-branches in the passage. When I say olive-branches, . . . I mean, our unpretending luggage' (ch. 6).

In the end such language and the people who use it cease altogether to be meaningful or human. 'Mind and matter', says one of the 'Literary Ladies' Martin meets in America, 'glide swift into the vortex of immensity. Howls the sublime, and softly sleeps the calm Ideal, in the whispering chambers of Imagination' (ch. 34). This is pure poetry, but pure poetry reduces itself for Dickens to pure lie, since it has dissociated itself altogether from the objective world, and no longer has any self-subsistent transcendent world on which to depend. Tigg has created the Anglo-Bengalee out of nothing, made it '[start] into existence one morning, not an Infant Institution, but a Grown-up Company running alone at a great pace, and doing business right and left' (ch. 27). He has done so as director of the 'ornamental department', 'the inventive and poetical department' of the company (ch. 27).

There is, then, a convergence of the themes of selfishness, of money, of false language, and of 'other-direction' in Dickens' novel. The selfishness of many characters is dramatized in their greed for money (Jonas, Anthony, Pecksniff, Tigg, the Americans), and the novel could be defined as Dickens' first elaborate attack on the money worship of commercialized man. His characterization of the Americans applies equally well to many of the Englishmen in the novel: 'All their cares, hopes, joys, affections, virtues, and associations, seemed to be melted down into dollars. Whatever the chance contributions that fell into the slow cauldron of their talk, they made the gruel thick and slab with dollars. Men were weighed by their dollars, measures gauged by their dollars; life was auctioneered, appraised, put up, and knocked down for its dollars' (ch. 16). But love of money is more than a symbol of the inturned selfishness which cuts the characters off from one another, or, rather, relates them to one another only through the impersonal bond of the 'cash-nexus'. It is because these people have submitted to money as the sole yardstick of value that they have only superficial and inauthentic identities. In *Martin Chuzzlewit* people are at once wholly turned in upon themselves and wholly dependent upon the value they have in other people's eyes. Like Anthony Chuzzlewit, they want to hoard more and more money, miser-like, and make it an expression of their self-contained value and substantiality. When they have amassed a great fortune, they can be independent of other people and sit in secret gloating over their gold. But at the same time they must recognize, even if only implicitly, that money has no value in itself. Its value lies only in the conventional ascription of worth agreed upon by society. The miser cannot, then, exist in secret, self-sufficiently. He has just that amount of value which society ascribes to the money he possesses, or is thought to possess. The founders of the Anglo-Bengalee recognize the factitiousness of money, and see that since money has no real substance in itself the appearance of wealth is exactly the equivalent of its real possession, so long as the fraud is not discovered. But here the theme of money approaches and merges into the theme of false language. Public language is a kind of paper currency. As long as people are willing to accept it as real, they will ascribe to the speaker the reality which ought to lie behind his language. The Anglo-Bengalee is created out of nothing through the prestidigitations of language, but this is only possible because the words are employed in a public realm where all measurement of value in terms of real substance has been replaced by the universal gauge of money. In a world where nothing is real, or in which everything has only the impalpable reality of money, the linguistic façade of the Anglo-Bengalee is as good as the real thing.

Moreover, the measurement of everything by its cash value tends to reduce all things and persons to anonymity. The uniqueness of personality is erased, and each person *is* whatever money he has. The use of debased language and the measurement of everything by money operate together to deprive the Americans of individuality. They have become like standardized and interchangeable coins. So Dickens can say that the ladies of America 'were strangely devoid of individual traits of character, insomuch that any one of them might have changed minds with the other, and nobody would have found it out' (ch. 16). If the minds of these ladies could be changed without discovery, it is really because they have no separate minds at all, but only a kind of mechanism of clichés. Their exterior appearances are interchangeable too. Each individual belongs to a certain conventional type, and, like the objects which appeared from the roof of Todgers' or to Tom Pinch in London, no individual has any separate value or identity. If one were to disappear, there would always be another to take his place, and nothing would be lost. It is a collective world, where any group is never a society, but merely another agglutinative compound of the same universal stuff: 'Here and there, some yawning gentlemen lounged up and down with their hands in their pockets; but within the house and without, wherever half a dozen people were collected together, there, in their looks, dress, morals, manners, habits, intellect, and conversation, were Mr Jefferson Brick, Colonel Diver, Major Pawkins, General Choke, and Mr La Fayette Kettle, over, and over, and over again. They did the same things; said the same things; judged all subjects by, and reduced all subjects to, the same standard' (ch. 21).

Dickens' comic vision of America culminates in a world of puppets who are reduced to their gestures, their grimaces, their imitations of one another. These puppets exist entirely as appearance, as a surface which rigidly and mechanically imitates life. Beneath the superficial façade which they have attained by submitting passively to a wholly public life there is nothing at all, an emptiness and silence of which the characters themselves are not even aware.

VII

Sometimes, however, such a character discovers his nonentity. This is most likely to happen if he finds that he is not even remaining the same public self from one day to the next. For if he depends altogether on other people in order to be, then other people can remake him as they will, and he may find himself undergoing a dizzying series of meta-morphoses within which there is no continuity, no persistence of anything which is the same. If he finds himself constantly in danger of becoming other, how can he believe in himself? Thus the boarders at Todgers' name and rename the servant boy at their pleasure. He is forced to become one after another a series of inconsistent avatars no one of which has any relation to what he is for himself: 'Benjamin was supposed to be the real name of this young retainer, but he was known by a great variety of names. Benjamin, for instance, had been converted into Uncle Ben, and that again had been corrupted into Uncle; which, by an easy transition, had again passed into Barnwell, in memory of the celebrated relative in that degree who was shot by his nephew George, while meditating in his garden at Camberwell. The gentlemen at Todgers's had a merry habit, too, of bestowing upon him, for the time being, the name of any notorious malefactor or minister; and sometimes when current events were flat, they even sought the pages of history for these distinctions; as Mr Pitt, Young Brownrigg, and the like' (ch. 9). Each of these 'selves' lasts only 'for the time being', and there is no predictable rationale in the transitions. Young Bailey is in the position of one who, when he goes to bed at night, does not know who he will find himself to be in the morning. No doubt the joke lies in the inappropriateness of all these names, the dissimilarity of each to the others, and more especially to Bailey himself. But can we not see a connection between Bailey's experience of an externally imposed transformation, and his decision to take matters into his own hands and be himself the source of an entirely new identity? It is no longer a question, when he does this, of creating a false protective surface behind which one hides, but of accepting the fact that he is what other people see, and of controlling and creating that self by an act of will. Having been passively a constant succession of different names, of different selves, he becomes himself the source of a new self and forces others to accept him, just as the earlier metamorphoses had been forced on him. He takes his revenge by appearing one day with a new job, new clothes, and a new self: 'Paul Sweedlepipe, the meek, was so perfectly confounded by his precocious self-possession, and his patronising manner, as well as by his boots, cockade, and livery, that a mist swam before his eyes, and he saw – not the Bailey of acknow-ledged juvenility, from Todgers's Commercial Boarding House, who had made his acquaintance within a twelvemonth, by purchasing, at sundry times, small birds at twopence each – but a highly-condensed embodiment of all the sporting grooms in London; an abstract of all the stable-knowledge of the time; a something at a high-pressure that must have had existence many years, and was fraught with terrible experiences' (ch. 26). Bailey has produced such a convincing façade that it is impossible not to believe that there is a corresponding reality within. The alternatives are 'to take Bailey for granted' or 'to go distracted' (ch. 26), go distracted because the whole technique by which one infers reality from the data of sensation is put in question. By a sheer effort of will, the 'high-pressure' of his inexhaustible vitality – 'And what a Life Young Bailey's was!' (ch. 49) says Sweedlepipe later – Bailey has 'eclipsed both time and space, cheated beholders of their senses, and worked on their belief in defiance of all natural laws' (ch. 26).

Bailey seems to have succeeded completely in controlling himself by controlling the vacillation of the self he is for others. But another similar transmogrification does not succeed so well. Montague Tigg becomes Tigg Montague and changes himself from a shabby beggar to the splendidly arrayed chairman of the Anglo-Bengalee: 'Flowers of gold and blue, and green and blushing red, were on his waistcoat; precious chains and jewels sparkled on his breast; his fingers, clogged with brilliant rings, were as unwieldy as summer flies but newly rescued from a honey-pot. The daylight mantled in his gleaming hat and boots as in a polished glass' (ch. 27). Tigg is the triumph of a multiple and dazzling surface, forbidding any access to the interior. And yet the deception does not work, or, rather, the façade, however changed it may be, is still recognizably a projection of the same false interior, still only a remodelling of the same substance: '. . . though changed his name, and changed his outward surface, it was Tigg. Though turned and twisted upside down, and inside out, as great men have been sometimes known to be; though no longer Montague Tigg, but Tigg Montague; still it was Tigg; the same Satanic, gallant, military Tigg. The brass was burnished, lacquered, newly-stamped: yet it was the true Tigg metal notwithstanding' (ch. 27). Doubtless this is a way of asserting the comfortable doctrine of the impossibility of substantial change in character. Dickens, as we have seen in *Oliver Twist*, holds firmly to the idea that each human being has an essence, a permanent nature which is born with him and persists through all the vicissitudes of his experience. In spite of the discovery of a subjective nothingness in the view from Todgers', Dickens believes that Tigg cannot cease to be himself however much he changes himself, any more than Oliver can cease to be virtuous and gentle whatever his experience. Indeed, since the public self which coerces belief from beholders has been chosen and created by Tigg himself, it cannot help but be an extension of himself, a new shape given to his own metal, arbitrary and unjustified, and depending on the subjective energy of the inner self for its existence.

Two extreme dangers, then, face the character who attempts to achieve an authentic self by accepting the necessity of being related to others. He may live in a constant state of inner tension resulting from the strain of sustaining an assumed identity in the eyes of those around him. Martin observes in Major Pawkins, as in other Americans, 'a peculiar air of quiet weariness, like [that of] a man who had been up all night' (ch. 16). What is this 'listlessness and languor' (ch. 16) if not spiritual exhaustion, consequence of a continually repeated act of self-creation?

Or, at the other extreme, a passive submission to other people will lead to complete spiritual paralysis. To let other people choose what one will be and to let them do all the work of bringing that identity into being is, in the end, to be nothing at all. Thus poor old Chuffey, the Chuzzlewit clerk, only lights up into a 'sentient human creature' when he is spoken to by old Anthony Chuzzlewit. If that does not happen, or if it ceases to happen, he relapses into total nothingness:

'. . . being spoken to no more, the light forsook his face by little and little, until he was nothing again' (ch. 11); '. . . breathing on his shrivelled hands to warm them, [he] remained with his poor blue nose immoveable about his plate, looking at nothing, with eyes that saw nothing, and a face that meant nothing. Take him in that state, and he was an embodiment of nothing. Nothing else' (ch. 11).

This collapse into nothing can take two forms. A loss of faith in someone other than oneself can cause the disintegration not only of that person, but of the entire world itself. Just as a person's removal from the center of a long-abiding world causes it to fall into fragments, so, for Tom Pinch, the loss of faith in Pecksniff, who had been, so to speak, the Platonic idea of his world, its organizing principle, causes a substantial change not only in his apprehension of Pecksniff, but in his apprehension of the whole world: 'But there was no Pecksniff; there never had been a Pecksniff, and the unreality of Pecksniff extended itself to the chamber, in which, sitting on one particular bed, the thing supposed to be that Great Abstraction had often preached morality with such effect, that Tom had felt a moisture in his eyes . . .' (ch. 31); 'Oh! what a different town Salisbury was in Tom Pinch's eyes to be sure, when the substantial Pecksniff of his heart melted away into an idle dream!' (ch. 36).

Or, the collapse may be of the character himself, an evaporation into the utter nonentity he has never really ceased to be. Like Chuffey, Pecksniff loses his positive existence when he is alone: 'But Mr Pecksniff . . . certainly did not appear to any unusual advantage, now that he was left alone. On the contrary, he seemed to be shrunk and reduced; to be trying to hide himself within himself; and to be wretched at not having the power to do it. His shoes looked too large; his sleeve looked too long; his hair looked too limp; his features looked too mean . . .' (ch. 30). And when he is denounced by old Martin at the end of the novel he collapses publicly and for good, like a deflated balloon: 'Not only did his figure appear to have shrunk, but his discomfiture seemed to have extended itself, even to his dress. His clothes seemed to have grown shabbier, his linen to have turned yellow, his hair to have become lank and frowsy; his very boots looked villainous and dim, as if their gloss had departed with his own' (ch. 52). Various critics have reproached Dickens for transforming Pecksniff into 'a drunken, squalid, begging-letter-writing man' (ch. 54), but it is only the permanent deflation of Pecksniff which will allow Dickens to make his point dramatically. Even in his greatest success and glory, as in the scene of the laying of the cornerstone of the building whose design he has stolen from Martin, Pecksniff has never possessed real substance. Like other characters in *Martin Chuzzlewit*, he struggles unsuccessfully to reconcile two radically incompatible needs.

There is no way, it seems, to combine simultaneously the two necessities of authentic individuality. If a person is simply what he is in the eyes of other people he is, in the end, something which has nothing to do with himself; hence he is nothing. But if he is something which derives wholly from himself he will rest on nothing outside himself, and, such is the unique peculiarity of the human condition, he will be nothing. However much Dickens believes that each person has an essence, a permanent intrinsic nature, he still also believes that he has a satisfactory identity only when that essence is recognized and accepted by something outside himself. Only if a man could be simultaneously independent *and* completely justified by something external could the void be filled and a stable identity attained. But whichever way they turn, whether by rejecting the existence of other people or by accepting it, the characters of *Martin Chuzzlewit* find themselves, at last, back in the same state of nonentity.

VIII

Everywhere in *Martin Chuzzlewit*, then, we find in the characters a vacillation between the desire to be wholly autonomous, and the even more intense desire to discover something outside themselves which will recognize their being.

The dramatic action of *Martin Chuzzlewit* is disentangled through a human relationship which represents an escape from this vacillation, the only escape which Dickens can discover at this time. The escape is *love*, the joining together of heroes and heroines which ends the novel, and sends the protagonists off to live happily ever after. Love is for Dickens that human relationship in which each partner, by giving himself unselfishly to the other, becomes the foundation and justification of the other's selfhood. But at this stage of Dickens' career love is shown from the outside, as a mystery. It brings the story happily to a close, but Dickens cannot really show how that happens. Love makes the Temple fountain sparkle and smile for John and Ruth, but not for Dickens. Nowhere is Dickens' self-betraying sentimentality more present here than in the treatment of the love affairs of his characters. All Dickens' attempts to get inside these relationships and show their reciprocity only move him (and the reader!) further and further away into the isolation of a self-generated emotion.

Furthermore, there is a very acute analysis, within the novel, of the way lovers are selfish in their relationship to other people. We remember how Tigg, speaking of commercial corporations, had said, 'We companies are all birds of prey' (ch. 27), and how Anthony Chuzzlewit had spoken of selfish cooperation as a way to escape impotent isolation: 'We are the two halves of a pair of scissors, when apart, Pecksniff; but together we are something. Eh?' (ch. 11). The intensely exclusive partnership of lovers is an unexpected repetition of this. The marriage of Mary and Martin means necessarily the eternal unfulfillment of Tom Pinch's love for Mary, and it was the fact that Mary and Martin had secretly and selfishly chosen one another which originally led old Martin to repudiate his grandson: 'he tortured himself with the reflection that they, so young, to whom he had been so kind a benefactor, were already like the world, and bent on their own selfish, stealthy ends' (ch. 52). Just as Martin's social sin was to attempt to be entirely self-sufficient in America, and to make his fortune independently, so his sin within the world of personal relations was to choose Mary for himself.

No doubt Dickens' intention, in this as in the treatment of Mark Tapley's unsuccessful and immoral attempt to find 'credit' in being jolly, was to show that there is a necessarily selfish element in all unselfishness, an element which must be accepted as in the nature of the moral life. But the problem cannot be so easily solved for his protagonists, since such a resolution would leave them still isolated from the human community. The solution offered brings the story to a close. It intertwines the social and personal issues, and reduces them both to the fundamental problem in Dickens' imaginative universe: How can the outcast find his way justifiably back into the human world?

Martin Chuzzlewit, like Pip, has 'great expectations': 'I have', he says, 'been bred up from childhood with great expectations, and have always been taught to believe that I should be, one day, very rich' (ch. 6). Again in *Martin Chuzzlewit*, as in *Oliver Twist*, we find centrally operative in the eventual fulfillment of these expectations the theme of the secret manipulation of the hero's life, the theme of a benevolent human providence. Apparently Martin is all alone. Throughout most of the story he has a consciousness of his isolation, of the fact that he must make his own way in the world. But his experiences in America portray the frustration of his attempt, both in his own total failure and in his discovery of the full implications of such aloneness. Dickens' Americans are a people without a past, a people who have made a code of going it alone after having made a clean sweep of all past institutions and beliefs. They are a people who have and are only what they have taken and made for themselves. Martin, disinherited by old Martin after he has chosen for himself the girl his grandfather wanted him to marry, is thrust into a world like that inhabited by the thieves of *Oliver Twist*, and when he goes to America he enters a whole nation full of people living in the isolation of the lonely crowd. But there is, it seems, no way out of this situation, once one is really in it, as the unhappy fates of the thieves in *Oliver Twist*, as well as the treatment of selfishness in *Martin Chuzzlewit*, show. The Americans cannot in any way escape from their isolation and from the fact that their every word and act is dishonest. They can never escape from the isolation of each man from all the others which makes society in America a game of subterfuge and a masquerade of false appearances. And they have no way to get even the necessities of life and a minimal identity without taking the one, and creating the other – and therefore possessing them illegitimately. Dickens' Americans are condemned to isolation and guilt.

Dickens devises for his hero an escape from this intolerable condition which is a variation of the resolution he used in *Oliver Twist*. Just as Oliver was in reality all along that which he tried to make himself by resisting the thieves, so Martin is all along secretly loved by old Martin. In the end Martin does not win a place for himself in the world, but has his original great expectations fulfilled from the outside by his grandfather. Old Martin, with unselfish abnegation, gives him Mary and a fortune. The handclasp which is to be in *Great Expectations* the symbol of human interrelationship and mutual responsibility appears already here, but it expresses not the free and unjustified choice of two lovers for one another, but rather the place of old Martin as a human providence who is the source and guarantee of human community: 'Martin took him [Tom Pinch] by the hand, and Mary too, and John, his old friend, stoutly too: and Mark, and Mrs Lupin, and his [Tom's] sister, little Ruth' (ch. 52). Only when old Martin gives his permission can this tableau give way to a handclasp and embrace between Martin and Mary.

Nevertheless, here again, just as Oliver only became himself, that is, the son of his real parents, because he was able to be himself without any external evidence of who he was, so Martin can be rewarded by old Martin and given a place in society only after he has learned the hard lesson of unselfishness in the isolation of an American swamp. This isolation is precisely to be defined by the fact that during that time he had no knowledge of anything outside himself on which he could depend to help him, reward him, or recognize him. Again Dickens contrives to have it both ways, to have his hero both responsible for what he is, and not guilty of creating himself. Like Oliver, Martin can only win so much because he has lost so much. Here too, there is an intervening testing period of isolation in which the hero makes himself by his own efforts what he is later constituted as being by some outside authority. The 'good' characters in Dickens' novels, at this stage of his career, are never left permanently in their condition of self-reliant isolation. Dickens does not yet have the courage to face the real implications of his view of human existence, and contrives a release for his hero which is only a sidestepping of the problems of his basic theme. Martin does not extricate himself; he is rescued by outside forces. And yet the whole bent of Dickens' nature drove him to discover a way in which the outcast could justifiably escape through his own efforts. In the novels which follow *Martin Chuzzlewit* we can see Dickens moving toward more unequivocal dramatizations of his sense of the world.

NOTES

1. Dorothy Van Ghent, in an excellent article, 'The Dickens World: A View from Todgers's', in *Sewanee Review*, LVIII 3 (1950) 419–38, uses this passage as her center of focus. Her interpretation, however, differs from mine.

2. 'The Dickens World', p. 421.

3. See F. O. Matthiessen's discussion of this in *American Renaissance* (New York, 1941) pp. 14–24, esp. 19–22. Matthiessen quotes the following passage from Edward Everett's address for Washington's birthday: '. . . the name and memory of Washington on that gracious night will travel with the silver queen of heaven through sixty degrees of longitude, nor part company with her till she walks in her brightness through the golden gate of California, and passes serenely on to hold midnight court with her Australian stars' (p. 20).

KATHLEEN TILLOTSON

Dombey and Son (1954)

I

Dombey and Son stands out from among Dickens's novels as the earliest example of responsible and successful planning; it has unity not only of action, but of design and feeling. It is also the first in which a pervasive uneasiness about contemporary society takes the place of an intermittent concern with specific social wrongs. These are the main reasons why this novel rather than *Martin Chuzzlewit* or *David Copperfield* is here chosen to represent Dickens in the 1840s; and these form the main headings – of unequal, but related importance – under which it will now be considered.

It is Dickens's seventh novel, and the fourth of those written in this decade. A gap unusually long for Dickens divides it from its predecessor; *Martin Chuzzlewit* was completed in July 1844, and the writing of *Dombey* was not begun until 27 June 1846.[1] The interval had been fully occupied in travel, theatricals, writing 'Christmas books', founding and for a short time editing the *Daily News*; at the end of May came what Forster calls the 'retreat to Switzerland', and it was at Geneva, Lausanne, and Paris that the first six numbers were written.[2] The writing was attended with many difficulties ('You can hardly imagine what infinite pains I take, or what extraordinary difficulty I find in getting on FAST'). He suffered from 'the absence of streets and number of figures' – required not as material, but as stimulus – and from the new problem of beginning a novel and writing a 'Christmas book' in the same months; but

> Invention, thank God, seems the easiest thing in the world; and I seem
> to have such a preposterous sense of the ridiculous after this long rest as
> to be constantly requiring to restrain myself from launching into extrava-
> gances in the height of my enjoyment.[3]

It was necessary for his illustrator to co-operate in avoiding 'extravagances' ('enormous care' is required with Dombey and Miss Tox, and 'the Toodle Family should not be too much caricatured, because of Polly').[4] He wrote the christening scene with 'the drag on', to avoid satire – 'malice in christening points of faith'.[5] There is evidence that he restrained himself especially in comic dialogue. When he had 'over-written' a number, it was the non-functional comic dialogue (between Miss Tox and Mrs Chick) that was cut, as the original proofs show: 'I have avoided unnecessary dialogue so far, to avoid overwriting; and all I *have* written is point.'[6]

This deliberate control of comic exaggeration and inventiveness marks one of the differences between *Dombey* and its predecessors; the comedy is in lower relief and is subordinate to the design of the whole.[7] The overflowing comic inventiveness is here kept within bounds; Dickens was setting himself new standards. His was the genius that 'progresses and evolves and does not spin upon itself'; it would have been easy (and remunerative) for him to repeat the happy improvisation of his early novels – but this no longer contented him. With *Dombey* he began to write novels founded on a theme, embodied in a relation between characters. This more conscious technique (contrast 'I thought of Mr Pickwick') and the particular theme chosen, with its gravity, and its subtle and various relevance to his own time, give *Dombey and Son* a peculiar interest.

II

Despite the gap, there is a significant relation between *Dombey and Son* and its predecessor. In *Martin Chuzzlewit*, says Dickens, in the Preface to the first edition, 'I have endeavoured to resist the temptation of the current Monthly Number, and to keep a steadier eye upon the general purpose and design. With this object in view I put a strong constraint upon myself.'

What was new was little more than the endeavour; the temptations were not always resisted nor the constraint effective. The origin of the book, we learn from Forster, lay in Pecksniff; 'the notion of taking Pecksniff for a type of character was really the origin of the book; the design being to show, more or less by every person introduced, the number and variety of humours and vices that have their root in selfishness'.[8] This is a very general 'purpose and design', leaving much room for improvisation and modification. There was no narrative plan, no dynamic view of the interaction of characters, such as we find in the long letter to Forster outlining the design of *Dombey*; evidence of foresight and design is found only after the writing, even the publication, is well under way. The plot of old Martin was drawn up when the third number was being written; Forster's comment on this bears upon *Dombey*: 'the difficulties he encountered in departing from other portions of his scheme were such as to render him, in his subsequent stories, more bent on constructive care at the outset, and on adherence as far as might be to any design he had formed'.

In *Dombey* he again had a 'general purpose and design', which is explicitly compared to that of *Chuzzlewit*; it is 'to do with Pride what its predecessor had done with Selfishness'.[9] Rather, what he had *meant* its predecessor to do; he would learn from its stumbling endeavour and work out the design of *Dombey* more precisely. This novel, even without its numerous surrounding documents – number-plans, letters to Forster and Browne, corrected manuscript and proofs – is eloquent of his far greater success. To say this is not to belittle *Chuzzlewit*; but it is doubtful there whether a reader lacking preface or biography would recognize that Selfishness, or even Hypocrisy (it is never quite clear which Dickens means) was its theme. Circumstances worked against him; sales of early numbers were disappointing, and 'America' was resorted to as an expedient to stimulate them. Although it is made relative to the theme (exposing Martin's selfishness, and magnificently illustrating the unconscious self-deception of another national character, which might be judged a kind of hypocrisy) it remains an expedient and an episode; 'a place Martin Chuzzlewit happens to go to'.[10] And throughout this novel the details mask the 'general purpose and design'; it is largely remembered and valued for single scenes and characters, either loosely attached to the theme or too expansively illustrative of it. Whereas *Dombey* has its firm centre, of theme, character, and scene, Pecksniff and Martin divide the centre, the one static, but giving out vitality, the other progressing, but uninteresting. There is no scenic centre, and no coherent impression of period; no one would select *Chuzzlewit* as especially representative or reflective of the early 1840s. We cannot mistake the earnestness of Dickens's moral and social concern to expose in Pecksniff a peculiarly English and contemporary vice,[11] as distinct from remediable and specific abuses. But for various reasons the exposure is not complete – far less so than in the smaller scale figures of Chadband and Podsnap. Dickens had not grasped the difficulty of having a hypocrite bearing the weight of a main character – he can hardly stand the strain if he is only to be exhibited, never analysed. We need to know, at least to suspect, how he appears to himself; we are told that Pecksniff had solitary thoughts by the fireside, but never what they were (ch. 9, which concludes no. III). Pecksniff exists mainly in the limelight of a series of superb scenes (and also as refracted in the contrasted natures of Tom and Martin); but under this continued exhibition, with its extravagantly comic dialogue, he becomes less not more repulsive. Dickens's comic inventiveness is still overflowing, neither subordinated to the general purpose nor fully contained by moral and social criticism. The resulting ambiguity is clearer still with Mrs Gamp, who is almost extraneous to the plot. We are less aware of the horrors of her ministrations than of the private world she blissfully inhabits, 'as light as any gash balloon', and which Dickens makes it seem a privilege to share. Contrast the continued yet unstrained harnessing of the comedy to the 'general purpose and design' in *Dombey*, where the absurd is on the side of the angels. Toots and Susan Nipper and Captain Cuttle and Miss Tox, all, by their natures and their share in the action, supply continuous moral comment on the evil represented in Mr Dombey; and they do so naturally and implicitly, without the copybook pointedness of Mark Tapley. So, from the other side, does Major Bagstock, whose function Dickens defined when he called him 'a kind of comic Mephistophelean power'[12] (with Mr Dombey as Faust?).

Not only the comedy, but all the characters and all the action are subordinated to Mr Dombey. This is the first novel of Dickens to be dominated by a leading idea, embodied in a single character. He is the origin, centre, and continuum of the novel, as no previous character of Dickens's had been. Before this is demonstrated in relation to the structural unity of the book it will be necessary to look into this idea and character, and the other character upon whom they chiefly act.

III

That the origin of the book lay in Mr Dombey is not indeed clearly attested by direct external evidence, as it is with Pickwick and Pecksniff; but everything even outside the novel itself points that way. Forster's

report that as first conceived 'it was to do with Pride what its predecessor had done with Selfishness';[13] Dickens's anxiety for secrecy – 'The
very name getting out, would be ruinous';[14] the 'outline of [his] immediate intentions' in the letter to Forster with the manuscript of
number 1;[15] his 'nervous dread of caricature in the face of his merchant-
hero'[16] – all these agree in their emphasis. It is safe to assume that the
originating idea took the form of a 'merchant-hero', in whom business
and family pride are twisted into a single hard knot; the continued
interplay between the affairs of the firm and the family is emphasized
by the early chapter-titles (see chs. 3, 13, 22) and 'shadowed forth' in
the semi-allegorical cover design; although in the working-out less is
made of the firm than Dickens seems to have intended. The title is its
epitome (there is no record of hesitation over this title as with most
others); and is also deliberately misleading – serving to keep the secret
of Paul's early death, and to point the irony of the book's true subject
– which is, of course, Dombey and Daughter.[17] The relation between
Mr Dombey and Florence is the backbone of the whole book; structurally, the relation between him and Paul, and that between Florence
and Paul, are only means of exposing and developing it.

> From that time [Paul's death], I purpose changing his feelings of in-
> difference and uneasiness towards his daughter into a positive hatred. . . .
> At the same time I shall change *her* feeling towards *him* for one of a greater
> desire to love him, and to be loved by him; engendered in her compassion
> for his loss, and her love for the dead boy whom, in his way, he loved so
> well too. So I mean to carry the story on, through all the branches and
> off-shoots and meanderings that come up; and through the decay and
> downfall of the house, and the bankruptcy of Dombey, and all the rest of
> it; when his only staff and treasure, and his unknown Good Genius always,
> will be this rejected daughter, who will come out better than any son at
> last, and whose love for him, when discovered and understood, will be
> his bitterest reproach.[18]

Through this changing relation works Mr Dombey's pride, the master-
motive of the novel, the mainspring of all its events. Much then depends upon the adequacy of these two characters, Mr Dombey and
Florence, to sustain this central interest, and especially upon Dickens's
power – not hitherto manifested – to draw a character undergoing
inner conflict.

This continued inner conflict was also a part of the original intention; the letter just quoted continues:

> For the struggle with himself, which goes on in all such obstinate natures, will have ended then; and the sense of his injustice, which you may be sure has never quitted him, will have at last a gentler office than that of only making him more harshly unjust.[19]

The last point alone shows Dickens's psychological insight; and it is repeated in the new Preface added by the author twelve years later – apparently in reply to criticism of the supposed 'violent change' in the hero.[20]

> The two commonest mistakes in judgment . . . are the confounding of shyness with arrogance . . . and the not understanding that an obstinate nature exists in a perpetual struggle with itself.
>
> Mr Dombey undergoes no violent change, either in this book, or in real life. A sense of his injustice is within him, all along. The more he represses it, the more unjust he necessarily is. Internal shame and external circumstances may bring the contest to a close in a week, or a day; but, it has been a contest for years, and is only fought out after a long balance of victory.[21]

The moment in the novel when the contest is nearest to the surface is in chapter 35, where Mr Dombey watches Florence, who believes him asleep. 'There are yielding moments in the lives of the sternest and harshest men, though such men often keep their secret well.' So begins the long paragraph in which his brief relenting is traced, and its hidden sources suggested. It ends with a dramatic turn; Edith enters, and, still unobserved, he witnesses her gentle and loving conversation with Florence – a double blow to his pride, and the stimulus to double revenge upon them.

'Such men often keep their secret well'; ' "Dombey", said the Major . . . "don't be thoughtful. . . . You are too great a man, Dombey, to be thoughtful" ' (ch. 20). The difficulty, especially to a writer more practised in exhibition than analysis, is to suggest the secret self-doubting of 'stiff-necked sullen arrogance'. Such suggestion is conveyed sometimes by the use of carefully timed silent pauses in the narrative, moments sharply presented to the sight and impressing the imagination: as when Mr Dombey watches Florence carrying Paul up 'the great, wide, vacant staircase' in the moonlight, and singing to him (ch. 8).[22] Or by a revealing but unannotated gesture: as when Mrs Chick, promoting the Brighton scheme, hesitantly submits that Florence must accompany Paul:

> 'It's quite an infatuation with him. He's very young, you know, and has his fancies.'
> Mr Dombey turned his head away, and going slowly to the bookcase, and unlocking it, brought back a book to read. (ch. 8)

In Mr Dombey Dickens achieves the remarkable feat of making us aware of the hidden depths of a character, while keeping them largely hidden; his method respects Mr Dombey's own proud reserve. The only times his thoughts are unrolled at length before us it is through the phantasmagoria of the railway journey (ch. 20, and see p. 175, below), where Dickens can 'analyse' as it were panoramically, with something of the picturesque freedoms of dream or allegory; and similarly again through the memories and visions called up when he roams through the silent house (ch. 59). Mr Dombey has 'lonely thoughts, bred late at night in the sullen despondency and gloom of his retirement' (ch. 20), but the reader is seldom admitted to them; yet he is often reminded, both by oblique reference and momentary pictures of that silent brooding presence, the shadow behind the figure which Mr Dombey presents to the world, 'self-important, unbending, formal, austere' (ch. 27). What makes him interesting is the moral suspense: although Florence may serve partly as an externalized conscience, a troublesome and even hated reminder of the whole world of feeling that his pride has forsworn, she does so because something within him responds to her. Before Paul's birth, he had been merely indifferent; afterwards this indifference turns to uneasiness and resentment (ch. 3), which increase after Paul's death.[23] But in this resentment there is an unadmitted sense of guilt, and even the seeds of repentance. His love for his son, involved though it is in 'a partial scheme of parental interest and ambition', is yet also the rift in the ice. We are aware of it even in the cruellest moment in which he repulses Florence's affection, and even aware of it as his justification for doing so; he watches her, silently and hopelessly ascending the stairs.

> The last time he had watched her, from the same place, winding up those stairs, she had had her brother in her arms. It did not move his heart towards her now, it steeled it: but he went into his room, and locked his door, and sat down in his chair, and cried for his lost boy. (ch. 18)

In his momentary relenting towards her (so abruptly terminated by a new jealousy) 'She became blended with the child he had loved, and he could hardly separate the two' (ch. 35). Such evidence keeps before us the 'contest [of] years, only fought out after a long balance of victory'; we can accept its bringing to a close, through 'internal shame and external circumstances', in a single chapter of the closing number (ch. 59). We may feel that for 'internal shame' to reach the purpose of self-murder, and for 'external circumstances' to bring Florence home in the nick of time, savours overmuch of the theatre; we may feel that the year's lapse between the last two numbers[24] has cheated us, or spared us, too much of the slow undermining of Mr Dombey's obstinate pride. But in the account of his days and nights of restless wandering through the desolate house, Dickens prevents us from feeling that the reconciliation is cheaply purchased. In a passage of no more than four pages he condenses Mr Dombey's history and his present state. And he does it, as always, by a combination of picture and analysis. The deserted rooms, the staircase (that recurring symbol) with its remembered footsteps, carry us backward in time. In Mr Dombey's thoughts, the whole of the original design of the novel is retraced. It is not a static view; the contest still continues. He has passed beyond Paul's death, the wreck of his marriage, his fallen fortunes:

> That which was his own work, that which he could so easily have wrought into a blessing, and had set himself so steadily for years to form into a curse: that was the sharp grief of his soul. . . .
>
> And yet—so proud he was in his ruin . . . that if he could have heard her voice in an adjoining room, he would not have gone to her. . . . He chiefly thought of what might have been, and what was not. What was, was all summed up in this: that she was lost, and he bowed down with sorrow and remorse.

Inevitably, the passage is introduced by a reiteration of the earlier prophecy: 'Let him remember it in that room, years to come' (ch. 18, 59). But the heavily emphasized pattern of sin, curse, retribution is not the 'figure in the carpet' of *Dombey and Son*. Dickens's impulse towards the cruder simplifications should not obscure from us that his hero is a character of tragic stature. Not seldom, towards the close of the novel, we think of another unbending but vulnerable man of affairs, who wished to stand 'as if a man were author of himself'; or of another proud father and banished daughter, Lear and Cordelia.

And no more than there is the forgiveness a sentimental concession; the famous criticism that Mr Dombey 'becomes the best of fathers, and spoils a fine novel',[25] is wide of the mark. It might have been ill judged if he were fully shown as 'the best of fathers'; but after this climax we see him only in the moral convalescence of physical illness, and in the afterglow of the epilogue.

IV

The contest for Mr Dombey's soul requires no more of Florence than a perfect goodness and persistent affection; in the words of a chapter-heading, 'The Study of a Loving Heart'. But the balance of the novel requires her to be prominent, and she is not completely absent from the scene for more than a single number (no. XVII, chs. 52, 54). A character conceived in terms of pure feeling, passive, innocent to the point of being almost 'incapable of her own distress', can hardly sustain this prominence. The dilemma, though it is doubtful if Dickens saw it as such, is clear. Conflict within her, introspection, or initiative, would mitigate the pathos of her situation; unmitigated, the pathos risks monotony, if not self-defeat. (It may even raise the more serious criticism that if her state of mind is not morbid, it is improbable;[26] and it is not within Dickens's range in *this* novel to regard it as morbid.)[27]

She has to be entirely lovable, in order to leave us in no doubt of the guilt of Mr Dombey (and his own sense of it); for the same reason, she has to be, with that noticeable exception, universally loved. The love according to their lights of almost all the other characters carries conviction, and at times Florence gains some reflected vitality from Susan Nipper, Mr Toots, and Captain Cuttle; even Mrs Chick was on one occasion struck into silence and 'lost . . . her presence of mind' at the sight of Florence grieving for Paul. But on the whole the effect is still of a space where Florence's character ought to be, with our attention drawn from the vacuum by the ring of admirers. Dickens's difficulties are not peculiar to him,[28] or to this novel; besides the time-less problem of making perfect virtue, and especially the passive virtues, attractive, he has his age's problem of vitalizing a heroine in a period of limiting ideals for girlhood.[29] Yet let the Victorian novel itself dictate our standards, and we see what is lacking in Florence as a heroine attracting the reader; that endearing solidity, even of appearance, that touch of individualizing charm, which Trollope was able to give to all the fifty or so of his young heroines;[30] and which Dickens was to find for his less perfect ones – Dora, Pet, Bella, and Rosa.

This is not to say that Florence fails; only that one must approach her differently from Mr Dombey, and see her as a character drawn wholly within the bounds of her situation; to an extent that she, and the pathos of that situation, are one and the same. Two approaches have at least the merit of being included in Dickens's own. First, by beginning with Florence as a child of six years old, he is able to sustain our pity and tenderness for her as a child, even after she grows to be seventeen. Because we have seen her 'pressing her small hands hard together' (ch. 3) as she timidly enters her father's room, or ragged and lost in the City streets, or clinging crying to Polly's skirts; because we have seen her through Paul's eyes, and Walter Gay's, we continue to think of her, when she is thirteen, fifteen, seventeen, as a child still. Her fear of Carker is of the same colouring as her fear of Good Mrs Brown; Walter is her 'brother'; flying from her home, she is once again the lost child. Not with the Esthers and Agneses or the child-wives, but with the children of Dickens's novels – Nell, and Oliver – should Florence be classed. There is one qualification. Though her feeling for Edith may begin as childish – the 'new mama' – it becomes more mature. When Florence, now sixteen, is drawn into the orbit of the unhappy domestic situation, Dickens does not leave her wholly innocent and bewildered. He attempts to suggest a transition from childhood (chs. 43, 47);[31] which is indeed necessary if he is to lead up to her flight from home – the sole occasion on which she is to act as well as suffer. But in the Dombey–Carker–Edith situation she is chiefly a pawn in the game; and the idiom in which it is conducted makes her less and not more alive.

The other approach is by way of the mysterious simplicities of fairy-tale, never far away in Dickens's work. Walter Gay, before ever he has seen Florence, is compared by his romantic uncle to Dick Whittington, who married his master's daughter (ch. 4); when he finds her as a lost child in the City streets, he feels like Cinderella's prince, and also 'not to say like Richard Whittington – that is a tame comparison – but like Saint George of England, with the dragon lying dead before him' (ch. 6).

The 'great dreary house' where Florence lives alone is like a 'magic

dwelling-place in magic story, shut up in the heart of a thick wood',
with the ironwork of the doorway instead of 'two dragon sentries';
but she 'bloomed there, like the king's fair daughter in the story'
(ch. 23). When she has taken refuge with Captain Cuttle, they are
compared to 'a wandering princess and a good monster in a story-
book' (ch. 49). With these as pointers,[32] we can discern other, unstated,
analogues: the recurring witch-figure (Good Mrs Brown, and Mrs
Pipchin, who has a black cat), the helpful animal (Diogenes attacking
Carker), and the comic knight and squire of the anti-masque (Toots
and the Game Chicken). The 'adult' characters, Mr Dombey, Edith,
and Carker, are clear of this tincture of romance, but the children (and
the fools) not wholly so. It affects us more than we are aware; and it
relates *Dombey* to the world of the earlier novels – *Oliver Twist*,
Nicholas Nickleby, and *The Old Curiosity Shop*. If we can see Florence
as the princess under a spell, or the unrecognized child of royal birth
from whom a strange light shines, or even as Spenser's Una, we may
come nearer Dickens's own intention. The presence of different modes
in a narrative is something we must accept in his novels, as in poetic
drama.

v

Two other major characters, Carker and Edith, belong to a different
mode again, and one which is nowadays less readily accepted in serious
novels. Of the second marriage and the machinations of the Manager[33]
the 'design' shows no prevision; but they cannot be reckoned among
the 'off-shoots and meanderings'. Both structurally and thematically
this part of the plot is justified, as I shall show. Nevertheless, in intro-
ducing a mode that is neither tragedy nor fairy-tale romance, though
allied to both – in fact, what is commonly called melodrama – it leads
to some disturbance of tone. As part of the plot, it has both necessity
and unity: it serves as counterplot – the means by which Mr Dombey's
downfall is brought about – and it is unified by the single but branching
motive of revenge, in both Carker and Edith. The irony is emphasized
by there being two of them, and by their revenge being partly directed
against Mr Dombey, partly against each other. Carker was the necessary active villain, slowly undermining Mr Dombey's security, both
in firm and family.[34] But his juxtaposition to Mr Dombey is valuable

in other ways. His unalloyed evil makes clearer by contrast the mixed nature of Mr Dombey (compare the effect of the cruder Jonas Chuzzlewit as against old Martin). His pride, concealed in false servility but militant and climbing, is contrasted with Mr Dombey's, self-evident, but dangerously complacent. This reveals other ironies in the situation: Mr Dombey is vulnerable, because in his pride he underrates others, believes them content in subservience; he is far too proud to be clever about people. Here is both motive and opening for the revenge-plot. Carker schemes revenge against Mr Dombey, for keeping him down and treating him as a tool; against Walter, for fear he should supplant him; against Edith, for despising him. This is the sum of his motivation, at least on the level of character. It is simple, but adequate for its purpose. Crafty and cat-like, his function is to scheme and be sinister; he requires no redeeming feature, no capacity for remorse. He might be, and is often taken for, an entirely 'flat' character, a mere stage villain – a black-hearted monster with a set of flashing white teeth attached – or a mere machine of the plot. But two things give him depth: Dickens's unquestioning assumption that humanity can produce characters wholly evil, which cannot be reformed, but must be wiped out; and his firm hold on his social theme – Carker the 'new man', the 'forerunner of the managerial revolution'.[35]

Melodrama is Carker's native air; but it is not Edith's. Perhaps the single flaw in this novel is that Dickens, having conceived a character so complex as hers – behaving so consistently with her nature and situation and yet producing such exciting turns of the action – allows her to be drawn into a sphere which distorts her effect. Her share in Mr Dombey's downfall springs from motives subtly compounded of passionate resentment and self-immolation. She, not Carker, is really Mr Dombey's 'mighty opposite'; not only because her pride, equal to his in strength but warm blooded where his is cold, is a cry against corruption; but because she is potentially his equal in stature and depth. 'Daughter who has been put through her paces, before countless marrying men, like a horse for sale – Proud and weary of her degradation, but going on, for it's too late now, to turn back.' That is her first appearance in Dickens's notes for the novel;[36] it is the promising basis of a character which never ceases to interest and surprise, and the starting-point for a complicated narrative pattern. From the impact of such a character on the existent characters and situations one could predict the serious conflict of tragic passions; or, almost equally, the high comedy of manners. (One spark of *wit* in her defiant awareness of her predicament, and Edith could have been a recognizable relative of Ethel Newcome.) The chapters in which she first appears do not falsify our hopes; but she is shown only in company, and the revelation of her own view of Mr Dombey's courtship is delayed. Mr Dombey has asked to call on her next day, evidently to propose; she is alone with her mother, who has schemed for the marriage.

> 'Why don't you tell me . . . that he is coming here tomorrow by appointment?'
> 'Because you know it,' returned Edith, 'Mother.'
> The mocking emphasis she laid on that one word!
> 'You know he has bought me,' she resumed. 'Or that he will, to-morrow. He has considered of his bargain; he has shown it to his friend; he is even rather proud of it; he thinks that it will suit him, and may be had sufficiently cheap; and he will buy to-morrow. God, that I have lived for this, and that I feel it!'
> Compress into one handsome face the conscious self-abasement, and the burning indignation of a hundred women, strong in passion and in pride; and there it hid itself with two white shuddering arms.
> 'What do you mean?' returned the angry mother. 'Haven't you from a child——'
> 'A child!' said Edith, looking at her. 'When was I a child? What childhood did you ever leave to me? I was a woman – artful, designing, mercenary, laying snares for men – before I knew myself, or you, or even understood the base and wretched aim of every new display I learnt. You gave birth to a woman. Look upon her. She is in her pride to-night.'
> And as she spoke, she struck her hand upon her beautiful bosom, as though she would have beaten down herself.
> . . . 'There is no slave in a market: there is no horse in a fair: so shown and offered and examined and paraded, Mother, as I have been, for ten shameful years,' cried Edith, with a burning brow, and the same bitter emphasis on the one word.

Edith's 'tone' is established, and is maintained to the end. Not a tragic heroine, but a tragedy queen. The curling lip, the flashing eyes, the burning brow, and the throbbing bosom monotonously recur with the phraseology that attaches to them; chapters in which she appears fall naturally into 'scenes', with all the stage directions supplied. This mode of treatment is perhaps rather wasteful than damaging. It does not distort the other characters by contact. Mr Dombey's own style is little affected – 'I beg that Mrs Granger's very different experiences may now come to the instruction of Mrs Dombey' (ch. 40) – and there are many moments when the truth of feeling breaks through the theatrical convention, and we lose sight of the too obtrusive hand of the producer. But that convention needs to be consciously disengaged before the seriousness of the design can be appreciated; no doubt many readers have been misled, and have missed Dickens's 'insight' because 'he chooses to speak in a circle of stage fire'.[37]

For this two excuses, though not a justification, may be tentatively offered. From the start Dickens had evidently planned to implicate Edith with Carker; he may have thought of them together, without distinguishing the melodramatic mode appropriate to Carker from the naturalistic mode which Edith really requires. And he thought of her as becoming – even while hating him – the mistress of Carker. His known change of plan here, resulting in the most effective 'scene' – the repudiation of Carker at Dijon – was made at a late stage.[38] Up to and including her departure from Mr Dombey's roof, Edith is designed to end as an adultress (and consequently, in death); though not to alienate the reader's sympathy. This role lent itself to the idiom and attitudes of melodrama. Moreover, that may have been the only way in which Dickens felt he could make the situation acceptable to the 'family reader'. The borrowed colouring of the contemporary theatre may have been a kind of necessary gloss upon such 'domestic relations'[39] as Dickens has to hint at in the Dombey household. This is not to say that he was writing against the grain; 'tremendous scenes' were thoroughly congenial to him. And finally one must admit that they were more congenial to his age than ours; nor necessarily an impediment to the serious treatment of passion.

Carker and Edith are the last of their kind in Dickens's novels;[40] and though no hint of doubt or self-criticism emerges in his comments on the writing of *Dombey*,[41] there is some evidence of it ten years later, in his criticism of another author's heroine:

> She is too convulsive from beginning to end. Pray reconsider, from this point of view, her brow, and her eyes, and her drawing herself up to her full height . . . also her asking people how they dare, and the like, on small provocation. . . . I am an impatient and impulsive person myself, but . . . it has been for many years the constant effort of my life to practise at my desk what I preach to you.[42]

VI

The 'minor' characters radiate from the centre of the novel, both in action and in theme. Each one is related, at not more than one remove, to the Dombey household or firm, or both; each one makes its comment, on pride and wealth. The novel could be broken up like a book of the *Faerie Queene*: family pride illustrated variously in Mrs Chick, the Toodle parents, Mrs Skewton, Cousin Feenix, and Good Mrs Brown (even Mr Perch and Mrs MacStinger contribute their mite); attitudes to wealth and property also in the two 'toadies', honest and dishonest (Miss Tox and Major Bagstock), in Captain Cuttle, and in Mr Toots. Their comments are dramatic rather than didactic; they could best be illustrated, along with the integration of structure, by the selection of single brief stages of the narrative. For just as there are no inactive characters in *Dombey*, none that are decorative marginal flourishes,[43] there is no episode which fails to advance the 'general purpose and design' and illustrate the theme both in its broadly human and its social implications. I shall take two separate chapters, one full of incident and one apparently discursive, as examples.

In the sixth chapter, 'Paul's Second Deprivation', we follow some members of the household into a new scene: Polly Toodle is the bridge between the grandiose gloom of Mr Dombey's house and the boisterous affection of the humble home in Staggs's Gardens, set in the confusion and poverty of a district hacked up by the railway. Other scenes and representatives of other groups of characters are linked together. Florence is lost in the back streets of Camden Town, captured and stripped by Good Mrs Brown, turned loose in rags to wander towards the Dombey firm in the City, to be rescued and brought home by Walter Gay, after a brief meeting with Carker the Junior and Sol Gills. With all its richness of detail, its variety of character and dialogue and its pointed social illustration of the contrasted 'two nations', this chapter is firmly tied at both ends to Mr Dombey's pride, though his appearance in person is brief. Polly has been forbidden to visit her own family, but her anxious affection has been made frantic by Mr Dombey's interference in enrolling her eldest son as a Charitable Grinder. Her intervention to protect the hapless Rob from his tormentors is the occasion of Florence's loss. Good Mrs Brown is at hand not entirely

by chance, nor does she strip Florence of her clothes in simple acquisi-
tiveness; as we learn much later,[44] she has deliberately 'hung about a
family', watching the Dombey household, and Carker, her daughter's
seducer; she remembers that daughter and her action is a symbolic
vengeance. (Already it is hinted that she knows the name and the home
of Dombey.) Walter's rescue of Florence initiates his relation to her,
already forecast (in ch. 4), and sharpens Mr Dombey's irrational
hostility to him by putting him under an obligation which leads
directly to his banishment (in the almost too aptly named 'Son and
Heir'). The most far-reaching and ironical result of the incident is set
down in the title; the infant Paul is deprived of his wet-nurse, and
Mr Dombey's parental ambition begins its long course of self-defeat.
At all points the social moral is pressed home: here first is clearly
emphasized the interdependence of the classes, the relation beyond the
cash nexus. Polly has feelings that wealth cannot buy; the heir of
Dombey and Son has needs which his father's pride rejects at his peril.
None of these links are insisted on; all are vital in the design. (Even
the new scene of Camden Town is not just any poor district; it is
deliberately chosen for its connexion with the coming railway, to be
developed in chapters 15 and 20.)[45] It is also an essential part of that
design that the single figure who never disappears from view in this
busily changing chapter is Florence: passively lost, and found, and little
noticed in the concluding scene. 'The entrance of the lost child made
a slight sensation, but not much. Mr Dombey, who had never found
her, kissed her once upon the forehead. . . .'

VII

My second instance of this integration is from a chapter which is
particularly important as a transition between two large phases of the
action; and which is also interesting because Dickens's notes show that
he here felt the need for restraint.[46]

In the twentieth chapter, which opens the seventh number, 'Mr
Dombey goes upon a Journey'. The devoting of a whole chapter to a
journey marks the transition; and in its course the inevitability of
coming events is built up, a new relation is defined and the moral
centres of the novel are clearly exposed. The main concern of the whole

number is the visit to Leamington,[47] and the setting in motion of Mr
Dombey's second marriage, to Edith Granger; of this event no hint
has yet appeared, and none is given in this chapter. Mr Dombey has
been in shadow since Paul's death, the only exhibited event being his
repulse of Florence. The second marriage apparently arises from a
chance visit, undertaken as an escape from sorrow. But we are to
assume that it belongs to his nature as well as to circumstance. Bluntly,
he has lost one son, and must seek another.[48] But deliberate action
would be as inconsistent with his pride as with his grief. There must
be an intermediary. Already a possible (but improbable) second marriage has been prepared for, the instigator Mrs Chick, and the candidate
Miss Tox. Against this issue Miss Tox's neighbour is already scheming;
the contrast of the unsuccessful and the successful sycophant, juxtaposed
in the desperate gentility of Princess's Place, is carried further at the
opening of this chapter. It is comic, but also serious. The grounds of
the Major's triumph over Miss Tox are soon to be made clear; in
addition to the advantages of his masculinity, in coarseness and heartlessness, he has something besides flattery to sell. By the standards of
the time, the retired Indian Army Major (Sandhurst, blue face, curry
and clubs complete) is at least on the edge of a class a cut above the
wealthy City merchant; his friendship marks an advance in Mr Dombey's dignified upward climb, whereas Miss Tox owed her temporary
elevation only to her insignificance (ch. 5). One of the functions of
this chapter is to plant the Major firmly in the picture as the coming
instigator of the second marriage; to groom him for the part of go-
between in the common exchange of wealth for 'blood'. His status
and his outlook are further defined in his treatment of the Native, his
anecdotes, his views on the education of the poor; another variety of
pride is set beside Mr Dombey's, supporting and encouraging it, but
differentiated. The Major's qualities, so freely exhibited in this chapter,
show why 'Mr Dombey was disposed to regard him as a choice spirit
who shone in society . . . a creditable companion . . . having an
air of gentlemanly ease about him that mixed well enough with his
own City character, and did not compete with it at all' (ch. 20).[49] In
his growing influence on his friend the Major is already adumbrated
as a 'comic Mephistophelean power', and the ease of this influence also
makes plain Mr Dombey's unworldliness. The subsequent chapters are
to show the great merchant as easy prey for the unscrupulous; one of
the ways in which he gains upon our sympathy is by appearing as a

lamb among wolves, hunted down almost without effort by the Major and Mrs Skewton, and always the dupe of Carker. Such unawareness, whatever its cause, has its own pathos.

The chapter includes a further breach in Mr Dombey's isolation, but one which he recognizes and resents. At the station he is accosted by the fireman of the engine, who is Mr Toodle; in him is concentrated Mr Dombey's recollection of his loss, and the humiliating knowledge that others are aware of it. A common human sympathy is offered, and repulsed; doubly repulsed, for Toodle's sad report of Rob the Grinder, 'gone wrong' after his charitable education, is greeted with a cynical generalization, 'The usual return!'

But the sight of the piece of crape on Toodle's cap rankles in Mr Dombey's mind. 'So! from high to low, at home or abroad, from Florence in his great house to the coarse churl who was feeding the fire then smoking before them, everyone set up some claim or other to a share in his dead boy, and was a bidder against him!'

The inner stage of his mind is now set for the rushing reverie that accompanies the violent motion of the train and the race of the passing landscape. The express train becomes on the one hand 'a type of the triumphant monster, Death'; on the other, of the oneness of society. As the train slows down among the black battered slums of an industrial city, the double allegory becomes clear: 'it is never in his thoughts that the monster who has brought him there has let the light of day in on these things: not made or caused them'. The 'monster', railway or death, merely revealed the social and spiritual desolation that was already there. Not grief, but guilt, is the cause of the storm in Mr Dombey's thoughts; 'he knew full well, in his own breast . . . that life had quite as much to do with his complainings as death'.

The haunting image of Florence deepens the gloom:

> More than once upon this journey, and now again as he stood pondering at this journey's end, tracing figures in the dust with his stick, the thought came into his mind, what was there he could interpose between himself and it?
> The Major, who had been blowing and panting all the way down. . . .

The chapter is nearly at its end, and we are now prepared for the second marriage; it is thus linked, from the outset, with Florence. It is one day only since he turned her from him; on the next day he meets Edith.

VIII

These two chapters have also illustrated Dickens's use of the railway, both as topical colouring[50] and as symbol, underlining the contemporary intention of the novel and its offered social commentary. (He must be one of the earliest Victorian writers to seize the railways imaginatively.) There are other recurrent symbols, and one, more obviously 'poetic' in itself and in intention, emphasizes rather the values of the 'other world' – not material progress or menace, but the mystery surrounding human life.

Through the whole novel echoes the sea; from the close of the first chapter, at the death of Mrs Dombey with Florence in her arms – 'Thus, clinging fast to that slight spar within her arms, the mother drifted out upon the dark and unknown sea that rolls round all the world' – to the very end, when 'autumn days are shining, and on the sea-beach' Florence and Mr Dombey walk together, with another Florence and Paul. In all its recurrences the sea is charged with its inevitable associations of separation and reunion, death and eternal life. Seen in their full context, the mysterious voice of the waves and the 'invisible country far away' of Paul's fancy are not a passing effect produced to intensify pathos; they are part of a larger design. In the Brighton chapters at least two further passages (chs. 12, 13) prepare for the 'waves' and the 'river that is always running on' of his dying hours; a much later chapter recalls them, not too explicitly – the last illness, death, and burial of Mrs Skewton at Brighton (ch. 41). The day-dreams of Solomon Gills, the supposed drowning of Walter Gay, the wedding voyage of Walter and Florence, all reinforce this covering symbol. Even though its verbal patterns are too pronounced for modern taste, they are at least based upon a perception of something profoundly natural, not factitious.

> And see the Children sport upon the shore,
> And hear the mighty waters rolling evermore.

This was a calculated means of unity; the sea – beyond what the actual incidents call for – is part of the semi-allegorical cover-design, and dominates the wholly allegorical frontispiece; the key phrases are often noted ahead in the notes for coming chapters. But it is a unity that includes much variety of tone. The shop of the Wooden Midshipman,

that landlocked harbour past which 'the human tide is still rolling
westward', is picturesque embroidery; Master Bitherstone's schemes
for reaching Bengal are more absurd than pathetic; and in one of Paul's
'old-fashioned' colloquies his sickly fancy is boldly juxtaposed to
comedy. Paul is gazing out of his window at Dr Blimber's:

> 'I say!' cried Toots, speaking the moment he entered the room, lest he
> should forget it; 'what do you think about?'
> 'Oh! I think about a great many things,' replied Paul.
> 'Do you, though?' said Toots, appearing to consider that fact in itself
> surprising.
> 'If you had to die,' said Paul, looking up into his face——
> Mr Toots stared, and seemed much disturbed.
> '——Don't you think you would rather die on a moonlight night, when
> the sky was quite clear, and the wind blowing, as it did last night?'
> Mr Toots said, looking doubtfully at Paul, and shaking his head, that
> he didn't know about that.
> 'Not blowing, at least,' said Paul, 'but sounding in the air like the sea
> sounds in the shells. . . . I got up and looked out. There was a boat over
> there, in the full light of the moon; a boat with a sail.
> The child looked at him so steadfastly, and spoke so earnestly, that
> Mr Toots, feeling himself called upon to say something about this boat,
> said 'Smugglers.' But with an impartial remembrance of there being two
> sides to every question, he added 'or Preventive.'
> 'A boat with a sail,' repeated Paul, 'in the full light of the moon. The
> sail like an arm, all silver. It went away into the distance, and what do you
> think it seemed to do as it moved with the waves?'
> 'Pitch,' said Mr Toots.
> 'It seemed to beckon,' said the child 'to beckon me to come!' (ch. 12)

The boldness is justified. Toots's literalness serves to 'distance' Paul's
fancies, suggesting a degree of detachment in the author (though
insufficient for the modern reader). It also emphasizes the irrational
bond between these two uncommunicative personalities, and this queer
association starts Toots off on his eccentric but firm career through the
narrative. He owes his very relation to the action to Paul's death, and
is continuously faithful to its memory, but nevertheless 'sinks into the
Silent Tomb with a gleam of joy'. Toots alone would justify Dickens's
new technique in comedy; always subordinated to the main design,
he yet gives ample elbow-room for Dickens's 'preposterous sense of
the ridiculous' . . . 'And all I have written is point'. Speech after

speech of Toots could be selected for its ludicrous but unerring penetration to the heart of a situation; 'children and fools speak the truth'. His schooldays remain his touchstone for experience – 'I never saw such a world. It's a great deal worse than Blimber's.' He carries their innocence through the novel, as well as their scars.

The child's view of the world is also a source of unity in this novel; it is more important than in *Oliver Twist* and *The Old Curiosity Shop*, though the children there are hero and heroine, and do not grow up. But the children now affect the adults more deeply; the childhood love of Paul and Florence haunts Mr Dombey, from the first chapter to the last. And their glance is more piercing. After *Dombey*, or even while writing it, Dickens was ready to write *David Copperfield*. The fourteenth chapter, 'Paul . . . goes home for the holidays', is almost in the first person; the single point of view is held throughout, with the child's lucid confusion. And since, for all his mystified intimations of mortality, he is still a normal child enjoying a party and being the centre of attention, it carries more conviction than the death-bed scene. The one has the mark of recovered experience on it; Dickens, after all, had never died. The essence of his childhood experience is of course already, in Oliver and Nell – the hapless, exploited child, tossed from place to place and from person to person. But in *Dombey* he began to use specific experience, and even to use it closely. Actual places and persons now appear, hardly disguised; Camden Town, and at least one of its denizens.

> I hope you will like Mrs Pipchin's establishment. It is from the life, and I was there – I don't suppose I was eight years old; but I remember it all as well, and certainly understood it as well, as I do now. We should be devilish sharp in what we do to children.[51]

The child's-eye view, bewildered, yet implacable, is impressed upon the Brighton chapters, and especially on Mrs Pipchin and her household. Perhaps some plausibility is here sacrificed; at least it needed a little manipulation to adjust this particular personal reminiscence to the much more prosperous Dombey family. The landlady takes a few steps up the social scale; her establishment is not in Camden Town, she has seen the better days which Susan Nipper pitied for having seen her, and no unpaid-for natural children[52] are mentioned among her boarders. The rest is evidently 'from the life'; hence Dickens's bitter disappointment over the illustration.[53] Mrs Roylance-Pipchin was the acknowledged breach in the wall that Dickens had built between himself and the darkest days of his childhood – a wall that is apt to crumble as middle age approaches, especially for a parent.[54] In the very letter which identifies Mrs Pipchin, he first broaches the notion of writing the story of his childhood; he wrote it in 1848, and then wove it into *David Copperfield*. There were other events to awaken recollections; in 1846–7 Dickens's beloved elder sister Fanny had entered her last illness;[55] (the 'Child's Dream of a Star',[56] avowedly written with her in mind, has its parallel in the relation of Paul and Florence). And he had as 'a very young child' fancied the moonlight on the water as the pathway to heaven.[57]

Dombey and Son is also a plea for children; generally, for their right to be treated as individuals, instead of appendages and hindrances to parental ambition, and particularly, against the wrongs done to them in the name of education. It is a measure of this novel's largeness of scope that it is not often thought of as an exposure of misconceived schooling; but it is not less so than *Nicholas Nickleby* and penetrates into more protected places.[58] While forwarding the general design Dickens has shown, incidentally and half-humorously but unmistakably, what is wrong with Dr Blimber's academy; what the plight of the cherished rich man's child[59] has in common with that of the foundling parish boy. Mr Dombey's other educational mistake[60] is more briefly but more angrily[61] exposed: the committing of Robin Toodle to the mercies of the Charitable Grinders. And here he can venture to admit the twisting of a character by mis-education;[62] if not beyond repair, since, restored to his parent and Miss Tox at the close, Rob is beginning to reform.

But Dickens is not here concerned to attack specific abuses. He is not so optimistic. In so far as *Dombey and Son* is a 'social' novel, its prevailing mood is one of deep disquiet about contemporary values, a suggestion that more is amiss with them than mere exposure and reform can hope to touch. Dickens had formerly presented the wealthy man as a benevolent fairy godmother or Father Christmas, in Mr Brownlow, Abel Garland, or the Cheeryble brothers. There would be no place for such characters here. *Dombey and Son* suggests the gloom of wealth (more strongly even than Thackeray was to do) and its capacity to petrify or poison human relations, in the family and in society. 'Papa, what's money? . . . It isn't cruel, is it?' Wealth is an evil, corrupting the heart; prosperity a house built on sand. The moral of the 'valuelessness in themselves of the greatest earthly possessions' commended by one critic[63] and patent to all readers, is inwoven with the main design. The potential cruelty, the emptiness, the cold isolation of a Mammonist society is repeatedly emphasized: but rarely in a didactic way. Dickens is not writing a tract for the times, even at the distance of allegory. There is no overt social reference in his draft of his general design, in his working notes, or his Preface; but in a letter written when he was halfway through he said: 'There is a great deal to do – one or two things among the rest that society will not be the worse, I hope, for thinking about a little.'[64] As we have seen, these 'one or two things' become a natural part of the narrative; still more effectively, they become part of the picture. House and firm together dominate the story, and the house, scenically central,[65] is also an emblem of the social theme.

The social intentions of the novel are pointed by the title, and the status of the hero. He is Palmerston's 'princely merchant in his counting house'; a character 'which could only be produced in a country whose commerce embraces the globe, whose merchants are potentates'.[66] Such a merchant-prince no longer, of course, lived in the City, nor even, like Mr Osborne and Mr Smedley, near its borders in Russell Square. He has followed the tide of fashion to 'the shady side of a tall, dark, dreadfully genteel street in the region between Portland-place and Bryanstone-square' . . . .[67] 'a house of dismal state'. We come to know all its appurtenances: the lustres, chandeliers, and marble floors, its statuary, its bookcase which 'repudiated all familiarities', 'glazed and locked'. The changing state of the house marks the movement of the narrative; we see its dreary magnificence abandoned to neglect in the months of Florence's solitude (ch. 23), then garishly revived in preparation for the second marriage (ch. 28), stripped by the auctioneers – 'the house is a ruin, and the rats fly from it' (ch. 59), and lastly 'frowning like a dark mute on the street; baulking any nearer inquiries with the staring announcement that the lease of this desirable Family Mansion was to be disposed of' (ch. 59).

The dreadful spectacle of that sad House of Pride.[68]

Compared with this distinctness and load of significance, the firm of 'Dombey and Son', 'wholesale, retail, and for exportation' is dimly treated;[69] it is the off-stage source of wealth, rather than the hub of activity, and its export trade is distinguished only by the dispatch of Walter Gay. It lives rather through the characters it involves. Firm and household are used skilfully to define the social pyramid, from the loftiest to the lowest, from Mr Carker the Manager down to Mr Perch the messenger, while the servants are 'carried through' – Dickens's own phrase – from beginning to end.[70] Every family event has its reverberations in the humming chorus of the servants' hall – 'misfortune in the family without feasting in these lower regions couldn't be'; below Susan, and Polly, and (later) Mrs Pipchin, is ranged the household hierarchy, from the lugubrious Towlinson to the young kitchenmaid in black stockings whose single recorded contribution marks the completeness of the collapse – 'Supposing the wages shouldn't be paid!' (ch. 59). More faintly indicated, the clerks' chorus is set in apposition to the servants' chorus in the closing act (chs. 51, 58, 59). Other houses, and one other business, contribute their variations on the theme; one, the town house of Cousin Feenix, confirms the dreariness and heartlessness of wealth with its 'black hatchments of pictures', its 'dark-brown dining-room, which no confectioner can brighten up, let him garnish the exhausted negroes with as many flowers and love-knots as he will' (ch. 31); others (the Toodles', the Wooden Midshipman) mark a contrast, with their cosy contrivances of ingenious frugality. Of these, the Wooden Midshipman is used with a twofold purpose of contrast; it is shown not only as a humble source of loyalty and affection, but as an outmoded retail concern representing a superseded past. No customers come to it – as Sol Gills laments, in almost too pointed exposition, 'Competition, competition – new invention, new invention . . . the world's gone past me'. (So much for the England of thirty years before – 'when that uniform was worn. . . . fortunes were to be made' (ch. 4).) This pocket of the past, in 'the immediate vicinity' of the offices of Dombey and Son, serves to emphasize the modernity and prosperity of the firm. (At the close, when the firm has fallen, 'Mr Gills's old investments are coming out wonderfully' and he was after all not 'behind the time' but 'a little before it' (ch. 62); a consummation perhaps wisely left vague.) One other recurrent 'place' deepens the contemporary picture. Four phases of the narrative are punctuated by scenes in the same church: Paul's christening, his funeral, Edith's wedding, and Florence's visit to Paul's grave before her own wedding (chs. 5, 18 (very briefly touched), 31, 57). In three of these the physical atmosphere is defined, in terms of chill and dust and wheeziness, with choric commentary from the two dried-up professional ministrants, Mr Sownds and Mrs Miff. Dickens spares nothing in his suggestion of a soulless society; he seems to point at house, firm, and church as three hollow shells of the established order.

Across the social picture are ruled the ruthless lines of the new order, symbolized in the railway. It links high and low, devastates Camden Town, uproots Staggs's Gardens, provides employment for Mr Toodle, bears Mr Dombey from grim past to grimmer future, and finally obliterates Carker. Its appearance on each of the four carefully spaced and placed occasions (chs. 6, 15, 20, 55) is emphasized by a volcanic upsurge in the style, by description much overflowing its narrative function. In these descriptions may be discerned the fascination of the new as well as the horror of the strange; but the tone is mainly that of dread. Twice the railway is used to highlight the darker thoughts of hero and villain, thoughts of fear and hate and death (chs. 20, 55). The train is seen only as destructive, ruthless, an 'impetuous monster', a 'fiery devil'. There is no suggestion of hope, of social progress. This colouring of gloom and horror may derive from the over-riding mood of the novel; it may be a picturesque reflection of contemporary doubts; but more probably, from the evidence of the later novels, it represents a persistent shade in Dickens's own social view, which contains at least as much pessimism as optimism, and always more of the visionary than of the reformer.

The social criticism in *Dombey and Son* cannot be abstracted from the novel, and even such disengaging as is attempted here perhaps distorts it. It is pervasive, unformulated; not documentary in origin or usefulness; no purposeful journeys or reading of newspaper reports lie behind it, and it is not a convenient source for social historians. Partly for this reason, that it is inseparable, it assists instead of disturbing the firm unity of the design. It is part of the 'Idea of the world' which protects Dickens from being 'prevailed over by the world's multitudinousness'.[71]

NOTES

1. John Forster, *The Life of Charles Dickens*, ed. J. W. T. Ley (1928) v 2; but it had been in his mind at least since the beginning of March (vi 2) and probably earlier (v 1).

2. As a result of his absence from England the early stages of *Dombey* are fairly fully documented in letters to Forster; quotations from these are scattered through v 2–7, vi 1–2.

3. Forster, v 5, letter of 30 Aug., written while at work on the second number.

4. Forster, v 3, letter of 18 July 1846; and *The Letters of Charles Dickens*, ed. Walter Dexter, 3 vols (Nonesuch Dickens: 1938) 1 768.

5. Forster, vi 2.

6. Forster, vi 2, letter of 6 Dec. 1846, written while at work on the fourth number.

7. On this, see Chesterton's Introduction to the Everyman edition of the novel, especially his remarks on Mrs Skewton.

8. Forster, iv 1.

9. Forster, vi 2.

10. Chesterton, loc. cit.

11. Cf. Dickens's Preface, and Forster, iv 2.

12. Letter to Browne, 10 March 1847; *Letters*, II 17.

13. Forster, vi 2; he is referring to what Dickens told him before he left England in May.

14. Forster, v 3; 18 July 1846.

15. Forster, vi 2; 25 July 1846.

16. Forster, vi 2; August 1846. To prevent caricature, Dickens asked for a sheet of sketches from which to select; this is reproduced by Forster.

17. In the original edition, and in all editions up to 1858, the 'turn' is emphasized by the closing words of no. v, chorically delivered by Miss Tox: 'To think . . . Dombey and Son should be a Daughter after all!' (cf. letter to Forster, 25 July; vi 2). When Dickens removed this sentence in 1859 (perhaps because it then seemed to him to mar the pathos of the conclusion) he forgot that it was echoed in ch. 59: 'And so Dombey and Son, as I observed upon a certain sad occasion . . . is indeed a daughter, Polly, after all.'

18. Letter of 25 July 1846.

19. Cf. ch. 59: 'obstinate and sullen natures . . . struggle hard to be such. Ground long undermined, will often fall down in a moment'.

20. See Forster, vi 2 (opening paragraph), and n. 25 below.

21. The Preface was added in the edition of 1858, and revised for the collected 'Charles Dickens' edition of 1867. I quote from the latter; in the passage quoted, the only differences are that 1858–62 read 'no violent internal change . . . or in life'; 'bring the contest to the surface'; and 'is only fought out then'. The Preface of 1848 is quite distinct – a brief farewell to readers, originally printed at the end of the concluding number.

22. The moment is openly recalled at the end of ch. 18, and again at the end of ch. 36.

23. Chs. 18, 20; and the reference to 'hatred' in ch. 40.

24. i.e. before ch. 58, 'After a lapse'. 'The year was out, and the great House was down.' In the first part of this chapter (balancing ch. 59) is concentrated much of the effect on Mr Dombey of the business failure, although he does not himself appear; and the better side of his pride is recognized by the unimpeachable Mr Morfin: 'He is a gentleman of high honour and integrity . . . resolved on payment to the last farthing of his means. . . . Ah, Miss Harriet, it would do us no harm to remember oftener than we do, that vices are sometimes only virtues carried to excess! His pride shows well in this.'

25. Taine, *History of English Literature* (Paris, 1863–4; trans. H. Van Laun, 1871) book v, ch. i §3 ii. Compare *Blackwood's* (Oct. 1848) p. 469: 'The entire change of character in Dombey is out of all nature.'

26. So more than one reviewer thought; e.g. *Blackwood's*, Oct. 1848: 'nor does the extraordinary affection of the daughter spring from any known principle of humanity' (p. 469).

27. Not that the emotional stresses of adolescent girlhood lay altogether outside Dickens's range; witness Tattycoram, also hungry for affection.

28. Though perhaps accentuated for him by the pressure of his idealized memory of Mary Hogarth, who died at sixteen.

29. 'Heroines are a sadly featureless class of well-intentioned young women in these days' (*Blackwood's*, April 1855, pp. 464–5).

30. 'It is a wonder how finely he discriminates them' (Henry James, 'Anthony Trollope', in *Partial Portraits*, 1888).

31. 'Florence's reflections', which open the former chapter, formulate the only doubt, the only complexity of feeling, which is ever attributed to her.

32. And others; Paul is compared to a changeling, Mrs Pipchin's establishment to an ogress's castle.

33. The cover design proves that they were thought of early: but not necessarily that they were part of the main design. (That was too 'secret' to be given away with the first number, and it is noticeable that Paul's death is not even 'shadowed forth'.) Perhaps Forster omitted some reference to this part of the plot when he quoted the early letter; his concern is to defend Dickens's design as it affects Mr Dombey and his children – and there are marks of omission.

34. He rises to prominence only after Paul's death (his position and character having been sufficiently expounded in ch. 13, where his designs against Walter Gay are already suggested), and his initial plan is to take the place of the lost son – as son-in-law. When the marriage to Edith seems to frustrate him there, he schemes against her, now using Florence as a tool.

35. I cannot now trace this quotation.

36. Manuscript of number-plan, no. VII.

37. Ruskin's comment on *Hard Times* in *Unto this Last* (quoted by Forster, vii 1).

38. Forster, vi 2; letter of 21 Dec. 1847 – that is, after ch. 47 had gone to press.

39. There are signs of anxiety over the number that included the chapter with this title (ch. 40): it 'requires to be so carefully done' (Forster, vi 1; letter of 12 Sept. 1847). The manuscript shows that ch. 47, 'The Thunderbolt', also caused difficulty.

40. As may be seen if we contrast Carker with Mr Tulkinghorn, Edith with Lady Dedlock.

41. Some deliberate restraint over Carker may be suggested in the memorandum, 'Be patient with Carker. Get him on very slowly, without incident' (no. XII, chs. 35–8), but on the whole the notes suggest satisfaction. Dickens was delighted with the way Phiz depicted Edith in the illustrations, and these emphasize her staginess.

42. Letter to Miss Jolly, rejecting a story submitted to *Household Words* (*Letters*, II 850).

43. Apparent exceptions among the very minor characters are there to give solidity and definition to others: the Game Chicken to Toots, the Reverend Melchizedek Howler to Mrs MacStinger, and she to Captain Cuttle. The thematic relevance of the characters is not necessarily always an advantage. With Alice Marwood, especially when she is revealed as Edith's 'natural' cousin, the diagram shows too starkly through the pattern. But at the climax, the doubling of the revenge-motif (Alice setting Mr Dombey in pursuit of Carker) contributes to narrative economy as well as poetic justice.

44. Ch. 34, in which this incident is recalled. It is Alice's cloak that she puts on to Florence; she spares her hair because it reminds her of Alice's.

45. Its association with Dickens's own childhood is an additional motive.

46. The manuscript number-plan has 'Take care of the Major'.

47. The first and fullest note concerns this, and the chapter-heads show that Dickens first planned to reach Leamington in the first chapter. Then comes the inspiration 'The Railroad Ride'.

48. Edith is a widow; he is careful to ascertain that she has borne a child.

49. The whole paragraph in which these words occur is an interesting analysis of their relationship.

50. Cf. ch. 15 (disappearance of Staggs's Gardens) and ch. 55 (death of Carker). The railway references supply the chronological limits, and define them as about 1835 to 1845.

51. Forster, vi 2; cf. i 2, where Mrs Roylance is described as 'a reduced old lady, long known to our family, in Little-College-street, Camden Town, who took children in to

board, and had once done so at Brighton . . .' Charles was lodged there while working at the blacking factory; later, on leaving the Marshalsea, the whole family went to live there for a time.

52. Forster, i 2.

53. Forster, vi 2; letter of Nov. 1846.

54. By 1846 Dickens had two daughters and four sons. Two of his sons were at a school where the master's daughter was 'a thorough classical scholar and assisted him', which 'suggested the Blimber notion' (Introduction by Charles Dickens, Jr, to edition of 1892).

55. Forster, v 7. She was the wife of Henry Burnett, and had two sons, one of whom, an invalid, is said to have been Paul's original. (The earliest evidence of this tradition seems to be in the recollections of a Manchester minister who had known them well: James Griffin, *Memories of the Past* (1883) p. 209.)

56. In the first number of *Household Words*, 30 March 1850. Forster links it with Fanny (vi 4, last paragraph).

57. *American Notes* (1842) ch. 16.

58. This was recognized by several contemporary reviewers (e.g. *Westminster Review*, XLVII (April 1847)) and by Edward Fitzgerald in a letter to Thackeray: 'a very fine account of the overcramming educational system, worth whole volumes of essays on the subject. . . . The boy who talks Greek in his sleep seems to me as terrible as Macbeth' (*The Letters and Private Papers of . . . Thackeray*, ed. Gordon N. Ray, 4 vols (Cambridge, Mass., 1945–6) II 226).

59. He defines the limits of Mr Dombey's obtuseness, however, by explicitly avoiding the public school; and has indicated his view of Sandhurst through Major Bagstock's grisly reminiscences (ch. 10).

60. Another novelist might have made something of the complete neglect of Florence's education!

61. Ch. 6, and ch. 20; and especially the last paragraph of ch. 38, given salience by being placed at the end of a number. Gissing calls Rob 'one of the most important of Dickens's social studies' (*Charles Dickens* (1898) p. 208).

62. Dickens was growing interested in gradual moral deterioration. His first design was to show Walter Gay going wrong; counselled against it by Forster, he remembered it in Richard Carstone, and Pip.

63. *English Review*, Dec. 1848, p. 271; and cf. *Christian Remembrancer*, Dec. 1847, p. 347.

64. Letter to Dr Hodgson, 4 June 1847; *Letters*, II 28.

65. Although there is much variety (Brighton, Leamington, Dijon outside London; Leadenhall St, Princess's Place, Brig Place, Brook St, Staggs's Gardens, and the Carker suburb within London), over a third of the chapters are set or partly set in the Dombey house, and these are among the 'high-lights' of the novel, such as chs. 3, 18, 23, 28, 36, 40, 43, 47–8, 51, and 59.

66. Taine, *History of English Literature* (Paris, 1863–4), trans. H. Van Laun (1871) book v, ch. i §3 ii.

67. And therefore well within the purview of Devonshire Terrace (opposite York Gate), which was Dickens's home when in London from 1839 to 1850.

68. *The Faerie Queene*, I v 53.

69. The 'exposition' in ch. 4 (through Walter Gay) and the description in ch. 13 stand almost alone; in the office scenes the details are never either sharply visual or symbolic.

70. Note in plan of no. x; cf. ch. 31. But this had begun much earlier; see the openings of chs. 3 and 18.

71. *Letters of Matthew Arnold to Arthur Hugh Clough*, ed. H. F. Lowry (1932) p. 97; letter of 1848.

MARK SPILKA

David Copperfield as Psychological Fiction (1959)

WHEN we speak of psychological fiction, we generally mean the use of probing methods, like introspection or analysis; or we mean enveloping techniques, like point of view and stream of consciousness, which simulate the flow of inner conflict. But there is another kind of fiction, the projective novel, in which surface life reflects the inner self. *David Copperfield* belongs to that tradition. As the hero views the world, his feelings fuse with outward action, and his selection of events advances inward meaning. Franz Kafka saw this when he called *Amerika* his 'Dickens novel' in method and detail. By 'method' he apparently meant the dream-effects in *Copperfield*: the infantile perspective on a world controlled by elders, and the hero's progress through that world toward ultimate redemption. As Kafka knew, the childlike view connects unconscious tensions with the conscious scene. Because the child lacks self-awareness, and because he fails to understand his elders, his bafflement aligns two realms of feeling; and in a world of harsh repression, his need for inner growth becomes directive and informing. In his early fiction, Kafka borrowed about six stages of that growth from *Copperfield*, plus two regressions. These 'imitations' alone suggest a formal sequence for the novel; but keeping them in reserve, consider simply the method which he so admired, especially as it strengthens early chapters.

In Kafka, inner states are projected through fantastic situations, then treated in precise detail; in Dickens, outer scenes are real, but are made to seem fantastic through projected feelings; in either case, the effect is of a surface charged with baffling implications. For Dickens, the creation of that surface came naturally, as part of his attempt to master childhood pain. In *Copperfield* he had summoned up the most anguished memories of youth: his wretched job in a blacking warehouse, his rejection by Maria Beadnell, and his earlier defeat within the home. With an artist's instinct, he had given form and texture to those episodes; and with genial and expansive humour, he had eased their pain and enlarged their meaning. Thus David's birth is to a world informed by sexual conflict – as heralded by his strident aunt, Miss Trotwood. Since her marriage to a younger man has ended badly, she has renounced the male sex and has even trained her maids to follow suit. Now she wants to train the approaching child, whose sex must be feminine and whose name must be her own: 'There must be no mistakes in life with *this* Betsey Trotwood. There must be no trifling with *her* affections.' But the babe's name is David, a mistake which makes her vanish 'like one of those supernatural beings' whom the boy is privileged to see by virtue of his birth on Friday midnight. From this renouncing spirit, he does see that marriage seldom works, and that the trouble seems to begin with sex in children; but her ghosthood is his own invention, and its comic form, his reaction to impending pain.

In chapter 2 the pain begins. His first memories are of his mother and nurse Peggotty, as loving protectors. A fierce cock makes him shiver, and he dreams at night of geese with stretching necks, as a man might dream of threatening lions. There are two parlours in the house: in one he sits with Peggotty and his mother, in complete security; in the other he feels doleful, for Peggotty has told him of his father's funeral there. When his mother reads to them, in the second parlour, 'how Lazarus was raised up from the dead', the boy becomes frightened; they are forced to quiet him, that night, by showing him the churchyard from his window, 'with the dead all lying in their graves at rest, below the solemn moon'. His father lies in one of those graves, and David fears his resurrection. Another night he suddenly asks about marriage: 'if you marry a person, and the person dies, why then you may marry another person, mayn't you, Peggotty?' He is worried about the man who walks his mother home from church. When she returns that night, the man is with her, and the boy is jealous of his touch. His name is Murdstone, which David's aunt compares with Murderer, to fit his surface role; but Murdstone also means the *murd*ered man beneath his grave*stone*, who has risen now to assert his rights – and Dickens makes the tie with conscious skill. One day the boy agrees to a ride with Murdstone. Seated before him on his horse, he looks up at his face and thinks him handsome, especially in his mother's eyes. Then they come to the hotel where Murdstone's friends are waiting:

> They both rolled on to their feet, in an untidy sort of manner, when we came in, and said, 'Halloa, Murdstone! We thought you were dead!'
>
> 'Not yet,' said Mr Murdstone.
>
> 'And who's this shaver?' said one of the gentlemen, taking hold of me.
>
> 'That's Davy,' returned Mr Murdstone. . . .
>
> 'What! Bewitching Mrs Copperfield's incumbrance?' cried the gentleman. 'The pretty little widow?'
>
> 'Quinion,' said Mr Murdstone, 'take care, if you please. Somebody's sharp.'
>
> 'Who is?' asked the gentleman, laughing. . . .
>
> 'Only Brooks of Sheffield,' said Mr Murdstone.
>
> I was quite relieved to find that it was only Brooks of Sheffield, for, at first, I really thought it was I. . . .
>
> 'And what is the opinion of Brooks of Sheffield, in reference to the projected business?'
>
> 'Why, I don't know that Brooks understands much about it at present,' replied Mr Murdstone; 'but he is not generally favourable, I believe.'
>
> There was more laughter at this, and Mr Quinion said he would ring the bell for some sherry in which to drink to Brooks. This he did; and when the wine came, he made me have a little, with a biscuit, and before I drank it, stand up and say, 'Confusion to Brooks of Sheffield!' The toast was received with great applause, and such hearty laughter that it made me laugh too; at which they laughed the more. In short, we quite enjoyed ourselves.

David is indeed confused by Murdstone's friends. That night he tells his mother of their talk, which pleases her immensely. Later, kneeling playfully by his bed, she makes him repeat their words, 'Bewitching Mrs Copperfield' and 'pretty little widow'. Again she responds with pleasure, and though she kisses him repeatedly, the scene conveys his bafflement at powers which keep her out of range, in areas where Murdstone is decidedly 'not dead'.

The next memory is of a trip to Yarmouth, arranged with special mystery. He meets Peggotty's family there, and the comedy turns on Mrs Gummidge, the 'lone lorn creetur' who exploits her husband's death for sympathy. With the orphan, little Em'ly, David soon achieves the security of childhood love, with no 'provision for growing older', and with greater purity and disinterestedness 'than can enter into the best love of a later time of life'. His ideal, then, is sexless love with Em'ly or his mother; he even indicates that Em'ly should have toppled into the sea one day, and joined her father beneath the waves, to avoid her sinful future. Thus Yarmouth scenes advance the major conflict: beneath the peaceful surface and light comedy, pain and loss continue; and on the return trip home, they erupt with sudden force. His nurse becomes so ill at ease, on nearing home, that David calls in fear for his mother. He believes she too is dead, but Peggotty cries No! and tries to explain her agitation:

> 'Master Davy,' said Peggotty, untying her bonnet with a shaking hand, and speaking in a breathless sort of way. 'What do you think? You have got a Pa!'
> I trembled, and turned white. Something – I don't know what or how – connected with the grave in the churchyard, and the raising of the dead, seemed to strike me like an unwholesome wind.
> 'A new one,' said Peggotty.
> 'A new one?' I repeated.
> Peggotty gave a gasp, as if she were swallowing something that was very hard, and putting out her hand, said:
> 'Come and see him.'
> 'I don't want to see him.'

The shock jars loose his graveyard fears. He now shakes hands with Lazarus and greets his mother, but he cannot face them. The house seems altered. Later, when he roams into the yard, his feelings suffer full projection: 'I very soon started back from there, for the empty dog-kennel was filled up with a great dog – deep-mouthed and black-browed like Him – and he was very angry at the sight of me, and sprang out to get me.'

This is brilliant psychological fiction. Murdstone has become the risen and revengeful father; his powers involve the mysteries of sex, and somehow pull the mother out of range. In the meantime, the boy's hostility and fear suffuse the outward scene. The projective artistry is unmatched, and most of it seems conscious; in chapter 4, moreover, it comes to full dramatic focus in a scene which Kafka found intriguing. Kept uninformed by nurse and mother, David has suffered deeply from the news of marriage. The shock might have been lessened if Murdstone had responded with encouragement. Instead he offers 'firmness' and distrust. Idyllic spelling lessons, once directed by the mother, become drudgery under Murdstone and his sister. David stumbles in their presence, and when Murdstone brings a cane to help his memory, the boy goes blank. In the struggle which follows, he bites the hand which touched his mother; he is beaten then with a vengeance and locked inside his room, where he rages helplessly upon the floor. Outside the wild household commotion is stilled. In the unnatural quiet, David crawls to the mirror and sees his face in the glass, 'so swollen, red, and ugly that it almost frightened me. My stripes were sore and stiff, and made me cry afresh, when I moved; but they were nothing to the guilt I felt. It lay heavier on my breast than if I had been the most atrocious criminal.'

This spectacle of a son locked in his room, shut off from his mother, and guilty of a crime against the father, appealed to Kafka; he used it in *The Metamorphosis* for his central situation, reshaping it to suit his needs – as the events themselves attest. Thus David lies by the window now, his head upon the sill, when Miss Murdstone brings in 'bread and meat and milk'. She glares at him with exemplary firmness, then locks him in again. His imprisonment lasts five days, which 'occupy the place of years' in his remembrance. He listens to the household sounds by day, confuses time at night, and feels weighed down on awakening 'by the stale and dismal oppression of remembrance'. He is ashamed to show himself at the window, lest the boys outside should see him. During evening prayers he is allowed to stand alone, near the parlour doors, and look out on the averted faces of the family. On the last night of his restraint, he hears his name repeated in a whisper. The voice is Peggotty's; it reaches him through the keyhole, to which he puts his own lips in response, so that a mouth-to-ear communication begins on David's future (at one point, mouth-to-mouth). Then both fall to kissing and patting the keyhole, and David feels within him an indefinable love for Peggotty. She has reached him, he asserts, with 'as much feeling and earnestness as a keyhole has ever been the medium of communicating'. Kafka seems to challenge this assumption with key-manipulations by his giant insect, whose shape derives from Dostoevsky, but whose crime and punishment begin with Dickens. The strange ordeal of Gregor Samsa, an older and certainly a more regressive outcast, repeats the intensities of guilt, exclusion and frustration which David undergoes; and the comparison affirms the unexpected depth of Dickens' 'method'.

After shock, whipping and exclusion, some kind of psychic damage seems inevitable, and the next ten chapters show its form. At Salem House, an older student, Steerforth, becomes the boy's protector.

David loves and admires him, and serves him by reciting stories, 'like the Sultana Scheherezade'. Steerforth seems to like this girlish adoration. 'If you had a sister', he tells him, 'I should think she would have been a pretty, timid, little, bright-eyed sort of girl. I should have liked to know her.' David's only 'sister', at this stage, is Em'ly; he will later bring these two together, and speak of his 'unconscious part' in their elopement. At the moment her budding womanhood disturbs him, and he is afraid to mention her. Steerforth's manhood is another matter; he admires him for his poise and charm, for powers which conquer elders. When Steerforth badgers Mr Mell, the master (Creakle) promptly fires his helper – and David cheers his hero. In Kafka's novel *Amerika* Steerforth's counterpart is Mr Mack, a sophisticated, patronizing figure who attracts and baffles young Karl Rossmann. Karl's attraction is an adolescent crush, like David's, but the sexual note has been enhanced by 'sharper lights . . . from the times', which show Mack in collusion with his elders. Still, the lights in *Copperfield* seem sharp enough: Steerforth later joins the fathers, as sadist and destroyer, and is now an adolescent sultan.

From Steerforth David seeks vicarious confidence, knowledge and seductive power; in the future, he will even blind himself to get them. But the projective paths to mother-love are varied. On his return from school, for instance, his route is more direct. Hearing his mother sing in the parlour, he remembers how she sang to him in infancy. When he finds her there with Murdstone's baby, she puts his head upon her bosom, 'near the little creature that was nestling there', and David longs for blissful death. He identifies himself with Murdstone's child, and with nurse and mother beside him, it seems 'as if the old days were come back'. Then the Murdstones return and break the spell. When he leaves for school again, his mother stands at the gate alone, holding the babe before her; and afterwards, in his sleep at Salem House, he sees her near his bed, 'looking at [him] with the same intent face – holding up her baby in her arms'. Her gesture seems to affirm his infant love, to fix it permanently in his mind. Thus, when mother and baby die, he remembers only 'the young mother of my earliest impressions, who had been used to wind her bright curls round and round her finger, and to dance with me at twilight in the parlour. . . . The mother who lay in the grave, was the mother of my infancy; the little creature in her arms, was myself, as I had once been, hushed for ever on her bosom.' In harsher terms, David has just appeased his guilt.

His projections take a comic turn with Barkis, the laconic carrier, who wants to marry Peggotty. When the boy first goes to school, Barkis waits in silence as the nurse embraces David and loads him down with pastry. Her buttons pop with every squeeze, and she leaves 'without a solitary button on her gown'; but Barkis, like a grownup child, is more concerned with cakes than sex. They have roused his marital appetite, and with David as protective agent, he can risk the cryptic message: 'Barkis is willing.' So too is David willing. In a later chapter, he waits outside with Em'ly, in vicarious embrace, while Barkis and the nurse are married. He dreams that night about dragons, and wakens, in the morning, with Peggotty calling from below, as if Barkis were a dream 'from first to last'. Such proxy dealings might have appealed to Kafka. In 'Wedding Preparations in the Country', young Eduard Raban wants to send his body ahead to meet his country sweetheart; in the meantime, he will rest in bed, as he had always done in childhood 'in matters that were dangerous'. Barkis too avoids the risks of courtship, like a frightened child; he also clings to boxes with the insecurity of Raban and Karl Rossmann, who seem to seek emotional support from baggage. Of course, he acts from slighter motives; but in marrying David's nurse, and in clinging to internal burdens, he reveals the boy's vicarious urges. In this sense, his death resembles that of Murdstone's child: it fixes David's attitude toward his nurse, just as Steerforth's death will fix his love for Em'ly. In each case, these characters die in their own right; but some of David's guilt dies with them, since they have allowed him to 'possess' his mother, nurse and 'sister' – all objects of the sexless love of childhood, with its hidden sexual base. Thus, as Barkis dies, he rests mutely on his box, which gives his form its only meaning; but at the last his mind begins to wander, as if under 'the mysterious influence' of David's presence: he talks of driving him to school, and then speaks his comic phrase, 'Barkis is willin' ', which carries hidden weight.

During the early phase, emotional growth is blocked by further punishment. At Salem House, David is forced to wear the placard, 'Take care of him. He bites', and the master whips him freshly for his crime. Mr Creakle is another Murdstone: he turns his son out for protesting cruelty in the school and 'usage of his mother'. He prides himself on firmness, tweaks ears to make his point, and bursts from his chair like Murdstone's dog. With the zest of a 'craving appetite', he delights in beating chubby boys like David. In London, David later works for Quinion, the manager of Murdstone's warehouse, who still refers to him as 'Brooks' and jokes about his sharpness. Through Creakle and Quinion, then, the father's power extends to realms beyond the home. This principle must have excited Kafka. In *Amerika* he joins David's 'menial labour' with his life at school, to create 'The Hotel Occidental'. Here Rossmann works for harsh parental figures, and sleeps in a dorm with other liftboys. His ultimate dismissal resembles Mr Mell's: for, in line with Dickens, the social scene repeats the indignities of childhood; the world belongs to fathers, and each phase of youth is an attempt to get beyond them.

This section of the novel ends with David's flight to Dover, a flight which seems to summarize his past. His trunk is stolen by a youth who calls him a 'pollis case' and threatens to expose him; he sleeps behind his school and dreams of Steerforth; an old-clothes dealer seizes him, with wild 'goroos', like Creakle gone berserk; and a tinker steals his kerchief, then beats a kindly wife, as if the world were full of Murdstones. Throughout the journey, he keeps before him an image of his mother 'in her youth and beauty'; but when he reaches Dover, where he hopes to find security with his aunt, the image disappears. In *Amerika* Karl Rossmann has troubles with his box, and with two unruly mechanics, on the road to Rameses. According to one critic, 'Karl's inner world determines the character of his experiences', while David's world is 'full of things and persons . . . essentially separate from his inward self, only temporarily and accidentally related to it'. Kafka's 'imitation' tells us otherwise: to integrate this journey, he drew from Dickens 'the story of the trunk' (involving David's fear of further confinement), the clothes-exchange (involving bestial treatment), a schoolroom scene (suggesting Creakle and Steerforth), the stolen kerchief (involving Murdstone and Clara), and the image of the mother (involving infancy), which disappears with an older woman's kindness (suggesting inner peace). In other words, he followed Dickens' scheme of psychic integration, which is neither accidental nor temporary, but part of the sustained method from which these fourteen chapters draw direction, power, depth and meaning: the method, in short, which yields a truly brilliant stretch of psychological fiction.

Admittedly, the stretch abruptly ends with David's 'new beginning' – and for the next five chapters, the novel seems to flounder. In his diaries, Kafka writes of 'passages of awful insipidity' in which Dickens

wearily repeats achieved effects; he speaks of 'heartlessness' behind his
sentimental style, and of rude characterizations which obstruct the
story. The indictment is severe, but such chapters seem to confirm it.
Thin characters like Mr Dick and Dr Strong, whose childlike traits
are overpraised, suggest a form of fake emotion; and the repetitious
effects are surely there. It seems more pertinent, however, that Dickens
loses power when the projective method stops: for in these five chapters David reaches psychic rest; his inner troubles cease, and his
connections with the outward scene are casual; at best, they extend
the *breadth* of the novel, as he puzzles over the marriage of an old man
and a young woman, a father's too-intense devotion to his daughter,
a scapegrace husband, and a badly treated sister. These problems are
thematic, but they leave him unengaged, and the novel seems impeded
by their weight. Still, the expansive quality of David's style, his use of
double perspective to forgive as parent while he errs as child, allows
for excess baggage. Light comedy is in order: there is room for the
Micawbers' economic dance, and for gargoyles like Uriah Heep. The
trouble is, the comedy thrives upon the original psychic thrust, and
Dickens' readers often miss the force behind it. One critic says the
story happens around the hero, not within him. But the projective
method shows otherwise: it provides the novel with its basic strength,
and sustains even the excess baggage – apt, crude, fresh, insipid – if
only by extended force.

Plainly the major plots relate to David's inner life. With Steerforth,
for instance, he is again obsessed with self-distrust. Before their
reunion, he is forced to yield his coach-seat to an older gentleman;
he passes by the lane where the 'goroo' man seized him; he passes
Salem House, where Creakle 'laid about him with a heavy hand'.
As on his first trip to school, a waiter treats him poorly. But with
Steerforth's appearance, the waiter knows his place. The hero has
returned in all his glory: hence David's shame at being beardless, his
rechristening as 'Daisy', and his regressions with the servant Littimer,
who makes him feel 'about eight years old'. At Steerforth's home,
these hints are clarified through Rosa Dartle, whose scarred lip signals
rage, and whose rage is based on sheer frustration. Brought up with
Steerforth, and jealously in love with him, she bears the hammermark
of his rejection. Once she strikes him, 'with the fury of a wildcat',
when he coaxes her to play the harp, then taunts her with the hope
of future love. Her scar pursues David to his bed, now, and even

invades his dreams, though he tries to escape it. Kafka's wildcat in *Amerika* is the amorous Clara Pollunder, who pursues Karl Rossmann to his bedroom, throws him down on the sofa, and nearly chokes him. Karl even calls her a wildcat, in his rage and shame. Later he plays the piano, when suddenly Mr Mack cajoles him from a near-by room, where he waits for Clara in his nightshirt. Like David, Karl is immersed in sexual ambiguity and violence, which fascinate and repel him – and highlight his incompetence. For David too is sexually inadequate: repelled by violence, and blinded by vicarious desire, he can only follow Steerforth to the shoreline at Yarmouth, where he links his childhood love for Em'ly with the hero's death. His long pursuit may run to melodramatic claptrap; but projection lends it strength and point.

Indulgent humour marks the Dora plot. Through the double per- spective, David's folly is accepted and forgiven. The doll-like Dora, the child-wife of the nineteenth century, is taken as a delightful hoax, a toy which breaks with possession, a sweet impossibility; and David's love is called 'the first mistaken impulses of an undisciplined heart'. But again the plot goes deeper. As critics often note, the girl resembles David's mother; her father, David's employer, is a businessman like Murdstone; and her paid companion is Miss Murdstone – as if Dickens had deliberately regrouped his early cast. In courting Dora, then, David re-enacts the terms of childhood tension. When Miss Murdstone intercepts his letters, she shows them to the employer-father. As with the early spelling lessons, these figures disapprove of David's words and cut him off from his beloved. By David's own confession: 'Miss Murdstone . . . looked so exactly as she used to look . . . in our parlour at Blunderstone, that I could have fancied I had been breaking down in my spelling lessons again, and that the dead weight on my mind was that horrible old spelling-book with oval woodcuts.' Here Dora joins the mother, nurse and sister as objects of forbidden love. David's folly, his blindness to her incompetence, begins with spelling lessons at Blunderstone, and ends with a disastrous marriage and another death. Kafka seems to have caught these implications. In *Amerika* Rossmann travels with a businessman, Mr Pollunder, to meet his daughter Clara. Clara herself resembles Rosa Dartle; but her sexual charade with Karl compares with David's country courtship. In each case, commercial bondage is expressed through sexual means; the fathers' powers have interfused, and the sons remain in double servitude.

In *Amerika* this theme extends to a later chapter, where Karl is trapped in an apartment drawn from Dickens' tenements. In the closing scene, however, he seems to find an escape from childhood. At the Nature Theatre of Oklahoma, he is accepted without question, just as David is received by Agnes Wickfield. Both endings seem unreal, and Kafka himself complains of Dickens' formal 'senselessness'. But his borrowed scenes belie him: they reveal projective loves and deaths which unify the novel and insure its progress. From his mother's death, through those of Barkis, Steerforth and Dora, David moves steadily away from childhood loves, and seems to reach maturity with Agnes. Dickens' authority here is weak, but so is Kafka's, in *Amerika*, when Rossmann seems to near adulthood. Significantly, both authors move toward darker novels. Pip, Richard Carstone and Arthur Clennam, Joseph K. and K., are older Karls and Davids whom the world imprisons. Here Dickens joins with other pioneer novelists, like Stendhal and Dostoevsky, for whom moral and spiritual maturity seem thwarted by the world's deficient fathers. One psychological critic undercuts this kinship; he holds that Copperfield 'is never a hero of a modern novel, never a Raskolnikov, nor a . . . Julien Sorel'. But as Kafka shows, David is another kind of modern hero – an Eduard Raban or Karl Rossmann, a younger Gregor Samsa; and Dickens' novel is one of our first and best examples of projective fiction. The wealth of comic action, the nostalgic tone, the author's great good humour, have made the novel popular; but like David's progress, they all relate to childhood anguish and help to ease its pain.

MONROE ENGEL

Bleak House (1959)

IN *Bleak House*, as in *Dombey and Son*, death functions as a touchstone
of reality. It is a measure of the wretchedness of man's earthly sojourn,
awful and profound, but – and this is much to the point – more kindly
than the torments imposed by society. One of Esther Summerson's
earlier memories is of a sombre birthday, the only recognition of
which was her godmother's remark after dinner: 'It would have been
far better, little Esther, that you had had no birthday; that you had
never been born!' When Caddy Jellyby gives her first confidence to
Esther, her misery bursts from her uncontrollably: 'I wish I was dead!
. . . I wish we were all dead. It would be a great deal better for us!'
The bricklayer's wife, Liz, thinking of her friend Jenny's dead baby,
says: 'Ah, Jenny, Jenny! . . . better so. Much better to think of dead
than alive, Jenny! Much better!' And of her own child, sleeping, she
says: 'If he should be turned bad, 'spite of all I could do, and the time
should come when I should sit by him in his sleep, made hard and
changed, an't it likely I should think of him as he lies in my lap now,
and wish he had died as Jenny's child died!' Mr Jarndyce, horrified to
find that Richard has based all his expectations on the outcome of
the chancery suit, says: 'Whatever you do on this side the grave, never
give one lingering glance towards the horrible phantom that has
haunted us so many years. Better to borrow, better to beg, better to
die!' Poor Mr Jellyby tells Caddy that she and her brothers and sisters
have been allowed to grow up like Indians, without care or teaching,
and that 'the best thing that could happen to them was, their being all
Tomahawked together'. Esther again, when she discovers the secret
of her parentage, feels and knows 'it would have been better and
happier for many people, if indeed I had never breathed'. And Jo,
when he is caught by Allan Woodcourt and Jenny, says: 'Can't you
never let such an unfortnet as me alone: An't I unfortnet enough for
you yet? How unfortnet do you want me fur to be? I've been a chivied

and a chivied, fust by one on you and nixt by another on you, till I'm
worritted to skins and bones. The Inkwhich wern't *my* fault. *I* done
nothink. He wos wery good to me, he wos; he was the only one I
knowed to speak to, as ever come across my crossing. It ain't wery
likely I should want him to be Inkwhich'd. I only wish I was myself.
I don't know why I don't go and make a hole in the water, I'm sure
I don't.'

Jo is an extreme example of a recurrent type in Dickens' novels:
the child already old with knowledge of the ways and miseries of the
world. Guppy and Smallweed are repellent examples of the same type.
But Jo, a far more extreme version, though repellent too, also stirs our
compassion. Among many other things, Jo knows about dying. When
Charley tells him he shouldn't sleep at the brick kiln, because people
die there, he says: 'They dies everywheres . . . They dies more than
they lives, according to what *I* see.' And when it comes Jo's time to
die, the fears he has are not of death. His only fear is of being taken
back to Tom-All-Alone's. He thinks of death as being 'moved on as
fur as ever I could go and couldn't be moved no furdur'. It is peace
for him, quiet, the end of the need to move on. Just before the end he
starts up, afraid that he will not get to the paupers' burying ground
in time – or that, once there, he will not be allowed to get in, that they
will not unlock it for him. But at last:

> The light is come upon the dark benighted way. Dead!
> Dead, your Majesty. Dead, my lords and gentlemen. Dead, Right
> Reverends and Wrong Reverends of every order. Dead, men and women,
> born with Heavenly compassion in your hearts. And dying thus around
> us every day.

Jo is a central character in *Bleak House*. He might, in fact, be called
the central character. In his notes for chapter 29, Dickens wrote: 'Then
connect Esther and Jo.' And by one means or another, Jo is 'connected'
with virtually all the characters of importance in *Bleak House*. This is
not accident, nor even the storymaker's simple and inevitable extension
of coincidence to tie his story together. The notes to *Bleak House* begin
with several lists of possible titles for the novel. Every list but the final
and deciding one starts with the title 'Tom-All-Alone's'. And in his
notes for chapter 16, Dickens indicated that Tom-All-Alone's was 'the
ruined property in Jarndyce and Jarndyce, already described by Mr
Jarndyce'.

Mr Jarndyce does describe the property which he prophesies quite correctly will no longer be anything but the means to pay the lawyers' costs in the case. 'It is a street of perishing blind houses, with their eyes stoned out, without a pane of glass, without so much as a window-frame, with the bare blank shutters tumbling from their hinges and falling asunder; the iron rails peeling away in flakes of rust; the chimneys sinking in; the stone steps to every door (and every door might be Death's Door) turning stagnant green; the very crutches on which the ruins are propped, decaying. These are the Great Seal's impressions . . . all over England – the children know them!'

Dickens is vehement against that moneyed world of fashion which is 'wrapped up in too much jeweller's cotton and fine wool, and cannot hear the rushing of the larger worlds, and cannot see them as they circle round the sun'. He insists that this ignorance does not just befall the well-to-do but that it is actually willed by them, that part of the *status quo* they wish to preserve is the *status quo* of their own ignorance, the peculiar ignorance of 'ladies and gentlemen . . . who have agreed to put a smooth glaze on the world, and to keep down all its realities. . . . Who have found out the perpetual stoppage.'

Such a 'perpetual stoppage' is, of course, as impossible as Dombey's 'double door of gold' to 'shut out all the world'. Truth has terrible ways to assert itself, and not even wealth, though it has many protections, is a barrier to infection. Tom-All-Alone's will have its revenge. 'Even the winds are his messengers, and they serve him in these hours of darkness. There is not a drop of Tom's corrupted blood but propagates infection and contagion somewhere. It shall pollute, this very night, the choice stream . . . of a Norman house, and his Grace shall not be able to say Nay to the infamous alliance. There is not an atom of Tom's slime, not a cubic inch of any pestilential gas in which he lives, not one obscenity or degradation about him, not an ignorance, not a wickedness, not a brutality of his committing, but shall work its retribution, through every order of society, up to the proudest of the proud, and to the highest of the high. Verily, what with tainting, plundering, and spoiling, Tom has his revenge.' Jo carries his fever about with him as he is hounded around the country. Charley catches it from him, and Esther Summerson catches it from Charley. They have been kind to Jo, but the realist Dickens knows that the fruits of social injustice are not distributed in any strict accordance with deserving. And at Jo's bedside, when he is dying, both Mr Jarndyce and

Allan Woodcourt think 'how strangely Fate has entangled this rough outcast in the web of very different lives'.

Epidemic is nature's counterpart for revolution. In Dickens' mind, disease and oppression were closely linked. In 1854, the year after he finished *Bleak House*, he warned Lady Burdett-Coutts of the danger the government faced if it did not take proper measures to control cholera:

> Let it [the cholera] come twice again, severely, – the people advancing all the while in the knowledge that, humanly speaking, it is, like Typhus Fever in the mass, a preventible disease – and you will see such a shake in this country as never was seen on Earth since Sampson pulled the Temple down upon his head.[1]

The misery that makes people long for death also and similarly breeds violence. By this time in the fifties, revolution seemed a dreadful and present possibility to Dickens. It is surely the possibility that lurks in the fog and mire of *Bleak House*.

When Richard asks Krook why his shop is called Chancery, the old man starts to explain directly; then is diverted by Ada's hair, and says he has three sacks of ladies' hair below in his shop; then finally does explain that he and the Lord Chancellor 'both grub on in a muddle'. By this time and through his inadvertence, we suspect what the human consequences of this grubbing and muddling are. When Krook dissolves of spontaneous combustion, Dickens tells us that this is the death 'of all Lord Chancellors in all Courts, and of all authorities in all places under all names soever, where false pretenses are made, and where injustice is done . . . [a death] inborn, inbred, engendered in the corrupted humours of the vicious body itself'.

A kind of inevitable dissolution is the hope, but how much is invested in this hope? Will the Dedlocks (surely the name is symbolic: dead-lock) break up or must they be broken up? Toward the end of *Bleak House* it is the suit of Jarndyce and Jarndyce that 'lapses and melts away', but not Chancery, and it is clear that Dickens has grave doubts that enough will happen by peaceful process. When Esther and Ada visit the bricklayers' house with Mrs Pardiggle, they both feel 'painfully sensible that between us and these people there [is] an iron barrier'. Miss Flite, who in her own flighty way is a social realist too, expects a judgment on the Day of Judgment when she will release or give flight to those birds, Hope, Joy, etc., which symbolize all that is frustrate and imprisoned in the hell of the world. Mr Boythorn says that the only possible way to reform Chancery is to blow it to atoms 'with ten thousand hundred-weight of gunpowder', and in the next instant he calls Sir Leicester Dedlock 'the most stiff-necked, arrogant, imbecile, pigheaded numskull, ever, by some inexplicable mistake of Nature, born in any station of life but a walking-stick's'.

It is the obduracy of the old bad system that makes the hope for gradual or peaceful improvement seem so small to Dickens – this obduracy, and terrible ignorance too, for the fog and mire of *Bleak House* are the fog and mire of ignorance. The wilful ignorance of the upper classes is based on a limited concept of self-interest; but middle-class ignorance is something else. Mr Turveydrop – in whose name the dropping that is a bow or curtsey and the dropping that is animal excrement become inextricably combined – is a genteelly impoverished and hypocritical worshipper of the upper classes, a gentlemen's gentleman, part of that middle class that Dickens describes as no class at all, but only a fringe on the mantle of the upper class. Mr Bayham Badger, another member of this no-class, prides himself ridiculously on the gentility of his wife's former husbands.

This pretentious ignorance, amounting to a failure of self-interest, is specially galling to Dickens, for he feels that there is nothing to hope from a man who fails to recognize even his own needs and reasonable claims, whose pretensions cause him to be ignorant of his own interests. In this cataloguing of kinds of ignorance, there is the self-deluding ignorance too of the Mrs Jellybys and Mrs Pardiggles, who find it easier to do good deeds at a distance than to do their duty close by. And there is Krook, who has his own brand of ignorance – the stubborn, self-destroying, and vicious but still comic ignorance of craft – and won't ask anyone to teach him to read because they might teach him wrong.

The most dangerous ignorance of all, though, is the ignorance of those too down-trodden in the world to know or care. A couple of years later, Dickens was to tell a friend that 'the alienation of the people from their own public affairs' was 'extremely like the general mind of France before the breaking out of the first Revolution'.[2] To every question addressed to him, Jo says '*I* don't know nothink [no-think?].' Dickens compares Jo to a vagabond dog, and says: 'Turn that dog's descendants wild . . . and in a very few years they will so degenerate that they will lose even their bark – but not their bite.' The logic of the drama scarcely requires Dickens' explanation.

Bleak House confronts authority – the authority of office, and of money, and of family – with the misery of the world. Mr Gridley asks who is responsible, and Esther tells Mr Skimpole that she fears 'everybody is obliged to be' responsible. Responsibility is part of Esther Summerson's great and revolting virtue. Most of the other impossible young women in Dickens' novels spring from the usual source for perfect young women in fiction, the area of erotic wish-fulfilment. But Esther stirs no chord of desire, and it is more likely that Dickens has created her as some kind of *alter ego* for himself, deprived of his aggressive force and talent but made kind and lovable instead. Lovable, too, for herself – not for her beauty, which for a time she loses, nor for her wealth and influence, which she never has. She starts as an unloved child, as Dickens at least fancied that he was himself, and there are certain aspects of her childhood that remind us of Pip and David Copperfield, the only other first-person narrators in Dickens' novels, and each in some sense a self-portrait. But Dickens had to take back all that he thought the world owed him for his lost childhood, and more, by the force of his own hand, whereas everything comes back to Esther Summerson through love. Yet it requires none of this speculation to see that Esther has a schematic place in the novel by being responsible: as John Jarndyce is, as Charley is, as Mrs Bagnet is, as Allan Woodcourt is, as Bucket is, as the Rouncewell family are; and as Skimpole, and Mrs Jellyby, and Mrs Pardiggle, and Mr Chadband are not. As Sir Leicester Dedlock is only by his own insufficient lights.

The attack on Chancery, and on the law and legal process, is an attack on irresponsibility. The law, we are told, takes no responsibility for anything but itself. Its first principle is 'to make business for itself'. It makes hypocritical claims, of course, to much more: Mr Tulking-horn talks of his devotion to Sir Leicester Dedlock, and Vholes talks always of putting his shoulder to the wheel, and of his responsibility to his growing daughters, and to his old father in the Vale of Taunton. But all this is mere sham, and what the legal gentlemen really intend is to enrich and dignify themselves. There are, too, many kinds of responsibility. Attractive responsibilities are easy, but it is the un-attractive ones that are the real test. The poor, Dickens knows and shows, are unattractive, like Jo:

> Dirty, ugly, disagreeable to all the senses, in body a common creature of the common streets. . . . Homely filth begrimes him, homely parasites

devour him, homely sores are in him, homely rags are on him: native ignorance, the growth of English soil and climate, sinks his immortal nature lower than the beasts that perish. Stand forth, Jo, in uncompromising colours! From the sole of thy foot to the crown of thy head, there is nothing interesting about thee.

It is easy to be responsible for pretty Rosa, or rosy Mrs Rouncewell. But who will be responsible for Jo, or for Nemo, the wretched nobody that Captain Hawdon becomes after he has failed in responsibility. For Esther's illegitimacy too is regarded in the light of responsibility, not of sexual morality, and both her father and her mother are made to pay a final price for their irresponsibility toward her.

The very point being made, and that helps substantiate this novel's realism, is that responsibility is difficult, indirect, often very obscure, but that the price of irresponsibility must be paid nonetheless. This is conveyed obviously by the fog-law analogy; less obviously but perhaps more tellingly by the indirect exactions made by disease, epidemic. Only when we have paid the price for our irresponsibilities – secret or unclear as they may be – can we 'begin the world'. Chancery is the set theme of this novel, death is the reality against which the foggy irresponsibility of legal process is assessed, and epidemic – moving by terrible indirection – symbolizes all too realistically the disaster that continued irresponsibility will bring.

NOTES

1. *Letters from Charles Dickens to Angela Burdett-Coutts*, ed. Edgar Johnson (1953) p. 273.
2. *The Letters of Charles Dickens* (in the Nonesuch Dickens: 1938) II 651; to Layard (10 April 1855).

W. J. HARVEY

Bleak House (1965)

DICKENS has often been likened to a Jacobean dramatist both for his vivid, exuberant, 'poetic' use of language and for his methods of characterization. There is a third point of likeness. Critics frequently discuss Jacobean plays in terms of 'episodic intensification'. By this they mean the impulse to exploit to the full possibilities of any particular scene, situation or action without too much regard for the relevance of such local intensities to the total work of art. Clearly much of Dickens's fiction is of the same order. To admit this is to risk the displeasure of much modern criticism of fiction which, largely deriving from James, lays great stress on the organic unity of the novel and demands that no part shall be allowed autonomy if this threatens the integrity of the whole.

We can defend in four ways the novel of episodic intensification from such criticism. First, we may admit that in some cases the work may fail as a whole while succeeding in some part. The result may be a dead or crippled work which yet intermittently achieves the vigour of a masterpiece. We may admire what we can and regret the waste of so much else. This, I think, is true of *Barnaby Rudge*. Second, we may deny the fiat of organic unity and maintain that in *some* cases a novel achieves no more than episodic intensification and yet possesses so much vitality that we are content simply to accept its greatness. In James's terms there must be room in the house of fiction for such 'loose, baggy monsters'. With much less certainty I would place *Pickwick Papers* in this category. Third, we may accept the idea of organic unity and yet maintain that by its standards Dickens's novels are entirely successful. Sometimes he achieves an economy, firmness, and clean-cut clarity of control that can only be called classical. This is surely true of *Great Expectations*. Finally, we may accept the idea of organic unity but argue that the criteria by which we judge its presence or absence have been too narrowly conceived and that there exist conventions and methods of organization which are non-Jamesian but still appropriate and effective. (James, unlike some more recent critics, admitted as much.) *Bleak House* is here a relevant example. Indeed, I would say that one of the reasons for its greatness is the extreme tension set up between the centrifugal vigour of its parts and the centripetal demands of the whole. It is a tension between the impulse to intensify each local detail or particular episode and the impulse to subordinate, arrange and discipline. The final impression is one of immense and potentially anarchic energy being brought – but only just – under control. The fact that the equipoise between part and whole is so precariously maintained is in itself a tribute to the energy here being harnessed.

How well does an examination of the novel's structure support this general view? *Bleak House* is for Dickens a unique and elaborate experiment in narration and plot composition. It is divided into two intermingled and roughly concurrent stories; Esther Summerson's first-person narrative and an omniscient narrative told consistently in the historic present. The latter takes up thirty-four chapters; Esther has one less. Her story, however, occupies a good deal more than half the novel. The reader who checks the distribution of these two narratives against the original part issues will hardly discern any significant pattern or correlation. Most parts contain a mixture of the two stories; one part is narrated by Esther and five parts entirely by the omniscient author. Such a check does, however, support the view that Dickens did not, as is sometimes supposed, use serial publication in the interest of crude suspense. A sensational novelist, for example, might well have ended a part issue with chapter 31; Dickens subdues the drama by adding another chapter to the number. The obvious exception to this only proves the rule; in the final double number the suspense of Bucket's search for Lady Dedlock is heightened by cutting back to the omniscient narrative and the stricken Sir Leicester. In general, however, Dickens's control of the double narrative is far richer and subtler than this. Through this technique, as I shall try to show, he controls the immense, turbulent and potentially confusing material of his novel. Indeed, the narrative method seems to me to be part of the very substance of *Bleak House*, expressive of what, in the widest and deepest sense, the novel is about.

Let us first examine the structural functions of Esther Summerson and her narrative. Esther has generally been dismissed as insipid, one

of Dickens's flat, non-comic good characters, innocent of imaginative
life, more of a moral signpost than a person. Even if we accept this
general judgment we may still find good reasons why Dickens had
necessarily to sacrifice vitality or complexity here in order to elaborate
or intensify other parts of his novel. If Dickens, far from failing to
create a lively Esther, is deliberately suppressing his natural exuberance
in order to create a flat Esther, then we may properly consider one of
Esther's functions to be that of a brake, controlling the runaway
tendency of Dickens's imagination – controlling, in other words, the
impulse to episodic intensification.

Can we possibly accept this view? The contrasting styles of the two
narratives, while they offer the reader relief and variety, also seem to
me evidence of Dickens's control in making Esther what she is, even
at the risk of insipidity and dullness. The omniscient style has all the
liveliness, fantastication and poetic density of texture that we typically
associate with Dickens. Esther's narrative is plain, matter-of-fact,
conscientiously plodding. Only very rarely does her style slip and
allow us to glimpse Dickens guiding her pen – as when, for instance,
she observes 'Mr Kenge, standing with his back to the fire, and casting
his eyes over the dusty hearthrug as if it were Mrs Jellyby's biography'
(ch. 4), or when, as Turveydrop bows to her, she could 'almost believe
I saw creases come into the white of his eyes' (ch. 14). Here one may
glimpse Dickens chafing at his self-imposed discipline. Such moments
apart, any stylistic vivacity or idiosyncrasy in Esther's prose comes
from the oddities and foibles of other characters. Dickens imagines
them; Esther merely reports them. Even when, at moments of emotional stress, her prose strays into the purple patch, one still feels that
this is the rhetoric of an amateur, not to be compared, for instance,
with the controlled crescendo of Jo's death. Similarly, whenever the
straightforward flow of Esther's narratives falters – as in her over-
casual mention of Allan Woodcourt at the end of chapter 14 – we
prefer to see this as appropriate to her character rather than to spot
Dickens signalling a new relationship to us behind her back. That, of
course, is precisely what he is doing, but the disguise of style persuades
us to focus on Esther and not on her creator. (There is, I think, a
corresponding and quite remarkable impersonality about the omniscient narrative. The general impression is of a vast, collective choric
voice brilliantly mimicking the varied life it describes, yet able to
generalize and comment without lapsing into the idiom of one man,

of Dickens himself. Obviously the style exploits and manipulates our sympathies; yet surprisingly rarely do we feel that Dickens is directly buttonholing us.)

As I have said, the two narratives are *roughly* concurrent. Deliberately so; Dickens juggles the two chronologies by keeping the details sufficiently vague. Only rarely do we feel any awkwardness in this temporal matching together and any obvious discontinuity generally has a specific narrative or dramatic point. Esther's tale, taken in isolation, plods forward in the simplest kind of sequence. Yet, being autobiographical, it is retrospective and was written, so we are told, at the very end, seven years after the main events. This simplicity is rarely disturbed; only occasionally does Esther sound the note of 'If I had known then what I know now'; only occasionally does she throw an anticipatory light forward into the shadowy future of her tale as, for example, she does at the end of chapter 37. The reason is that, despite the retrospective nature of her story, Esther must *seem* to be living in a dramatic present, ignorant of the plot's ramifications. Dickens is *really* omniscient in the other narrative; god-like he surveys time as though it were an eternal present and Esther must seem to belong to that present. It is a convention most readers readily accept.

In what ways does Esther's tale throw light on its teller? During his later period Dickens showed considerable interest in the possibilities of the first-person narrative. In some cases – *David Copperfield*, *Great Expectations* – the adult narrator judges, implicitly or explicitly, his growth towards maturity. Esther is clearly not in this category; she swiftly advances from child to woman and scarcely changes at all. We feel that she was 'born old' – a feeling reflected in the nicknames given her, though in fact she is little older than Ada Clare. On the other hand, she cannot be classed with Miss Wade, of *Little Dorrit*, whose story is taken by some critics as an early exercise in that kind of point-of-view technique which dramatizes a limited or crippled consciousness so that what is conveyed to the reader differs radically from the intention of the narrator. Clearly, we are meant to take Esther on trust. If what she tells us is wrong or limited this signifies no moral blindspot in her, no flaw in her sensibility but only her necessary innocence of the full ramifications of the plot. Dickens's treatment of Esther is devoid of irony. We have only to imagine what narrative would have resulted if the teller had been Skimpole – or even Richard Carstone – to see that Esther's responses, attitudes, and actions are never qualified or criticized. She is, in short, thoroughly idealized.

One result of the idealizing process is the static nature of Esther's character, the essentials of which we quickly come to know. These never change; her story merely exhibits them in a variety of situations in which she is generally the patient rather than the agent. That is, Esther *does* very little in the sense of initiating a chain of actions by a deliberate choice. Things are done to her or because of her rather than by her. Devastating things happen to Esther from the moment of her birth, but she generally emerges with her usual placidity and acceptance of duty. Indeed, at times Dickens takes care to subdue the effect on the reader of these crises through which Esther as patient must pass. The chapter which deals, for example, with the recognition scene between Esther and her mother closes in fact with Esther's reunion with Ada. The curious thing is the feelings aroused by the Esther–Ada relationship seem more intense – and intensely rendered – than those aroused by the Esther–Lady Dedlock encounter.

Esther then is static, consistent, passive. She is also good. The difficulties of combining these qualities to produce a compelling character are so immense that we should wonder not that Dickens fails, but that his failure is so slight. Still, he does fail. The exigencies of the narrative force him to reveal Esther's goodness in a coy and repellent manner; she is, for instance, continually imputing to others qualities which the author transparently wishes us to transfer to her. Esther's goodness is most acceptable when she is least conscious of its effects radiating out to impinge on others. Similarly, her narrative is most acceptable when she is pushed from the centre of the stage by the typical inhabitants of the Dickens world. Happily, this is usually so. In other words, Dickens has to reconcile in Esther the demands of a narrator and a main character and he chooses to subdue Esther as a character in the interests of her narrative function. We do not, so to speak, look *at* Esther; we look *through* her at the teeming Dickensian world. This viewpoint is no Jamesian dramatization of a particular consciousness; Esther is as lucid and neutral as a clear window. We look through at a human landscape but we are not, as with James, constantly aware that the window is limited by its frame or that it has a scratch here and an opaque spot there. The penalty Dickens pays for this is the insipidity of Esther's character. But then, *Bleak House* is a thickly populated novel; each character claims his own share of attention and all are connected by a complicated series of interlocking actions. There is no single centre, no Jamesian *disponsible*; rather we have a complex field of force, of interacting stresses and strains. Given this complication it would be too much to ask of the reader that he concentrate on the perceiver as well as the perceived. Were Esther to be complicated the novel would have to be correspondingly simplified and the Dickens world depopulated. Who would wish it so? If the real subject-matter of a novel is a subtly dramatized consciousness then the objects of that consciousness will tend to the sparse refinements of the closet drama. Dickens is the opposite of this; he is to Shakespeare as James is to Racine.

While this, I hope, explains the necessary limitations of Esther's character, it only pushes the real problem one stage further back. Why was it necessary to have a narrator of this kind at all? Any adequate answer must also take into account the omniscient narrative as well. The two narratives are the systole and diastole of the novel and between them they produce the distinctive effect of *Bleak House*; something that I can only call, in a crudely impressionistic manner, the effect of *pulsation*, of constant expansion and contraction, radiation and convergence.

The famous first chapter of *Bleak House* has had more than its fair share of critical attention; at the risk of tedium, therefore, I wish to isolate two striking features of Dickens's method. The omniscient eye which surveys the scene is like the lens of a film camera in its mobility. It may encompass a large panoramic view or, within a sentence, it may swoop down to a close scrutiny of some character or local detail. Closely related to this mobility is the constant expansion and contraction from the omniscient eye to Esther's single viewpoint. Closely related again is the constant expansion and contraction of the total narrative; now concentrating at great length on some episode, now hustling the plot along with a rapid parade of characters. Dickens's narrative skill is nowhere more evident than in his control of tempo.

All this I mean by *pulsation*. But chapter 1 displays yet another related effect. The scene contracts to the Court of Chancery at the heart of the fog, but suddenly this process is reversed; Chancery monstrously expands to encompass the whole country:

> This is the Court of Chancery; which has its decaying houses and its blighted lands in every shire; which has its worn-out lunatic in every madhouse, and its dead in every churchyard. . . .

The heart of Chancery in this respect is Tom All Alone's the breeding-ground of disease (again the radiation of infection). The two are appropriately linked, for Chancery *is* a disease and is constantly described in these terms.

This theme is, of course, abundantly worked out in the novel – in Miss Flite, in Gridley, and above all, in Richard Carstone. The idea of corruption radiating out from a rotten centre (Chancery *and* Tom All Alone's) is reflected, in geographical terms, in the constant to-and-fro movement between London, Bleak House, and Chesney Wold. But this idea is counterpointed, in plot terms, by the sense one has of convergence, especially the sense of something closing-in on Lady Dedlock. Geography and plot coalesce in the final constriction of the chase and the discovery of Lady Dedlock dead near her lover's tomb.

This pulsation, this interaction of radiation and convergence, is also temporal. The case of Jarndyce and Jarndyce does not merely fan out in the present to enmesh innocent and remote people; it also has a terrible history:

> Innumerable children have been born into the cause; innumerable young people have married into it; innumerable old people have died out of it. Scores of persons have deliriously found themselves made parties in Jarndyce and Jarndyce, without knowing how or why; whole families have inherited legendary hatreds with the suit.

Diverse pressures from the past converge to mould the present; Jarndyce and Jarndyce bears down on Richard Carstone; the past catches up with Esther and finally with her mother. This temporal convergence is reflected in the structure of the novel as a whole and locally, in its parts. Thus the first chapter given to Esther (ch. 3) quickly brings us from her childhood back to the dramatic present already described in the omniscient first chapter. Sometimes the dramatic present is illuminated by a shaft driven back into the past; thus both Boythorn and Miss Barbary are in some sense enlarged by the revelation of their abortive love long ago. Or again, the dramatic present will be left unexplained until time has passed and many pages have been turned; thus, on a small scale, the mystery of Jo's disappearance from Bleak House or, on a large scale, Bucket's uncovering of Tulkinghorn's murderess.

Granted the extremely complicated tangle of effects I have labelled *pulsation*, the desirability of a simple, lucid, straightforward narrative

such as Esther's should be obvious. It offers us stability, a point of rest
in a flickering and bewildering world, the promise of some guidance
through the labyrinth. The usual novel may be compared to a pebble
thrown into a pool; we watch the ripples spread. But in *Bleak House*
Dickens has thrown in a whole handful of pebbles and what we have
to discern is the immensely complicated tracery of half a dozen circles
expanding, meeting, interacting. Esther – to change the metaphor – has
the stability of a gyroscope; by her we chart our way.

She is, of course, much more than this. She is, as well, a moral
touchstone; her judgments are rarely emphatic but we accept them.
She can see Richard more clearly than Ada; through her Skimpole is
revealed in his true colours and the Growlery becomes a sign of
Jarndyce's obtuseness. She is also the known constant by which we
judge all the other variables of character. Through her we can see the
horrifyingly vivid rotation of decay and infection that signals the slow
process of Richard's destruction. (Among other things, the intertwining
of the two narratives enables Dickens, drastically to foreshorten and
mould the *apparent* time sequence here.) Again, by her consistency
Esther contributes to the wonderfully skilful characterization of Sir
Leicester and Guppy, who change by fits and starts throughout the
novel. Because these characters demand very different reactions from
us at different times we impute complexity and development to them.
In fact they are not so much complex as discontinuous. Dickens's art
lies in masking this discontinuity and Esther in large part provides a
convincing façade; because she is a simple unity we are conjured into
believing that the heterogeneity of Guppy or Sir Leicester is a unified
complexity.

Finally – and perhaps most important – by intertwining the two
narratives Dickens compels us to a double vision of the teeming,
fantastic world of *Bleak House*. We – and Esther – are within; we –
and the omniscient author – are outside. This double perspective forces
us as readers to make connections which as I have said, because *we*
make them have more validity than if Dickens had made them for
us. The most crucial instance is Esther's ignorance of so much that
surrounds her. What she sees she sees clearly; but she cannot see more
than a fraction of the whole. In this she is not alone; one of the triumphs
of the novel is the delicacy with which Dickens handles the knowledge,
suspicions, guesses, and mistakes of the various characters. Some of
them are limited to one or other of the narrative streams; Esther is

never seen by the omniscient eye, nor does Tulkinghorn ever appear personally in Esther's narrative. This corresponds to their limited knowledge; Tulkinghorn, for all his plotting, never knows of Esther's relation to Lady Dedlock while there is no substantial evidence that Esther knows anything of her father until after her mother's death.

Granted this, the opportunities for dramatic irony are clearly enormous and it is to Dickens's credit as an artist that with great tact he refuses many of the chances for irony offered by the interlocking narratives. How close – all unknowing – is Esther to meeting her father during her first visit to Krook's? Yet we scarcely perceive this, even on a re-reading of the novel. A lesser artist would have wrung dry the irony of such an incident, but Dickens is sound in his refusal to do so. For the novel, as it stands, is so taut, so potentially explosive, that to expatiate on, or to underline, its implications would make it quite intolerable. Of course the irony is there but it is kept latent and, so to speak, subcritical; it does not explode in the reader's conscious attention. In this, of course, its effect is almost the opposite of that which Mann achieves in *Death in Venice*. Mann's story depends largely on its insistently schematic nature, whereas Dickens's problem – like that of most novelists – is to avoid over-schematization, to control the complex and manifold life of the novel without drawing too much attention to the art involved. In this he is again helped by his chosen mode of narration. Through the double narrative Dickens refracts, reflects, varies, distorts, reiterates his major themes, and the disturbing resonance thus set up is expressive of his deepest sense of what life is like. *Bleak House* is so dense with examples of this process that I will quote only one, very minor example. In chapter 25, Mrs Snagsby is suspicious:

> Mrs Snagsby screws a watchful glance on Jo, as he is brought into the little drawing-room by Guster. He looks at Mr Snagsby the moment he comes in. Aha! Why does he look at Mr Snagsby? Mr Snagsby looks at him. Why should he do that, but that Mrs Snagsby sees it all? Why else should that look pass between them; why else should Mr Snagsby be confused, and cough a signal cough behind his hand. It is as clear as crystal that Mr Snagsby is that boy's father.

Mrs Snagsby's magnificent illogicality is a comic analogue, a parody of the dominant atmosphere of the book, that of hints, guesses, suspicions, conspiracies. It is also a distorted echo of one of the novel's major themes, that of parents and children. Even here, in an insignificant corner of the book, its major concerns are repeated and echoed in a different key; this abundance of doubling, parallelling, contrasting, this constant modulation from sinister to pathetic or comic, serves to create a density of life providing a context for those vivid scenes of episodic intensification. We accept these, take them on trust as more than brilliant but isolated moments, because we know they mesh with that complicated web of human affairs which entangles all the characters, even the most trivial. We weave this web, this pattern, as the tale shuttles to and fro between its two tellers and, of course, it is a pattern which gradually and continuously develops and emerges.

HUMPHRY HOUSE

Hard Times (1941)

IN all the work of the early fifties the idea of muddle is spreading over wider and wider social fields. *Hard Times* came out between April and August 1854, and Stephen Blackpool's reiterated comment, "Tis a' a muddle' is superficially the least hopeful moral to be got from any novel Dickens wrote. Discussion of the book has often centred too much on Macaulay's condemnation of it as 'sullen socialism', and the almost exaggerated praise that Ruskin gave it in *Unto this Last*; for it is the least read of the novels and probably also the least enjoyed by those who read it. Even Mr Edwin Pugh called it 'dry', 'hard', and 'the least alluring' of them all. The most common general explanation of the book's failure is that Dickens was writing of people and things quite outside the range of his own experience. This is, in itself, of course, no explanation at all, or *A Tale of Two Cities* would stand equally condemned; but the decision to write just when he did about industrial Lancashire with no more experience than deliberate copy-hunting could give him was peculiar in several ways. The fashion for industrial novels was already passing: *Martin Armstrong*, *Helen Fleet-wood*, *Sybil*, *Mary Barton*, and forgotten stories by such people as Camilla Toulmin, belong to the late thirties and forties, the period of Chartism, terrific unemployment and angry strikes. The experience and motives behind their authors were very various. Mrs Trollope, who had to write for money and had made her name with social criticism, found a topical subject and approached it with an average sense of decency and justice; Mrs Tonna was inspired by her evangelical faith to a hatred of the factory system and its child employment even more passionate than Ashley's; Disraeli was caught for a moment by an image of feudalism and found his experience in official reports; Mrs Gaskell lived every day among the things she wrote of, and only discovered her talent because she thought the experience had to be used.

It has often been said that Dickens was a good deal influenced by *Mary Barton* in writing *Hard Times*: it might even be added that he was influenced by Elizabeth Gaskell herself[1] – it is impossible that he should have known her without being half in love – for his editorial letters about her work show an affectionate care abnormal even for him. But there was never any question of a conscious and deliberate imitation of her, or of Carlyle, or of anybody else. The strange thing is that though most readers find *Hard Times* dry and brain-spun, Dickens said of it himself that he had not meant to write a new story for a year, when the idea laid hold of him by the throat in a very violent manner.

What this central idea was there is no means of knowing; but it is plain that *Hard Times* is one of Dickens's most thought-about books. One of the reasons why, in the fifties, his novels begin to show a greater complication of plot than before, is that he was intending to use them as a vehicle of more concentrated sociological argument. All his journalism shows too that he was *thinking* much more about social problems, whereas earlier he had been content to feel mainly, and to record a thought, when it occurred, in emotional dress. The objection to such a character as Gradgrind is not just that he is a burlesque and an exaggeration – so are Squeers and Pecksniff – but rather that in him the satire is directed against a kind of thought: he is in fact the only major Dickens character who is meant to be an 'intellectual': 'His character was not unkind, all things considered; it might have been a very kind one indeed if he had only made some round mistake in the arithmetic that balanced it, years ago.' Dickens was caught with the idea of a man living by a certain philosophy, as in the past he had often been caught with the idea of a man living by a master vice such as miserhood or hypocrisy or pride. Such vices he understood, but he did not understand enough of any philosophy even to be able to guy it successfully. But he obviously felt during the fifties, when Public Health and Administrative Reform were keeping him so closely to social-political problems, that there must be some essential flaw in the reasoning of such a man as Bright. The creation of Gradgrind is an attempt to track it down. The despondent atmosphere of the whole book reflects the failure to do so.

This atmosphere is concentrated in Stephen Blackpool. In him Dickens tried to rescue the idea of personality in an individual industrial worker. Stephen's successive defeats by the Law, by the Trade Union, and by his employer might have become the material of genuine tragedy, if Dickens had been prepared to accept his death from the beginning as inevitable and unanswerable; but he was hankering all the time after a way to avoid the proper tragic solution, and the result is nothing but a slow record of inglorious misery and defeat. Dickens did not want to admit that Stephen's bargaining power – whether against Bounderby, his marriage, or life itself – was negligible, but wrote as if there might be an unexpected solution at every turn. There is no difficulty about Stephen's relation to the Law or about his relation to Bounderby;[2] the true crux is in the part of the plot that deals with the Trade Union, and in making it so Dickens was apparently trying to work out, in the actual writing of the book, the implications of his old ideal of *man to man* benevolence in the relations between employers and labour in large-scale industry. Three points were emphasized in the treatment of the Union – Stephen's inexplicable obstinacy in refusing to join it; Dickens's hatred of Slackbridge; and the difference of mood and attitude of the other workers towards Stephen as men and as Union members under Slackbridge's influence.

For the Union meeting itself he did a thing which was very rare for him – he deliberately went in search of copy, to Preston, to watch the effects of a strike of the cotton workers there which had dragged on for weeks. He seems to have gone expecting to find discontent, disorder, and even rioting, and his first impression caused surprise and a sort of sentimental gladness that everything was so quiet and the men generally so well-behaved. When he came to write up the visit for the article *On Strike* in *Household Words* (11 Feb. 1854) there was overlaid upon this first impression a certain horror at the idleness. He seemed to be asking whether these were perhaps after all the lazy poor, in whose existence he had never believed. The article describes the two meetings of the strikers that he attended, and they are obviously the foundation for the Union meeting in *Hard Times*: it stresses their order and courtesy, the efficiency of the business and the competence of the men's local leaders; it decries the influence of an outside orator who is a prototype of Slackbridge; it makes clear that the men fully believed in the justice of their case, but that, at the same time, they had no hatred or resentment for most of the employers: it does, however, quote one example of a threatening notice against a particular man, together with various other placards and verses: the moral approval seems to be all on the side of the strikers. But the political conclusion is not that the strike is right:

> In any aspect in which it can be viewed, this strike and lock-out is a deplorable calamity. In its waste of time, in its waste of a great people's energy, in its waste of wages, in its waste of wealth that seeks to be employed, in its encroachment on the means of many thousands who are laboring from day to day, in the gulf of separation it hourly deepens between those whose interests must be understood to be identical or must be destroyed, it is a great national affliction. But, at this pass, anger is of no use, starving out is of no use – for what will that do, five years hence, but overshadow all the mills in England with the growth of a bitter remembrance? – political economy is a mere skeleton unless it has a little human covering and filling out, a little human bloom upon it, and a little human warmth in it.

The only practical suggestion is that the dispute should be submitted immediately to impartial arbitrators agreed upon by both sides. This paragraph is extremely important and interesting, because in it Dickens accepts the fundamental ethical and political proposition of the political economy he generally so much deplores. The interests of employers and employed must be assumed to be identical or must be destroyed. The doctrine of the identity of interests was common to the utilitarians and the economists: on the question of *theory* there is no real difference between Dickens and W. R. Greg:[3] he is not in the least a Socialist.

This paragraph also helps to explain why the satire of Mr Gradgrind is comparatively ineffective; for Dickens is not even intending to attack the whole philosophy which he thought was represented in the Manchester men; he is only attacking the excessive emphasis on statistics; in fact he is repeating Mr Filer over again, and he seems to have no uneasiness about whether such satire is adequate or important. He is through all these years, however, extremely uneasy in his attempts to find a channel through which the desires and needs of an ordinary decent working-man like Blackpool can find expression. Why, when he recognized the capacity of such men for conducting their own business, did he reject the Trade Union solution, and reject it as emphatically as a Manchester man like Greg?

On the whole the 'Combinations' of the thirties and forties, whether organized locally, by trades, or nationally, had avowed revolutionary aims. The extent to which their members advocated the use of physical force was less important than the fact that they were widely believed to do so; but, physical force aside, they were revolutionary in the sense that they did not accept the doctrine of the natural identity of interests between Capital and Labour, and were in their political activities more or less conscious of a class-struggle; and this consciousness was shared by their opponents. The Chartist failure of '48 meant widespread disillusionment in the possibilities of working-class political action, and the reviving unions of the fifties concentrated more on the immediate problem of collective bargaining within particular trades than on the formation of huge amalgamations with political aims.[4] Dickens seems to have realized that this change was happening, but he shared two common popular misconceptions about it; the first was that the leaders of such unions were bound to be demagogic frauds like Gruffshaw and Slackbridge; and the second was that the unions were likely to violate liberty by being exclusive and tyrannical towards workers who refused to join them:[5] both points were heavily underlined in *Hard Times*. The first of these objections was a legacy from the earlier amalgamating, revolutionary period, and was very largely justified. For in the period of Chartism and the large national unions the working-class movement was grotesquely top-heavy and therefore unstable: the middle-class mistrust of 'demagogues' and 'paid agitators', whatever its motives may have been, was justified in the sense that national leadership had not developed out of solidly organized cells of local opinion. Local organization even in the fifties was likely, as in the Preston strike, to be an *ad hoc* affair called into being by a particular dispute; and Dickens was faithful in his reporting, in *On Strike*, of the way that outside influence was likely to be overridden; but in *Hard Times* he regarded local opinion as dynamically inferior to Slackbridge's bluster; he meant to imply that Stephen was socially boycotted in spite of a predominating feeling in his favour, and the other workers bamboozled out of their better selves; and he made the distortion seem more serious by giving Stephen no better reason for not joining them than a mysterious promise. The objection to unions on the ground of exclusiveness and tyranny followed inevitably from the general mis-understanding of their nature: Dickens realized that when Stephen had been both boycotted by his fellow-workers and sacked by Bounderby he had no chance of getting another job; but he did not draw from this the conclusion that an individual worker *cannot* be the equal of an employer in bargaining power, and that the ideal bargaining for labour-price talked of by the economists only had any meaning when the bargaining was done by a unanimous combination. His emotional admiration for the conscientious blackleg was not based on any alternative argument. But he did not abandon all hope of finding some means other than the unions by which such men as Stephen might be politically and socially articulate; he was still groping after it later in the year in the address *To Working Men* and his other articles on Public Health.

However, the failure of *Hard Times* in two main strands of its plot and in so many of its major characters does not lessen the force of the mixture of fascination and repulsion that Dickens felt for the industrial scene in which the book was set. The fascination, which appears in the descriptions of the night railway journey out from Coketown to Bounderby's house, of the people surging to the mills in the morning, and returning at night to their various homes, has the interest in life and movement, which is plain everywhere in his work, heightened by greater speed and tension. The repulsion is generally more marked, as it is in the Black Country parts of *The Old Curiosity Shop*; the dismal appearance of the competing chapels, the rigidity of the Bounderby bank and the grim business discipline which intrudes on every detail even of domestic life, express once more the Southerner's dismay at what he could not assimilate; but underlying it there is unresting indignation at the impoverishment of human life that such things implied. This indignation is not crude and immature anger, but rather a disturbed mood that colours every perception, contributing a great deal to the unpopularity of *Hard Times*. The book is ultimately unsatisfying and oddly uncomfortable to nearly all its readers; but this very fact is the main thing that has to be considered in assessing its value as a novel; unanswerable disquiet was normal among the very few who were not misled into the easy optimism in which Bagehot typifies the fifties; Ruskin's exaggerated praise of *Hard Times* may be understood as a recognition that a work of art, by conveying this at least to others, might make up for many other imperfections; and even those writers whose economics and social criticism were more solid and thoughtful than Dickens's betray in their own ways shifting of opinion and misplacement of emphasis – Mill, Ruskin, and Arnold are examples – which equally, express the practical embarrassment of the time.

NOTES

1. From his letter of 21 April 1854, it is plain that he had talked over the story with her in some detail when he was in the North.

2. Ruskin's judgement that Bounderby was merely a 'dramatic monster, instead of a characteristic example of a worldly master' is probably more or less true if we assume Coketown to be Manchester and Bounderby a man of the local prominence that Dickens gives him. But if Coketown was some smaller place, a monster of that kind might well have got such power over its life. Mr and Mrs Hammond have, for instance, found a possible original (*The Town Labourer* (1917) p. 302): 'P——d, the Beggar-maker, who sits on the destinies of the Poor, we have made a Man of him, whose Mother hawked about the Streets a small Basket; on two Spinners being deputed to ask for a small advance of Price, had the audacity to thrust one of them from him with an Umbrella and discharged them both' (Letter from Committee of Manchester Weavers, 1823, *Home Office Papers*, XL 18). Such a man might well have grown into Bounderby by the fifties.

3. See especially Greg's long review of *Mary Barton*, of 1849, reprinted in *Mistaken Aims and Attainable Ideals of the Artizan Class* (1876), and his *English Socialism* (1850). Both essays are directed against the impatient philanthropy of 'feeling' as compared with the long-distance philanthropy of the economists. The cures for labour disputes are that the working-class should be more provident and should, by the study of political economy, realize the necessary identity of their interests with those of the employers.

4. The Amalgamated Society of Engineers, for instance, was founded in 1851, and played a very important part in the development of Unionism in the next twenty years.

5. Even Kingsley, when calling himself a Socialist, wrote to a Manchester friend, 28 March 1856: 'I admire your boldness in lifting up your voice to expose the tyranny of "Union" Strikes. From my own experience of demagogues . . . I can well believe every word you say as to the "humbug" connected with the inner working of them.'

LIONEL TRILLING

Little Dorrit (1953)

Little Dorrit is one of the three great novels of Dickens' great last period, but of the three it is perhaps the least established with modern readers. When it first appeared – in monthly parts from December 1855 to June 1857 – its success was even more decisive than that of *Bleak House*, but the suffrage of later audiences has gone the other way, and of all Dickens' later works it is *Bleak House* that has come to be the best known. As for *Our Mutual Friend*, after having for some time met with adverse critical opinion among the enlightened – one recalls that the youthful Henry James attacked it for standing in the way of art and truth – it has of recent years been regarded with ever-growing admiration. But *Little Dorrit* seems to have retired to the background and shadow of our consciousness of Dickens.

This does not make an occasion for concern or indignation. With a body of works as large and as enduring as that of Dickens, taste and opinion will never be done. They will shift and veer as they have shifted and veered with the canon of Shakespeare, and each generation will have its special favorites and make its surprised discoveries. *Little Dorrit*, one of the most profound of Dickens' novels and one of the most significant works of the nineteenth century, will not fail to be thought of as speaking with a peculiar and passionate intimacy to our own time.

Little Dorrit is about society, which certainly does not distinguish it from the rest of Dickens' novels unless we go on to say, as we must, that it is *more* about society than any other of the novels, that it is about society in its very essence. This essential quality of the book has become apparent as many of the particular social conditions to which it refers have passed into history. Some of these conditions were already of the past when Dickens wrote, for although imprisonment for debt was indeed not wholly given up until 1869, yet imprisonment for small debts had been done away with in 1844, the prison of the

Marshalsea had been abolished in 1842 and the Court of the Marshalsea in 1849. Bernard Shaw said of *Little Dorrit* that it converted him to socialism; it is not likely that any contemporary English reader would feel it appropriate to respond to its social message in the same way. The dead hand of outworn tradition no longer supports special privilege in England. For good or bad, in scarcely any country in the world can the whole art of government be said to be How Not To Do It. Mrs General cannot impose the genteel discipline of Prunes and Prisms, and no prestige whatever attaches to 'the truly refined mind' of her definition – 'one that will seem to be ignorant of the existence of anything that is not perfectly proper, placid, and pleasant'. At no point, perhaps, do the particular abuses and absurdities upon which Dickens directed his terrible cold anger represent the problems of social life as we now conceive them.

Yet this makes *Little Dorrit* not less but more relevant to our sense of things. As the particulars seem less immediate to our case, the general force of the novel becomes greater, and *Little Dorrit* is seen to be about a problem which does not yield easily to time. It is about society in relation to the individual human will. This is certainly a matter general enough – general to the point of tautology, were it not for the bitterness with which the tautology is articulated, were it not for the specificity and the subtlety and the boldness with which the human will is anatomized.

The subject of *Little Dorrit* is borne in upon us by the symbol, or emblem, of the book, which is the prison. The story opens in a prison in Marseilles. It goes on to the Marshalsea, which in effect it never leaves. The second of the two parts of the novel begins in what we are urged to think of as a sort of prison, the monastery of the Great St Bernard. The Circumlocution Office is the prison of the creative mind of England. Mr Merdle is shown habitually holding himself by the wrist, taking himself into custody, and in a score of ways the theme of incarceration is carried out, persons and classes being imprisoned by their notions of their predestined fate or their religious duty, or by their occupations, their life schemes, their ideas of themselves, their very habits of language.

Symbolic or emblematic devices are used by Dickens to one degree or another in several of the novels of his late period, but nowhere to such good effects as in *Little Dorrit*. The fog of *Bleak House*, the dust heap and the river of *Our Mutual Friend* are very striking, but they scarcely equal in force the prison image which dominates *Little Dorrit*. This is because the prison is an actuality before it is ever a symbol;[1] its connection with the will is real, it is the practical instrument for the negation of man's will which the will of society has contrived. As such, the prison haunted the mind of the nineteenth century, which may be said to have had its birth at the fall of the Bastille. The genius of the age, conceiving itself as creative will, naturally thought of the prisons from which it must be freed, and the trumpet call of the 'Leonore' overture sounds through the century, the signal for the opening of the gates, for a general deliverance, although it grows fainter as men come to think of the prison not as a political instrument merely but as the ineluctable condition of life in society. 'Most men in a brazen prison live' – the line in which Matthew Arnold echoes Wordsworth's 'shades of the prison-house begin to close / Upon the growing boy' – might have served as the epigraph of *Little Dorrit*. In the mind of Dickens himself the idea of the prison was obsessive, not merely because of his own boyhood experience of prison life through his father's three months in the Marshalsea (although this must be given great weight in our understanding of his intense preoccupation with the theme), but because of his own consciousness of the force and scope of his will.

If we speak of the place which the image of the prison occupied in the mind of the nineteenth century, we ought to recollect a certain German picture of the time, inconsiderable in itself but made significant by its use in a famous work of the early twentieth century. It represents a man lying in a medieval dungeon; he is asleep, his head pillowed on straw, and we know that he dreams of freedom because the bars on his window are shown being sawed by gnomes. This picture serves as the frontispiece of Freud's *Introductory Lectures on Psychoanalysis* – Freud uses it to make plain one of the more elementary ideas of his psychology, the idea of the fulfilment in dream or fantasy of impulses of the will that cannot be fulfilled in actuality. His choice of this particular picture is not fortuitous; other graphic representations of wish-fulfilment exist which might have served equally well his immediate didactic purpose, but Freud's general conception of the mind does indeed make the prison image peculiarly appropriate. And Freud is in point here because in a passage of *Little Dorrit* Dickens anticipates one of Freud's ideas, and not one of the simplest but nothing less bold and inclusive than the essential theory of the neurosis.

The brief passage to which I make reference occurs in the course

of Arthur Clennam's pursuit of the obsessive notion that his family is
in some way guilty, that its fortune, although now greatly diminished,
has been built on injury done to someone. And he conjectures that the
injured person is William Dorrit, who has been confined for debt in
the Marshalsea for twenty years. Clennam is not wholly wrong in his
supposition – there is indeed guilt in the family, incurred by Arthur's
mother, and it consists in part of an injury done to a member of the
Dorrit family. But he is not wholly right, for Mr Dorrit has not been
imprisoned through the wish or agency of Mrs Clennam. The reasoning by which Arthur reaches his partly mistaken conclusion is of the
greatest interest. It is based upon the fact that his mother, although
mentally very vigorous, has lived as an invalid for many years. She has
been imprisoned in a single room of her house, confined to her chair,
which she leaves only for her bed. And her son conjectures that her
imprisoning illness is the price she pays for the guilty gratification of
keeping William Dorrit in *his* prison – that is, in order to have the
right to injure another, she must unconsciously injure herself in an
equivalent way: 'A swift thought shot into [Arthur Clennam's] mind.
In that long imprisonment here [i.e. Mr Dorrit's] and in her long
confinement to her room, did his mother find a balance to be struck?
I admit that I was accessory to that man's captivity. I have suffered it
in kind. He has decayed in his prison; I in mine. I have paid the penalty.'

I have dwelt on this detail because it suggests, even more than the
naked fact of the prison itself, the nature of the vision of society of
Little Dorrit. One way of describing Freud's conception of the mind is
to say that it is based upon the primacy of the will, and that the
organization of the internal life is in the form, often fantastically
parodic, of a criminal process in which the mind is at once the criminal,
the victim, the police, the judge, and the executioner. And this is a
fair description of Dickens' own view of the mind, as, having received
the social impress, it becomes in turn the matrix of society.

In emphasizing the psychological aspects of the representation of
society of *Little Dorrit* I do not wish to slight those more immediate
institutional aspects of which earlier readers of the novel were chiefly
aware. These are of as great importance now as they ever were in
Dickens' career. Dickens is far from having lost his sense of the cruelty
and stupidity of institutions and functionaries, his sense of the general
rightness of the people as a whole and of the general wrongness of
those who are put in authority over them. He certainly has not moved

to that specious position in which all injustice is laid at the door of the original Old Adam in each of us, not to be done away with until we shall all, at the same moment, become the new Adam. The Circumlocution Office is a constraint upon the life of England which nothing can justify. Mr Dorrit's sufferings and the injustice done to him are not denied or mitigated by his passionate commitment to some of the worst aspects of the society which deals with him so badly.

Yet the emphasis on the internal life and on personal responsibility is very strong in *Little Dorrit*. Thus, to take but one example, in the matter of the Circumlocution Office Dickens is at pains to remind us that the responsibility for its existence lies even with so good a man as Mr Meagles. In the alliance against the torpor of the Office which he has made with Daniel Doyce, the engineer and inventor, Mr Meagles has been undeviatingly faithful. Yet Clennam finds occasion to wonder whether there might not be 'in the breast of this honest, affectionate, and cordial Mr Meagles, any microscopic portion of the mustard-seed that had sprung up into the great tree of the Circumlocution Office'. He is led to this speculation by his awareness that Mr Meagles feels 'a general superiority to Daniel Doyce, which seemed to be founded, not so much on anything in Doyce's personal character, as on the mere fact of [Doyce's] being an originator and a man out of the beaten track of other men'.

Perhaps the single best index of the degree of complexity with which Dickens views society in *Little Dorrit* is afforded by the character of Blandois and his place in the novel. Blandois is wholly wicked, the embodiment of evil; he is, indeed, a devil. One of the effects of his presence in *Little Dorrit* is to complicate our response to the theme of the prison, to deprive us of the comfortable, philanthropic thought that prisons are nothing but instruments of injustice. Because Blandois exists, prisons are necessary. The generation of readers that preceded our own was inclined, I think, to withhold credence from Blandois – they did not believe in his aesthetic actuality because they did not believe in his moral actuality, the less so because they could not account for his existence in specific terms of social causation. But events have required us to believe that there really are people who seem entirely wicked, and almost unaccountably so; the social causes of their badness lie so far back that they can scarcely be reached, and in any case causation pales into irrelevance before the effects of their actions; our effort to 'understand' them becomes a mere form of thought.

In this novel about the will and society, the devilish nature of Blandois is confirmed by his maniac insistence upon his gentility, his mad reiteration that it is the right and necessity of his existence to be served by others. He is the exemplification of the line in *Lear*: 'The prince of darkness is a gentleman.' The influence of Dickens upon Dostoevski is perhaps nowhere exhibited in a more detailed way than in the similarities between Blandois and the shabby-genteel devil of *The Brothers Karamazov*, and also between him and Smerdyakov of the same novel. It is of consequence to Dickens as to Dostoevski that the evil of the unmitigated social will should own no country, yet that the flavor of its cosmopolitanism should be 'French' – that is, rationalistic and subversive of the very assumption of society. Blandois enfolds himself in the soiled tatters of the revolutionary pathos. So long as he can play the game in his chosen style, he is nature's gentleman dispossessed of his rightful place, he is the natural genius against whom the philistine world closes its dull ranks. And when the disguise, which deceives no one, is off, he makes use of the classic social rationalization: Society has made him what he is; he does in his own person only what society does in its corporate form and with its corporate self-justification. 'Society sells itself and sells me: and I sell society.'[2]

Around Blandois are grouped certain characters of the novel of whose manner of life he is the pure principle. In these people the social will, the will to status, is the ruling faculty. To be recognized, deferred to, and served – this is their master passion. Money is of course of great consequence in the exercise of this passion, yet in *Little Dorrit* the desire for money is subordinated to the desire for deference. The Midas figure of Mr Merdle must not mislead us on this point – should, indeed, guide us aright, for Mr Merdle, despite his destructive power, is an innocent and passive man among those who live by the social will. It is to be noted of all these people that they justify their insensate demand for status by some version of Blandois' pathos; they are confirmed in their lives by self-pity, they rely on the great modern strategy of being the insulted and injured. Mr Dorrit is too soft a man for his gentility mania ever to be quite diabolical, but his younger daughter, Fanny, sells herself to the devil, damns herself entirely, in order to torture the woman who once questioned her social position. Henry Gowan, the cynical, incompetent gentleman-artist who associates himself with Blandois in order to *épater* society, is very nearly as diabolical as his companion. From his mother – who must dismiss once and for all any lingering doubt of Dickens' ability to portray what Chesterton calls the delicate or deadly in human character – he has learned to base his attack on society upon the unquestionable rightness of wronged gentility. Miss Wade lives a life of tortured self-commiseration which gives her license to turn her hatred and her hand against everyone, and she imposes her principle of judgment and conduct upon Tattycoram.

In short, it is part of the complexity of this novel which deals so bitterly with society that those of its characters who share its social bitterness are by that very fact condemned. And yet – so much further does the complexity extend – the subversive pathos of self-pity is by no means wholly dismissed, the devil has not wholly lied. No reader of *Little Dorrit* can possibly conclude that the rage of envy which Tattycoram feels is not justified in some degree, or that Miss Wade is wholly wrong in pointing out to her the insupportable ambiguity of her position as the daughter-servant of Mr and Mrs Meagles and the sister-servant of Pet Meagles. Nor is it possible to read Miss Wade's account of her life, 'The History of a Self Tormentor', without an understanding that amounts to sympathy. We feel this the more – Dickens meant us to feel it the more – because the two young women have been orphaned from infancy, and are illegitimate. Their bitterness is seen to be the perversion of the desire for love. The self-torture of Miss Wade – who becomes the more interesting if we think of her as the exact inversion of Esther Summerson of *Bleak House* – is the classic maneuver of the child who is unloved, or believes herself to be unloved; she refuses to be lovable, she elects to be hateful. In all of us the sense of injustice precedes the sense of justice by many years. It haunts our infancy, and even the most dearly loved of children may conceive themselves to be oppressed. Such is the nature of the human will, so perplexed is it by the disparity between what it desires and what it is allowed to have. With Dickens as with Blake, the perfect image of injustice is the unhappy child, and, like the historian Burckhardt, he connects the fate of nations with the treatment of children. It is a commonplace of the biography and criticism of Dickens that this reflects his own sense of having been unjustly treated by his parents, specifically in ways which injured his own sense of social status, his own gentility; the general force of Dickens' social feelings derives from their being rooted in childhood experience, and something of the special force of *Little Dorrit* derives from Dickens' having discovered its matter in the depths of his own social will.

At this point we become aware of the remarkable number of false and inadequate parents in *Little Dorrit*. To what pains Dickens goes to represent delinquent parenthood, with what an elaboration of irony he sets it forth! 'The Father of the Marshalsea' – this is the title borne by Mr Dorrit, who, preoccupied by the gratification of being the First Gentleman of a prison, is unable to exercise the simplest paternal function; who corrupts two of his children by his dream of gentility; who will accept any sacrifice from his saintly daughter Amy, Little Dorrit, to whom he is the beloved child to be cherished and forgiven. 'The Patriarch' – this is the name bestowed upon Mr Casby, who stands as a parody of all Dickens' benevolent old gentlemen from Mr Pickwick through the Cheerybles to John Jarndyce, an astounding unreality of a man who, living only to grip and grind, has convinced the world by the iconography of his dress and mien that he is the repository of all benevolence. The primitive appropriateness of the strange – the un-English! – punishment which Mr Pancks metes out to this hollow paternity, the cutting off of his long hair and the broad brim of his hat, will be understood by any reader with the least tincture of psychoanalytical knowledge. Then the Meagles, however solicitous of their own daughter, are, as we have seen, but indifferent parents to Tattycoram. Mrs Gowan's rearing of her son is the root of his corruption. It is Fanny Dorrit's complaint of her enemy, Mrs Merdle, that she refuses to surrender the appearance of youth, as a mother should. And at the very center of the novel is Mrs Clennam, a false mother in more ways than one; she does not deny love but she perverts and prevents it by denying all that love feeds on – liberty, demonstrative tenderness, joy, and, what for Dickens is the guardian of love in society, art. It is her harsh rearing of her son that has given him cause to say in his fortieth year, 'I have no will.'

Some grace – it is, of course, the secret of his birth, of his being really a child of love and art – has kept Arthur Clennam from responding to the will of his mother with a bitter, clenched will of his own. The alternative he has chosen has not, contrary to his declaration, left him no will at all. He has by no means been robbed of his ethical will, he can exert energy to help others, and for the sake of Mr Dorrit or Daniel Doyce's invention he can haunt the Circumlocution Office with his mild, stubborn, 'I want to know . . .' But the very accent of that phrase seems to forecast the terrible 'I prefer not to' of Bartleby the Scrivener in Melville's great story of the will in its ultimate fatigue.

It is impossible, I think, not to find in Arthur Clennam the evidence of Dickens' deep personal involvement in *Little Dorrit*. If we ask what Charles Dickens has to do with poor Clennam, what The Inimitable has to do with this sad depleted failure, the answer must be: nothing, save what is implied by Clennam's consciousness that he has passed the summit of life and that the path from now on leads downward, by his belief that the pleasures of love are not for him, by his 'I want to know . . .', by his wish to negate the will in death. Arthur Clennam is that mode of Dickens' existence at the time of *Little Dorrit* which makes it possible for him to write to his friend Macready, 'However strange it is never to be at rest, and never satisfied, and ever trying after something that is never reached, and to be always laden with plot and plan and care and worry, how clear it is that it must be, and that one is driven by an irresistible might until the journey is worked out.' And somewhat earlier and with a yet more poignant relevance: 'Why is it, that as with poor David, a sense always comes crushing upon me now, when I fall into low spirits, as of one happiness I have missed in life, and one friend and companion I have never made?'

If we become aware of an autobiographical element in *Little Dorrit*, we must of course take notice of the fact that the novel was conceived after the famous incident of Maria Beadnell, who, poor woman, was the original of Arthur Clennam's Flora Finching. She was the first love of Dickens' proud, unfledged youth; she had married what Dickens has taught us to call Another, and now, after twenty years, she had chosen to come back into his life. Familiarity with the story cannot diminish our amazement at it – Dickens was a subtle and worldly man, but his sophistication was not proof against his passionate sentimentality, and he fully expected the past to come back to him, borne in the little hands of the adorable Maria. The actuality had a quite extreme effect upon him, and Flora, fat and foolish, is his monument to the discovered discontinuity between youth and middle age; she is the nonsensical spirit of the anticlimax of the years. And if she is in some degree forgiven, being represented as the kindest of foolish women, yet it is not without meaning that she is everywhere attended by Mr F's Aunt, one of Dickens' most astonishing ideas, the embodiment of some rage and spite, flinging to the world the crusts of her buttered toast. 'He has a proud stomach, this chap,' she cries when poor Arthur hesitates over her dreadful gift. 'Give him a meal of chaff!' It is the voice of one of the Parcae.

It did not, of course, need the sad comedy of Maria Beadnell for Dickens to conceive that something in his life had come to an end. It did not even need his growing certainty that, after so many years and so many children, his relations with his wife were insupportable – this realization was as much a consequence as it was a cause of the sense of termination. He was forty-three years old and at the pinnacle of a success unique in the history of letters. The wildest ambitions of his youth could not have comprehended the actuality of his fame. But the last infirmity of noble mind may lead to the first infirmity of noble will. Dickens, to be sure, never lost his love of fame, or of whatever of life's goods his miraculous powers might bring him, but there came a moment when the old primitive motive could no longer serve, when the joy of impressing his powers on the world no longer seemed delightful in itself, and when the first, simple, honest, vulgar energy of desire no longer seemed appropriate to his idea of himself.

We may say of Dickens that at the time of *Little Dorrit* he was at a crisis of the will which is expressed in the characters and forces of the novel, in the extremity of its bitterness against the social will, in its vision of peace and selflessness. This moral crisis is most immediately represented by the condition of Arthur Clennam's will, by his sense of guilt, by his belief that he is unloved and unlovable, by his retirement to the Marshalsea as by an act of choice, by his sickness unto death. We have here the analogy to the familiar elements of a religious crisis. This is not the place to raise the question of Dickens' relation to the Christian religion, which was a complicated one. But we cannot speak of *Little Dorrit* without taking notice of its reference to Christian feeling, if only because this is of considerable importance in its effect upon the aesthetic of the novel.

It has been observed of *Little Dorrit* that certain of Dickens' characteristic delights are not present in their usual force. Something of his gusto is diminished in at least one of its aspects. We do not have the amazing thickness of fact and incident that marks, say, *Bleak House* or *Our Mutual Friend* – not that we do not have sufficient thickness, but we do not have what Dickens usually gives us. We do not have the great population of characters from whom shines the freshness of their autonomous life. Mr Pancks and Mrs Plornish and Flora Finching and Flintwinch are interesting and amusing, but they seem to be the fruit of conscious intention rather than of free creation. This is sometimes explained by saying that Dickens was fatigued. Perhaps so, but if we are aware that Dickens is here expending less of one kind of creative energy, we must at the same time be aware that he is expending more than ever before of another kind. The imagination of *Little Dorrit* is marked not so much by its powers of particularization as by its powers of generalization and abstraction. It is an imagination under the dominion of a great articulated idea, a moral idea which tends to find its full development in a religious experience. It is an imagination akin to that which created *Piers Plowman* and *Pilgrim's Progress*. And, indeed, it is akin to the imagination of *The Divine Comedy*. Never before has Dickens made so full, so Dantean, a claim for the virtue of the artist, and there is a Dantean pride and a Dantean reason in what he says of Daniel Doyce, who, although an engineer, stands for the creative mind in general and for its appropriate virtue: 'His dismissal of himself [was] remarkable. He never said, I discovered this adaptation or invented that combination; but showed the whole thing as if the Divine Artificer had made it, and he had happened to find it. So modest was he about it, such a pleasant touch of respect was mingled with his quiet admiration of it, and so calmly convinced was he that it was established on irrefragable laws.' Like much else that might be pointed to, this confirms us in the sense that the whole energy of the imagination of *Little Dorrit* is directed to the transcending of the personal will, to the search for the Will in which shall be our peace.

We must accept – and we easily do accept, if we do not permit critical cliché to interfere – the aesthetic of such an imagination, which will inevitably tend toward a certain formality of pattern and toward the generalization and the abstraction we have remarked. In a novel in which a house falls physically to ruins from the moral collapse of its inhabitants, in which the heavens open over London to show a crown of thorns, in which the devil has something like an actual existence, we quite easily accept characters named nothing else than Bar, Bishop, Physician. And we do not reject, despite our inevitable first impulse to do so, the character of Little Dorrit herself. Her untinctured goodness does not appall us or make us misdoubt her, as we expected it to do. This novel at its best is only incidentally realistic; its finest power of imagination appears in the great general images whose abstractness is their actuality, like Mr Merdle's dinner parties, or the Circumlocution Office itself, and in such a context we understand Little Dorrit to be the Beatrice of the *Comedy*, the Paraclete in female form. Even the physical littleness of this grown woman, an attribute which is insisted on and which seems likely to repel us, does not do so, for we perceive it to be the sign that she is not only the Child of the Marshalsea, as she is called, but also the Child of the Parable, the negation of the social will.

NOTES

1. Since writing this, I have had to revise my idea of the actuality of the symbols of *Our Mutual Friend*. Professor Edgar Johnson's biography of Dickens – *Charles Dickens: A Biographical and Critical Study*, 2 vols. (New York, 1952; London, 1953) – has taught me much about the nature of dust heaps, including their monetary value, which was very large, quite large enough to represent a considerable fortune: I had never quite believed that Dickens was telling the literal truth about this. From Professor Dodd's *The Age of Paradox* I have learned to what an extent the Thames was visibly the sewer of London, of how pressing was the problem of the sewage in the city as Dickens knew it, of how present to the mind was the sensible and even the tangible evidence that the problem was not being solved. The moral *disgust* of the book is thus seen to be quite adequately comprehended by the symbols which are used to represent it.

2. This is in effect the doctrine of Balzac's philosophical-anarchist criminal, Vautrin. But in all other respects the difference between Blandois and Vautrin is extreme. Vautrin is a 'noble' and justified character; for all his cynicism, he is on the side of virtue and innocence. He is not corrupted by the social injustices he has suffered and perceived, by the self-pity to which they might have given rise; his wholesomeness may be said to be the result of his preference for power as against the status which Blandois desires. The development of Blandois from Vautrin – I do not know whether Dickens' creation was actually influenced by Balzac's – is a literary fact which has considerable social import.

JOHN GROSS

A Tale of Two Cities (1962)

A Tale of Two Cities ends fairly cheerfully with its hero getting killed; Dickens's previous novel, *Little Dorrit*, ends in deep gloom with its hero getting married. Violence offers Dickens a partial release from the sense of frustration and despondency which crept over him during the 1850s; the shadow of the Marshalsea lifts a little with the storming of the Bastille, and everyone remembers *A Tale of Two Cities* above all for the intoxication of its crowd scenes. In fact they take up less space than one supposes in retrospect, and for the most part the atmosphere is every bit as stifling as that of *Little Dorrit*. Dickens originally thought of calling the book 'Buried Alive', and at its heart lie images of death and, much less certainly, of resurrection: themes which foreshadow *Our Mutual Friend*.

The story opens with the feeblest of resurrections, the recall to life of Doctor Manette. His daughter is afraid that she is going to meet his ghost, a fear that is almost justified when she actually sees his spectral face and hears his voice, so faint and lacking in life and resonance that it is 'like the last feeble echo of a sound made long and long ago . . . like a voice underground' (bk 1 ch. 6). The whole novel is thronged with ghosts; from the mist moving forlornly up the Dover Road 'like an evil spirit seeking rest and finding none' to the gunsmoke which as it clears suggests Madame Defarge's soul leaving her body, there are scores of references to spectres, phantoms, and apparitions. The penniless émigrés haunt Tellson's like familiar spirits; Lorry sees the likeness of the Lucie whom he once knew pass like a breath across the pier-glass behind her; the fountains of the château show ghostly in the dawn – but it would be tedious to compile a catalogue.

Such ghostliness suggests, first of all, a sense of unreality, of the death in life to which men are reduced by imprisonment, psychological or actual. To Darnay, the prisoners in La Force, going through the motions of elegance and pride in the midst of squalor, are ghosts all, 'waiting their dismissal from the desolate shore', and the scene simply 'the crowning unreality of his long unreal ride' (bk III ch. 1). But ghosts are also the creatures of false or, at any rate, imperfect resurrection: the grave gives up its dead reluctantly, and the prisoner who has been released is still far from being a free man. The inmates of the Bastille, suddenly given their liberty by 'the storm that had burst their tomb', are anything but overjoyed: 'all scared, all lost, all wondering and amazed, as if the Last Day were come, and those who rejoiced around them were all lost spirits' (bk II ch. 21). Even the phlegmatic Darnay, after his Old Bailey acquittal, 'scarcely seems to belong to this world again'. As for Doctor Manette, he has been as deeply scarred by his prison experience as William Dorrit. Lucie's love is not enough in itself to stop him from retreating into his shoe-making, and it takes a symbolic act of violence to complete the cure; he is fully restored to himself only after Mr Lorry has hacked to pieces his cobbler's bench, 'while Miss Pross held the candle as if she were assisting at a murder' (bk II ch. 19). But by this time the centre of interest in the book has shifted unmistakably to Sydney Carton.

The prison and the grave are linked in Dickens's mind with the idea that 'every human creature is constituted to be that profound secret and mystery to every other'. We live in essential isolation; in each heart there is, 'in some of its imaginings, a secret to the heart nearest it. Something of the awfulness, even of death itself, is referable to this . . . In any of the burial-places of this city through which I pass, is there a sleeper more inscrutable than its busy inhabitants are, in their innermost personality, to me, or than I am to them?' (bk I ch. 3). On his journey to greet the newly released Manette, Mr Lorry feels as if he is going to unearth a secret as well as dig up a dead man; in his dream the grave is confused with the underground strong-rooms at Tellson's, and he fancies himself digging 'now with a spade, now with a great key, now with his hands'. In his hotel room, the two tall candles are reflected on every leaf of the heavy dark tables, 'as if *they* were buried in deep graves of dark mahogany, and no light to speak of could be expected of them until they were dug out' (bk I ch. 4).

This oppressive sense of mystery generates suspicion and fear. 'All secret men are soon terrified', Dickens tells us in connection with Barsad, the police spy; but we are in a world where everyone is a secret man, a world of whispers and echoes. On the Dover Mail 'the guard suspected the passengers, the passengers suspected one another and the guard, they all suspected everybody else'; when Darnay returns to France, 'the universal watchfulness so encompassed him, that if he had been taken in a net, or were being forwarded to his destination in a cage, he could not have felt his freedom more completely gone' (bk III ch. 1). Even in the haven established for Doctor Manette near Soho Square there is foreboding in the air, in the echoes which Lucie makes out to be 'the echoes of all the footsteps that are coming by and by into our lives'. An accurate enough premonition of the noise of feet and voices pouring into the Paris courtyard which first draws her attention to the bloodstained grindstone, or of the troubled movement and shouting round a street-corner which herald the Carmagnole. Carton's last impression, too, is to be of 'the pressing on of many footsteps' on the outskirts of the crowd round the guillotine. Footsteps suggest other people, and in *A Tale of Two Cities* other people are primarily a threat and a source of danger. The little group around Doctor Manette is as self-contained as any in Dickens, but it enjoys only a precarious safety; the emblematic golden arm on the wall at Soho Square is always capable of dealing a poisoned blow.

A Tale of Two Cities is a tale of two heroes. The theme of the double has such obvious attractions for a writer preoccupied with disguises, rival impulses, and hidden affinities that it is surprising that Dickens didn't make more use of it elsewhere. But no one could claim that his handling of the device is very successful here, or that he has managed to range the significant forces of the novel behind Carton and Darnay. Darnay is, so to speak, the accredited representative of Dickens in the novel, the 'normal' hero for whom a happy ending is still possible. It has been noted, interestingly enough, that he shares his creator's initials – and that is pretty well the only interesting thing about him. Otherwise he is a pasteboard character, completely undeveloped. His position as an exile, his struggles as a language-teacher, his admiration for George Washington are so many openings thrown away.

Carton, of course, is a far more striking figure. He belongs to the line of cultivated wastrels who play an increasingly large part in Dickens's novels during the second half of his career, culminating in Eugene Wrayburn; his clearest predecessor, as his name indicates, is the luckless Richard Carstone of *Bleak House*. He has squandered his gifts and drunk away his early promise; his will is broken, but his intellect is unimpaired. In a sense, his opposite is not Darnay at all, but the aggressive Stryver, who makes a fortune by picking his brains. Yet there is something hollow about his complete resignation to failure; his self-abasement in front of Lucie, for instance. ('I am like one who died young . . . I know very well that you can have no tenderness for me . . .') For, stagy a figure though he is, Carton does suggest what Thomas Hardy calls 'fearful unfulfilments'; he still has vitality, and it is hard to believe that he has gone down without a struggle. The total effect is one of energy held unnaturally in check: the bottled-up frustration which Carton represents must spill over somewhere.

Carton's and Darnay's fates are entwined from their first meeting, at the Old Bailey trial. Over the dock there hangs a mirror: 'crowds of the wicked and the wretched had been reflected in it, and had passed from its surface and this earth's together. Haunted in a most ghastly manner that abominable place would have been, if the glass could ever have rendered back its reflections, as the ocean is one day to give up its dead' (bk II ch. 2). After Darnay's acquittal we leave him with Carton, 'so like each other in feature, so unlike in manner, both reflected in the glass above them'. Reflections, like ghosts, suggest unreality and self-division, and at the end of the same day Carton stares at his own image in the glass and upbraids it: 'Why should you particularly like a man who resembles you? There is nothing in you to like: you know that. Ah, confound you! . . . Come on, and have it out in plain words! You hate the fellow' (bk II ch. 4). In front of the mirror, Carton thinks of changing places with Darnay; at the end of the book, he is to take the other's death upon him. Dickens prepares the ground: when Darnay is in jail, it is Carton who strikes Mr Lorry as having 'the wasted air of a prisoner', and when he is visited by Carton on the rescue attempt, he thinks at first that he is 'an apparition of his own imagining'. But Dickens is determined to stick by Darnay: a happy ending *must* be possible. As Lorry and his party gallop to safety with the drugged Darnay, there is an abrupt switch to the first person: 'The wind is rushing after us, and the clouds are flying after us, and the moon is plunging after us, and the whole wild night is in pursuit of us; but so far, we are pursued by nothing else' (bk III ch. 13). *We* can make our escape, however narrowly; Carton, expelled from our system, must be abandoned to his fate.

But the last word is with Carton – the most famous last word in

Dickens, in fact. Those who take a simplified view of Dickens's radicalism, or regard him as one of nature's Marxists, can hardly help regretting that *A Tale of Two Cities* should end as it does. They are bound to feel, with Edgar Johnson, that 'instead of merging, the truth of revolution and the truth of sacrifice are made to appear in conflict'. A highly personal, indeed a unique crisis cuts across public issues and muffles the political message. But this is both to sentimentalize Dickens's view of the revolution, and to miss the point about Carton. The cynical judgment that his sacrifice was trifling, since he had nothing to live for, is somewhat nearer the mark. Drained of the will to live, he is shown in the closing chapters of the book as a man courting death, and embracing it when it comes. 'In seasons of pestilence, some of us will have a secret attraction to the disease – a terrible passing inclination to die of it. And all of us have like wonders hidden in our breasts, only needing circumstances to evoke them' (bk III ch. 6). It is Carton rather than Darnay who is 'drawn to the loadstone rock'.[1] On his last walk around Paris, a passage which Shaw cites in the preface to *Man and Superman* as proof of Dickens's essentially irreligious nature, his thoughts run on religion: 'I am the Resurrection and the Life.' But his impressions are all of death: the day comes coldly, 'looking like a dead face out of the sky', while on the river 'a trading boat, with a sail of the softened colour of a dead leaf, then glided into his view, floated by him, and died away' (bk III ch. 9). His walk recalls an earlier night, when he wandered round London with 'wreaths of dust spinning round and round before the morning blast, as if the desert sand had risen far away and the first spray of it in its advance had begun to overwhelm the city' (bk II ch. 5). Then, with the wilderness bringing home to him a sense of the wasted powers within him, he saw a momentary mirage of what he might have achieved and was reduced to tears; but now that the city has been overwhelmed in earnest, he is past thinking of what might have been. 'It is a far, far better thing that I do, than I have ever done' – but the 'better thing' might just as well be committing suicide as laying down his life for Darnay. At any rate, he thinks of himself as going towards rest, not towards resurrection.

By this time the Revolution has become simply the agency of death, the storm that overwhelms the city. Or rather, all the pent-up fury and resentment that is allowed no outlet in the 'personal' side of the

book, with Carton kow-towing to Stryver and nobly renouncing
Lucie, boils over in revolutionary violence: Dickens dances the
Carmagnole, and howls for blood with the mob. Frightened by the
forces which he has released, he views the revolution with hatred and
disgust; he doesn't record a single incident in which it might be shown
as beneficent, constructive or even tragic. Instead, it is described time
and again in terms of pestilence and madness. Dickens will hear nothing
of noble aspirations; the disorder of the whole period is embodied in
the dervishes who dance the Carmagnole – 'no fight could have been
half so terrible'. Confronted with the crowd, Dickens reaches for his
gun; he looks into eyes 'which any unbrutalized beholder would have
given twenty years of life, to have petrified with a well-directed gun'
(bk III ch. 2). That 'well-directed' has the true ring of outraged rate-
paying respectability, while the image seems oddly out of place in a
book which has laid so much stress on the stony faces and petrified
hearts of the aristocracy.

   Dickens can only deal with mob-violence in a deliberately picturesque story set in the past. But *A Tale of Two Cities*, written by a
middle-aged man who could afford a longer perspective at a time
when Chartism was already receding into history, is not quite analogous to *Barnaby Rudge*. There, however contemptible we are meant
to find the world of Sir John Chester, the riots are an explosion of
madness and nothing more. But the French Revolution compels
Dickens to acquire a theory of history, however primitive: 'crush
humanity out of shape once more, under similar hammers, and it will
twist itself into the same tortured forms' (bk III ch. 15). The revolu-
tionaries return evil for evil; the guillotine is the product not of innate
depravity but of intolerable oppression. If Dickens's sympathies shift
towards the aristocrats as soon as they become victims, he can also
show a grim restraint; he underlines the horror of Foulon's death,
strung up with a bunch of grass tied to his back (how his imagination
pounces on such a detail!), but he never allows us to forget who
Foulon was. Nor does he have any sympathy with those who talk of
the Revolution 'as though it were the only harvest under the skies
that had never been sown', although he himself is at times plainly
tempted to treat it as an inexplicable calamity, a rising of the sea (the
gaoler at La Force has the bloated body of a drowned man, and so
forth) or a rising of fire: the flames which destroy the château of St
Evrémonde 'blow from the infernal regions', convulsing nature until

the lead boils over inside the stone fountains. But cause and effect are never kept out of sight for long; Dickens is always reminding himself that the Revolution, though 'a frightful moral disorder', was born of 'unspeakable suffering, intolerable oppression, and heartless indifference'. Society was diseased before the fever broke out: the shattered cask of wine which at the outset falls on the 'crippling' stones of Saint Antoine is scooped up in little mugs of 'mutilated' earthenware.

But to grasp a patient's medical history is not to condone his disease, and Dickens is unyielding in his hostility to the crowd. The buzzing of the flies on the scent for carrion at the Old Bailey trial and the mass-rejoicing at Roger Cly's funeral are early indications of what he feels. The courtroom in Paris is also full of buzzing and stirring, but by this time the atmosphere has become positively cannibalistic; a jury of dogs has been empanelled to try the deer, Madame Defarge 'feasts' on the prisoner, Jacques III, with his very Carlylean croak, is described as an epicure.

Whatever Dickens's motives, a good deal of this is no doubt perfectly valid; morbid fantasies can still prompt shrewd observations, as when we are shown Darnay, the prisoner of half an hour, already learning to count the steps as he is led away to his cell. In particular, Dickens recognizes the ways in which a period of upheaval can obliterate the individual personality; there is no more telling details in the book than the roll-call of the condemned containing the names of a prisoner who has died in jail and two who have already been guillotined, all of them forgotten. Insane suspicion, senseless massacres, the rise to power of the worst elements: in the era of Gladstonian budgets Dickens understands the workings of a police state.

But it would be ludicrous to claim very much for the accuracy of Dickens's account of the French Revolution as such. There are scarcely any references to the actual course of events, and no suggestion at all that the revolution had an intellectual or idealistic content, while the portrayal of fanaticism seems childish if we compare it even with something as one-sided as *The Gods are Athirst*. For the purposes of the novel, the revolution is the Defarges, and although Carton foresees that Defarge in his turn will perish on the guillotine, he has no inkling of how the whole internecine process will ever come to a halt. As for Madame Defarge, she is as much driven by fate as the stony-hearted Marquis, with his coachmen cracking their whips like the Furies: the time has laid 'a dreadfully disfiguring hand upon her'. Her last entry

is her most dramatic. Miss Pross is bathing her eyes to rid herself of
feverish apprehensions, when she suddenly appears – materializes, one
might say – in the doorway: 'The basin fell to the ground broken, and
the water flowed to the feet of Madame Defarge. By strange stern
ways, and through much staining blood, those feet had come to meet
that water' (bk III ch. 14). We are reminded, by rather too forcible
a contrast, of the broken cask of red wine which prefaces Madame
Defarge's first appearance in the novel. Her element, from the very
start, is blood.

Still, *A Tale of Two Cities* is not a private nightmare, but a work
which continues to give pleasure. Dickens's drives and conflicts are
his raw material, not the source of his artistic power, and in itself the
fact that the novel twists the French Revolution into a highly personal
fantasy proves nothing: so, after all, does *The Scarlet Pimpernel*.
Everything depends on the quality of the writing – which is usually
one's cue, in talking about Dickens, to pay tribute to his exuberance
and fertility. Dickens's genius inheres in minute particulars; later we
may discern patterns of symbolism and imagery, a design which lies
deeper than the plot, but first we are struck by the lavish heaping-up
of acute observations, startling similes, descriptive flourishes, circum-
stantial embroidery. Or such is the case with every Dickens novel
except for the *Tale*, which is written in a style so grey and unadorned
that many readers are reluctant to grant it a place in the Canon at all.
Dickens wouldn't be Dickens if there weren't occasional touches like
the 'hospital procession of negro cupids, several headless and all
cripples', which Mr Lorry notices framing the mirror in his hotel (or
the whitewashed cupid 'in the coolest linen' on the ceiling of his Paris
office, which makes its appearance three hundred pages later). But for
the most part one goes to the book for qualities which are easier to
praise than to illustrate or examine: a rapid tempo which never lets
up from the opening sentence, and a sombre eloquence which saves
Carton from mere melodrama, and stamps an episode like the running-
down of the child by the Marquis's carriage on one's mind with a
primitive intensity rarely found after Dickens's early novels, like an
outrage committed in a fairy-tale.

But it must be admitted that the *Tale* is in many ways a thin and
uncharacteristic work, bringing the mounting despair of the 1850s
to a dead end rather than ushering in the triumphs of the sixties. In no

other novel, not even *Hard Times*, has Dickens's natural profusion been so drastically pruned. Above all, the book is notoriously deficient in humour. One falls – or flops – back hopefully on the Crunchers, but to small avail. True, the comic element parodies the serious action: Jerry, like his master, is a 'Resurrection-Man', but on the only occasion that we see him rifling a grave it turns out to be empty, while his son's panic-stricken flight with an imaginary coffin in full pursuit is nightmarish rather than funny. As comic characters the Crunchers are forced and mechanical; such true humour as there is in the book is rather to be found in scattered observations, but settings and characters are colourful rather than grotesque. Obviously Dickens's humour is many things, but it is usually bound up with a sense of almost magical power over nature: to distort, exaggerate, yoke together or dissolve is to manipulate and control external reality. In Dickens people are always taking on the qualities of objects with which they come into contact, and *vice versa*; a basic Dickensian trick of style, which makes its appearance as early as the opening pages of *Sketches by Boz*, where there is a fine passage ('Our Parish', ch. 7) on the 'resemblance and sympathy' between a man's face and the knocker on his front door. Such transformations are not unknown in *A Tale of Two Cities* – there is the obstinate door at Tellson's with the weak rattle in its throat, for example – but they occur less frequently than in any other Dickens novel, and there is a corresponding lack of power for which a neatly constructed plot is small compensation.

Contrary to what might be expected, this absence of burlesque is accompanied by a failure to present society in any depth: *A Tale of Two Cities* may deal with great political events, but nowhere else in the later work of Dickens is there less sense of society as a living organism. Evrémondes and Defarges alike seem animated by sheer hatred; we hear very little of the stock social themes, money, hypocrisy, and snobbery. Tellson's, musty and cramped and antiquated, makes an excellent Dickensian set-piece, but it is scarcely followed up. Jarvis Lorry, too, is a sympathetic version of the fairy-godfather, a saddened Cheeryble who repines at spending his days 'turning a vast pecuniary mangle', but this side of his character is only lightly sketched in. He may glance through the iron bars of his office-window 'as if they were ruled for figures too, and everything under the clouds were a sum', but he is more important as a protective, reassuring figure: in times of revolution Tellson's mustiness becomes a positive virtue.

The lack of social density shows up Dickens's melodrama to dis-advantage. This is partly a question of length, since in a short novel everything has to be worked in as best it can: Barsad will inevitably turn out to be Miss Pross's long-lost brother, Defarge has to double as Doctor Manette's old servant, and so forth. But there is a deeper reason for feeling more dissatisfaction with the artificial plot here than one does with equally far-fetched situations elsewhere in Dickens. Where society is felt as an all-enveloping force, Dickens is able to turn the melodramatic conventions which he inherited to good use; how-ever preposterous the individual coincidences, they serve an important symbolic function. The world is more of a piece than we suppose, Dickens is saying, and our fates are bound up, however cut off from one another we may appear: the pestilence from Tom-All-Alone's really will spread to the Dedlock mansion, and sooner or later the river in which Gaffer Hexam fishes for corpses will flow through the Veneering drawing-room. In a word, we can't have Miss Havisham without Magwitch. But without a thick social atmosphere swirling round them, the characters of *A Tale of Two Cities* stand out in stark melodramatic isolation; the spotlight is trained too sharply on the implausibilities of the plot, and the stage is set for Sir John Martin-Harvey and *The Only Way*. So, too, the relentless workings of destiny are stressed rather clumsily by such a bare presentation; Madame Defarge points the finger of fate a little too vigorously, and there is a tendency towards heavy repetitions and parallelisms, brought out by the chapter-headings, 'A Hand at Cards' and 'The Game Made', 'Dusk' and 'Darkness', and so forth.

Yet despite the dark mood in which it was conceived, the *Tale* isn't a wholly gloomy work; nor is the final impression which it leaves with us one of a wallow of self-pity on the scaffold. We are told of Darnay in the condemned cell (or is it Carton?) that

> his hold on life was strong, and it was very, very hard to loosen; by gradual efforts and degrees unclosed a little here, it clenched the tighter there; and when he brought his strength to bear on that hand and it yielded, this was closed again. There was a hurry, too, in all his thoughts, a turbulent and heated working of his heart, that contended against resignation. (bk III ch. 13)

And near the end, as Miss Pross grapples with Madame Defarge, Dickens speaks of 'the vigorous tenacity of love, always so much stronger than hate'. The gruesome events of the book scarcely bear out such a judgment, yet as an article of faith, if not as a statement of the literal truth, it is curiously impressive. For all the sense of horror which he must have felt stirring within him when he wrote *A Tale of Two Cities*, Dickens remained a moralist and a preacher, and it was his saving strength. But if the author doesn't succumb with Carton, neither does he escape with Darnay. At the end of the book 'we' gallop away not to safety and Lucie, but to the false hopes of Pip, the thwarted passion of Bradley Headstone, the divided life of John Jasper. Nothing is concluded, and by turning his malaise into a work of art Dickens obtains parole, not release: the prison will soon be summoning him once more.

NOTE

1. Darnay, who only comes to life in the face of death, is nevertheless obsessed with the guillotine. He has 'a strange besetting desire to know what to do when the time came, a desire gigantically disproportionate to the few swift moments to which it referred; a wondering that was more like the wondering of some other spirit within his, than his own' (bk III ch. 13). Carton's spirit, perhaps; through the exigencies of the plot, Dickens has got the wires crossed.

DOROTHY VAN GHENT

Great Expectations (1953)

The distinguishing quality of Dickens's people is that they are solitaries. They are people caught living in a world of their own. They soliloquize in it. They do not talk to one another; they talk to themselves. The pressure of society has created fits of twitching in mind and speech, and fantasies in the soul. . . . The solitariness of people is paralleled by the solitariness of things. Fog operates as a separate presence, houses quietly rot or boisterously prosper on their own . . . Cloisterham believes itself more important than the world at large, the Law sports like some stale and dilapidated circus across human lives. Philanthropy attacks people like a humor or an observable germ. The people and the things of Dickens are all out of touch and out of hearing of each other, each conducting its own inner monologue, grandiloquent or dismaying. By this dissassociation Dickens brings to us something of the fright of childhood . . .[1]

Some of the most wonderful scenes in *Great Expectations* are those in which people, presumably in the act of conversation, raptly soliloquize; and Dickens' technique, in these cases, is usually to give the soliloquizer a fantastic private language as unadapted to mutual understanding as a species of pig Latin. Witness Mr Jaggers' interview with Joe Gargery, in which the dignified lawyer attempts to compensate Joe financially for his part in Pip's upbringing, and Joe swings on him with unintelligible pugilistic jargon.

> Which I meantersay . . . that if you come into my place bullbaiting and badgering me, come out! Which I meantersay as sech if you're a man, come on! Which I meantersay that what I say, I meantersay and stand or fall by!

Or Miss Havisham's interview with Joe over the question of Pip's wages; for each question she asks him, Joe persists in addressing his reply to Pip rather than herself, and his replies have not the remotest relation to the questions. Sometimes, by sheer repetition of a phrase, the words a character uses will assume the frenzied rotary unintelligibility of an idiot's obsession, as does Mrs Joe's 'Be grateful to them which brought you up by hand', or Pumblechook's mincing 'May I? – May I?' The minimal uses of language as an instrument of communication and intellectual development are symbolized by Pip's progress in the school kept by Mr Wopsle's great-aunt, where the summit of his education consists in his copying a large Old-English 'D', which he assumes to be the design for a belt buckle; and by Joe's pleasure in the art of reading, which enables him to find three J's and three O's and three 'J-O, Joes' in a piece of script.

> Give me [he says] a good book, or a good newspaper, and sit me down afore a good fire, and I ask no better. Lord! when you *do* come to a J and a O, and says you, 'Here, at last, is a J-O, Joe,' how interesting reading is!

There is, perhaps, no purer expression of solipsism in literature. The cultivation of the peculiar Dickensian values of language reaches its apogee when the convict Magwitch, with a benefactor's proud delight, asks Pip to read to him from a book in a foreign language, of which he understands no syllable.

From *Don Quixote* on, [novels] . . . have frequently drawn our attention to the ambiguities of language and the varieties of its expressive relationship to life – from the incongruities between Quixote's and Sancho's understanding of the meaning of words, to the hopeless lapse of verbal understanding between Walter and Toby Shandy, and to the subtly threatening divergencies of meaning in the constricted language of Jane Austen's characters. Language as a means of communication is a provision for social and spiritual order. You cannot make 'order' with an integer, one thing alone, for order is definitively a relationship among things. Absolute noncommunication is an unthinkable madness for it negates all relationship and therefore all order, and even an ordinary madman has to create a kind of order for himself by illusions of communication. Dickens' soliloquizing characters, for all their funniness (aloneness is inexorably funny, like the aloneness of the man who slips on a banana peel, seen from the point of view of togetherness), suggest a world of isolated integers, terrifyingly alone and unrelated.

The book opens with a child's first conscious experience of his aloneness. Immediately an abrupt encounter occurs – Magwitch suddenly comes from behind a gravestone, seizes Pip by the heels, and suspends him upside down. ' "Hold your noise!" cried a terrible voice, as a man started up from among the graves at the side of the church porch. "Keep still, you little devil, or I'll cut your throat!" '

Perhaps, if one could fix on two of the most personal aspects of Dickens' technique, one would speak of the strange languages he concocts for the solitariness of the soul, and the abruptness of his tempo. His human fragments suddenly shock against one another in collisions like those of Democritus' atoms or of the charged particles of modern physics. Soldiers, holding out handcuffs, burst into the blacksmith's house during Christmas dinner at the moment when Pip is clinging to a table leg in an agony of apprehension over his theft of the pork pie. A weird old woman clothed in decayed satin, jewels and spider webs, and with one shoe off, shoots out her finger at the bewildered child, with the command: 'Play!' A pale young gentleman appears out of a wilderness of cucumber frames, and daintily kicking up his legs and slapping his hands together, dips his head and butts Pip in the stomach. These sudden confrontations between persons whose ways of life have no habitual or logical continuity with each other suggest the utmost incohesion in the stuff of experience.

Technique is vision. Dickens' technique is an index of a vision of life that sees human separatedness as the ordinary condition, where speech is speech *to* nobody and where human encounter is mere collision. But the vision goes much further. Our minds are so constituted that they insist on seeking in the use of language an exchange function, a delivery and a passing on of perceptions from soul to soul and generation to generation, binding them in some kind of order; and they insist on finding cause and effect, or *motivation*, in the displacements and encounters of persons or things. Without these primary patterns of perception we would not have what we call minds. And when these patterns are confused or abrogated by our experience, we are forced, in order to preserve some kind of psychic equilibrium, to seek them in extraordinary explanations – explanations again in terms of mutual exchange and cause and effect. Dickens saw his world patently all in pieces, and as a child's vision would offer some reasonable explanation of why such a world was that way – and, by the act of explanation, would make that world yield up a principle of order, however obscure or fantastic – so, with a child's literalism of imagination, he discovered organization among his fragments.

Dickens lived in a time and an environment in which a full-scale demolition of traditional values was going on, correlatively with the uprooting and dehumanization of men, women, and children by the millions – a process brought about by industrialization, colonial imperialism, and the exploitation of the human being as a 'thing' or an engine or a part of an engine capable of being used for profit. This was the 'century of progress' which ornamented its steam engines with iron arabesques of foliage as elaborate as the antimacassars and aspidistras and crystal or cut-glass chandeliers and bead-and-feather portieres of its drawing rooms, while the human engines of its welfare groveled and bred in the foxholes described by Marx in his *Capital*. (Hauntingly we see this discordance in the scene in *Great Expectations* where Miss Havisham, sitting in her satin and floral decay in the house called Satis, points her finger at the child and outrageously tells him to 'play'. For though the scene is a potent symbol of childish experience of adult obtuseness and sadism, it has also another dimension as a social symbol of those economically determined situations in which the human soul is used as a means for satisfactions not its own, under the gross and transparent lie that its activity is its happiness, its welfare and fun and 'play' – a publicity instrument that is the favorite of manufacturers and insurance agencies, as well as of totalitarian strategists, with their common formula, 'We're just a happy family.') The heir of the 'century of progress' is the twentieth-century concentration camp, which makes no bones about people being 'things'.

Dickens' intuition alarmingly saw this process in motion, a process which abrogated the primary demands of human feeling and rationality, and he sought an extraordinary explanation for it. People were becoming things, and things (the things that money can buy or that are the means for making money or for exalting prestige in the abstract) were becoming more important than people. People were being de-animated, robbed of their souls, and things were usurping the prerogatives of animate creatures – governing the lives of their owners in the most literal sense. This picture, in which the qualities of things and people were reversed, was a picture of a daemonically motivated world, a world in which 'dark' or occult forces or energies operate not only in people (as modern psychoanalytic psychology observes) but also in things: for if people turn themselves or are turned into things, metaphysical order can be established only if we think of things as turning themselves into people, acting under a 'dark' drive similar to that which motivates the human aberration.

There is an old belief that it takes a demon to recognize a demon, and the saying illustrates the malicious sensibility with which things, in Dickens, have felt out and imitated, in their relationship with each other and with people, the secret of the human arrangement. A four-poster bed in an inn, where Pip goes to spend the night, is a despotic monster that straddles over the whole room, 'putting one of his arbitrary legs into the fireplace, and another into the doorway, and squeezing the wretched little washing-stand in quite a Divinely Righteous manner'. Houses, looking down through the skylight of Jaggers' office in London, twist themselves in order to spy on Pip like police agents who presuppose guilt. Even a meek little muffin has to be 'confined with the utmost precaution under a strong iron cover', and a hat, set on a mantelpiece, demands constant attention and the greatest quickness of eye and hand to catch it neatly as it tumbles off, but its ingenuity is such that it finally manages to fall into the slop basin. The animation of inanimate objects suggests both the quaint gaiety of a forbidden life and an aggressiveness that has got out of control – an aggressiveness that they have borrowed from the human economy and an irresponsibility native to but glossed and disguised by that economy.

Dickens' fairly constant use of the pathetic fallacy (the projection of human impulses and feelings upon the nonhuman, as upon beds and houses and muffins and hats) might be considered as incidental stylistic embellishment if his description of people did not show a reciprocal metaphor: people are described by nonhuman attributes, or by such an exaggeration of or emphasis on one part of their appearance that they seem to be reduced wholly to that part, with an effect of having become 'thinged' into one of their own bodily members or into an article of their clothing or into some inanimate object of which they have made a fetish. Dickens' devices for producing this transposition of attributes are various. To his friend and biographer, Forster, he said that he was always losing sight of a man in his diversion by the mechanical play of some part of the man's face, which 'would acquire a sudden ludicrous life of its own'. Many of what we shall call the 'signatures' of Dickens' people – that special exaggerated feature or gesture or mannerism which comes to stand for the whole person – are such dissociated parts of the body, like Jaggers' huge forefinger which he bites and then plunges menacingly at the accused, or Wemmick's post-office mouth, or the clockwork apparatus in Magwitch's throat that clicks as if it were going to strike. The device is not used arbitrarily or capriciously. In this book, whose subject is the etiology of guilt and of atonement, Jaggers is the representative not only of civil law but of universal Law, which is profoundly mysterious in a world of dissociated and apparently lawless fragments; and his huge forefinger, into which he is virtually transformed and which seems to act like an 'it' in its own right rather than like a member of a man, is the Law's mystery in all its fearful impersonality. Wemmick's mouth is not a post-office when he is at home in his castle but only when he is at work in Jaggers' London office, where a mechanical appearance of smiling is required of him. And as Wemmick's job has mechanized him into a grinning slot, so oppression and fear have given the convict Magwitch a clockwork apparatus for vocal chords.

Or this general principle of reciprocal changes, by which things have become as it were daemonically animated and people have been reduced to thing-like characteristics – as if, by a law of conservation of energy, the humanity of which people have become incapable had leaked out into the external environment – may work symbolically in the association of some object with a person so that the object assumes his essence and his 'meaning'. Mrs Joe wears a large apron, 'having a square impregnable bib in front, that was stuck full of pins and needles' – she has no reason to wear it, and she never takes it off a day in her life. Jaggers flourishes a large white handkerchief – a napkin that is the mysterious complement of his blood-smeared engagements. Estella – who is the star and jewel of Pip's great expectations – wears jewels in her hair and on her breast; 'I and the jewels', she says, as if they were interchangeable. This device of association is a familiar one in fiction; what distinguishes Dickens' use of it is that the associated object acts not merely to *illustrate* a person's qualities symbolically – as novelists usually use it – but that it has a necessary metaphysical function in Dickens' universe: in this universe objects actually usurp human essences; beginning as fetishes, they tend to – and sometimes quite literally do – devour and take over the powers of the fetish-worshiper.

The process of conversion of spirit into matter that operates in the Dickens world is shown working out with savage simplicity in the case of Miss Havisham. Miss Havisham has been guilty of aggression against life in using the two children, Pip and Estella, as inanimate instruments of revenge for her broken heart – using them, that is, as if they were not human but things – and she is being changed retributively into a fungus. The decayed cake on the banquet table acts, as it were, by homeopathic magic – like a burning effigy or a doll stuck with pins; its decay parallels the necrosis in the human agent. 'When the ruin is complete', Miss Havisham says, pointing to the cake but referring to herself, she will be laid out on the same table and her relatives will be invited to 'feast on' her corpse. But this is not the only conversion. The 'little quickened hearts' of the mice behind the panels have been quickened by what was Miss Havisham, carried off crumb by crumb.

The principle of reciprocal changes, between the human and the nonhuman, bears on the characteristic lack of complex 'inner life' on the part of Dickens' people – their lack of a personally complex psychology. It is inconceivable that the fungoid Miss Havisham should have a complex inner life, in the moral sense. But in the *art* of Dickens (distinguishing that moral dialectic that arises not solely from the characters' in a novel but from all the elements in the aesthetic structure) there is a great deal of 'inner life', transposed to other forms than that of human character: partially transposed in this scene, for instance, to the symbolic activity of the speckle-legged spiders with blotchy bodies and to the gropings and pausings of the black beetles on Miss Havisham's hearth. Without benefit of Freud or Jung, Dickens saw the human soul reduced literally to the images occupying its 'inner life'.

Through the changes that have come about in the human, as humanity has leaked out of it, the atoms of the physical universe have become subtly impregnated with daemonic aptitude. Pip, standing waiting for Estella in the neighborhood of Newgate, and beginning dimly to be aware of his implication in the guilt for which that establishment stands – for his 'great expectations' have already begun to make him a collaborator in the generic crime of using people as means to personal ends – has the sensation of a deadly dust clinging to him, rubbed off on him from the environs, and he tries to beat it out of his clothes. Smithfield, that 'shameful place', 'all asmear with filth and fat and blood and foam', seems to 'stick to him' when he enters it on his way to the prison. The nettles and brambles of the graveyard where Magwitch first appears 'stretch up cautiously' out of the graves in an effort to get a twist on the branded man's ankles and pull him in. The river has a malignant potentiality that impregnates everything upon it – discolored copper, rotten wood, honeycombed stone, green dank deposit. The river is perhaps the most constant and effective symbol in Dickens, because it establishes itself so readily to the imagination as a daemonic element, drowning people as if by intent, disgorging unforeseen evidence, chemically or physically changing all it touches, and because not only does it act as an occult 'force' in itself but it is the common passage and actual flowing element that unites individuals and classes, public persons and private persons, deeds and the results of deeds, however fragmentized and separated. Upon the river, one cannot escape its action; it may throw the murderer and his victim in an embrace. At the end of *Great Expectations*, it swallows Compeyson, while, with its own obscure daemonic motivation, though it fatally injures Magwitch, it leaves him to fulfill the more subtle spiritual destiny upon which he has begun to enter. The river scene in this section, closely and apprehensively observed, is one of the most memorable in Dickens.

It is necessary to view Dickens' 'coincidences' under the aspect of this wholesale change in the aptitudes of external nature. Coincidence is the violent connection of the unconnected. Life is full of violent connections of this sort, but one of the most rigorous conventions of fictional and dramatic art is that events should make a logically sequential pattern; for art is the discovery of order. Critics have frequently deplored Dickens' use of coincidences in his plots. But in a universe that is nervous throughout, a universe in which nervous ganglia stretch through both people and their external environment, so that a change in the human can infect the currents of the air and the sea, events and confrontations that seem to abrogate the laws of physical mechanics can logically be brought about. In this sense, the apparent coincidences in Dickens actually obey a causal order – not of physical mechanics but of moral dynamics. 'What connection can there be', Dickens asks in another novel, 'between many people in the innumerable histories of this world, who, from opposite sides of great gulfs, have, nevertheless, been very curiously brought together!'

What brings the convict Magwitch to the child Pip, in the graveyard, is more than the convict's hunger; Pip (or let us say simply 'the child', for Pip is an Everyman) carries the convict inside him, as the negative potential of his 'great expectation' – Magwitch is the concretion of his potential guilt. What brings Magwitch across the 'great gulfs' of the Atlantic to Pip again, at the moment of revelation in the story, is their profoundly implicit compact of guilt, as binding as the convict's leg-iron which is its recurrent symbol. The multiplying likenesses in the street as Magwitch draws nearer, coming over the sea, the mysterious warnings of his approach on the night of his reappearance, are moral projections as 'real' as the storm outside the windows and as the crouched form of the vicious Orlick on the dark stairs. The conception of what brings people together 'coincidentally' in their seemingly uncaused encounters and collisions – the total change in the texture of experience that follows upon any act, public or private, external or in thought, the concreteness of the effect of the act not only upon the conceiving heart but upon the atoms of physical matter, so that blind nature collaborates daemonically in the drama of reprisal – is deep and valid in this book.

In a finely lucid atmosphere of fairy tale, Dickens uses a kind of montage in *Great Expectations*, a superimposing of one image upon another with an immediate effect of hallucination, that is but one more way of representing his vision of a purely nervous and moral organization of reality. An instance is the scene in which Estella walks the casks in the old brewery. Estella's walking the casks is an enchanting ritual dance of childhood (like walking fence rails or railroad ties), but inexplicably present in the tableau is the suicidal figure of Miss Havisham hanging by her neck from a brewery beam. Accompanying each appearance of Estella – the star and the jewel of Pip's expectations – is a similarly disturbing ghost, an image of an unformed dread. When Pip thinks of her, though he is sitting in a warm room with a friend, he shudders as if in a wind from over the marshes. Her slender knitting fingers are suddenly horribly displaced by the marred wrists of a murderess. The technique of montage is that of dreams, which know with awful precision the affinities between the guilt of our desires and the commonplaces of our immediate perceptions.

This device, of doubling one image over another, is paralleled in the handling of character. In the sense that one implies the other, the glittering frosty girl Estella, and the decayed and false old woman, Miss Havisham, are not two characters but a single one, or a single essence with dual aspects, as if composed by montage – a spiritual continuum, so to speak. For inevitably wrought into the fascinating jewel-likeness of Pip's great expectations, as represented by Estella, is the falsehood and degeneracy represented by Miss Havisham, the soilure on the unpurchased good. The boy Pip and the criminal Magwitch form another such continuum. Magwitch, from a metaphysical point of view, is not outside Pip but inside him, and his apparition is that of Pip's own unwrought deeds: Pip, having adopted 'great expectations', will live by making people into Magwitches, into means for his ends. The relationship between Joe Gargery, saintly simpleton of the folk, and Orlick, dark beast of the Teutonic marshes (who comes 'from the ooze'), has a somewhat different dynamics, though they too form a spiritual continuum. Joe and Orlick are related not as two aspects of a single moral identity, but as the opposed extremes of spiritual possibility – the one unqualified love, the other unqualified hate – and they form a frame within which the actions of the others have their ultimate meaning. A commonplace of criticism is that, as Edmund Wilson puts it, Dickens was usually unable to 'get the good and bad together in one character'.[2] The criticism might be valid if Dickens' were a naturalistic world, but it is not very relevant to Dickens' daemonically organized world. In a naturalistic world, obeying mechanical laws, each character is organically discrete from every other, and presumably each contains a representative mixture of 'the good and bad'. But in Dickens' thoroughly nervous world, that does not know the laws of mechanics but knows only spiritual law, one simple or 'flat' character can be superimposed upon another so that together they form the representative human complexity of good-in-evil and evil-in-good.

Two kinds of crime form Dickens' two chief themes, the crime of parent against child, and the calculated social crime. They are formally analogous, their form being the treatment of persons as things; but they are also inherent in each other, whether the private will of the parent is to be considered as depraved by the operation of a public institution, or the social institution is to be considered as a bold concert of the depravities of individual 'fathers'. In *Great Expectations* the private crime against the child is Mrs Joe's and Pumblechook's and Wopsle's, all 'foster parents' either by necessity or self-conceit; while the social crime is the public treatment of Magwitch. That the two kinds of crime are inherent in each other we are made aware of as we are led to identify Magwitch's childhood with Pip's; the brutality exercised toward both children was the same brutality, though the 'parents' in the one case were private persons, and in the other, society itself. Complicating the meaning of 'the crime' still further, Magwitch also has taken upon himself the role of foster parent to Pip, and whether, as parent, he acts in charity or impiousness, or both, is a major ambiguity which the drama sets out to resolve.

'The crime', in Dickens, is evidently a permutation of multiple
motivations and acts, both public and private, but always with the same
tendency to convert people into things, and always implying either
symbolically or directly a child-parent situation. The child-parent
situation has been disnatured, corrupted, with the rest of nature; or
rather, since the child-parent situation is the dynamic core of the
Dickens world, the radical disnaturing here is what has corrupted the
rest. His plots seldom serve to canalize, with the resolution of the
particular set of plotted circumstances, the hysteria submerged in his
vision of a nature gone thoroughly wrong; the permutations of the
crimes are too many, and their ultimate cause or root is evasive, unless
one would resort to some dramatically unmanageable rationale such
as original sin. The Dickens world requires an act of redemption. A
symbolic act of this kind is again and again indicated in his novels, in
the charity of the uncherished and sinned-against child for the inadequate or criminal father – what might be called the theme of the
prodigal father, Dickens' usual modification of the prodigal son theme.
But the redemptive act should be such that it should redeem not only
the individual 'fathers', but society at large. One might almost say –
thinking of Dickens' caricatures of the living dead, with their necrotic
members and organs, their identifications of themselves with inanimate
objects – that it should be such as to redeem the dead. *Great Expectations*
is an exception among his novels in that here the redemptive act is
adequate to and structural for both bodies of thematic material – the
sins of individuals and the sins of society.

Pip first becomes aware of the 'identity of things' as he is held suspended heels over head by the convict; that is, in a world literally
turned upside down. Thenceforth Pip's interior landscape is inverted
by his guilty knowledge of this man 'who had been soaked in water,
and smothered in mud, and lamed by stones, and cut by flints, and
stung by nettles, and torn by briars'. The apparition is that of all
suffering that the earth can inflict, and that the apparition presents itself
to a child is as much as to say that every child, whatever his innocence,
inherits guilt (as the potential of his acts) for the condition of man. The
inversion of natural order begins here with first self-consciousness: the
child is heir to the sins of the 'fathers'. Thus the crime that is always
pervasive in the Dickens universe is identified in a new way – not
primarily as that of the 'father', nor as that of some public institution,
but as that of the child – the original individual who must necessarily

take upon himself responsibility for not only what is to be done in the present and the future, but what has been done in the past, inasmuch as the past is part and parcel of the present and the future. The child is the criminal, and it is for this reason that he is able to redeem his world; for the world's guilt is his guilt, and he can expiate it in his own acts.

The guilt of the child is realized on several levels. Pip experiences the psychological *form* (or feeling) of guilt before he is capable of voluntary evil; he is treated by adults – Mrs Joe and Pumblechook and Wopsle – as if he were a felon, a young George Barnwell (a character in the play which Wopsle reads on the night when Mrs Joe is attacked) wanting only to murder his nearest relative, as George Barnwell murdered his uncle. This is the usual nightmare of the child in Dickens, a vision of imminent incarceration, fetters like sausages, lurid accusatory texts. He is treated, that is, as if he were a thing, manipulable by adults for the extraction of certain sensations: by making him feel guilty and diminished, they are able to feel virtuous and great. But the psychological *form* of guilt acquires spiritual *content* when Pip himself conceives the tainted wish – the wish to be like the most powerful adult and to treat others as things. At the literal level, Pip's guilt is that of snobbery toward Joe Gargery, and snobbery is a denial of the human value of others. Symbolically, however, Pip's guilt is that of murder; for he steals the file with which the convict rids himself of his leg-iron, and it is this leg-iron, picked up on the marshes, with which Orlick attacks Mrs Joe; so that the child does inevitably overtake his destiny, which was, like George Barnwell, to murder his nearest relative. But the 'relative' whom Pip, adopting the venerable criminality of society, is, in the widest symbolic scope of intention, destined to murder is not Mrs Joe but his 'father', Magwitch – to murder in the socially chronic fashion of the Dickens world, which consists in the dehumanization of the weak, or in moral acquiescence to such murder. Pip is, after all, the ordinary mixed human being, one more Everyman in the long succession of them that literature has represented, but we see this Everyman as he develops from a child; and his destiny is directed by the ideals of his world – toward 'great expectations' which involve the making of Magwitches – which involve, that is, murder. These are the possibilities that are projected in the opening scene of the book, when the young child, left with a burden on his soul, watches the convict limping off under an angry red sky, toward the black marshes, the gibbet, and the savage lair of the sea, in a still rotating landscape.

In Dickens' modification of the folk pattern of the fairy wishing, Magwitch is Pip's 'fairy godfather' who changes the pumpkin into a coach. Like all the 'fathers', he uses the child as a thing in order to obtain through him vicarious sensations of grandeur. In relation to society, however, Magwitch is the child, and society the prodigal father; from the time he was first taken for stealing turnips, the convict's career has duplicated brutally and in public the pathos of the ordinary child. Again, in relation to Pip, Magwitch is still the child; for, spiritually committed by his 'great expectations' to that irresponsibility which has accounted for the Magwitches, Pip is projectively, at least, answerable for Magwitch's existence and for his brutalization. Pip carries his criminal father within him; he is, so to speak, the father of his father. The ambiguities of each term of the relationship are such that each is both child and father, making a fourfold relationship; and the act of love between them at the end is thus reinforced fourfold, and the redemption by love is a fourfold redemption: that is to say, it is symbolically infinite, for it serves for all the meanings Dickens finds it possible to attach to the central child-father situation, the most profound and embracing relationship that, in Dickens' work, obtains among men.

As the child's original alienation from 'natural' order is essentially mysterious, a guilty inheritance from the fathers which invades first awareness, so the redemptive act is also a mysterious one. The mysterious nature of the act is first indicated, in the manner of a motif, when Mrs Joe, in imbecile pantomime, tries to propitiate her attacker, the bestial Orlick. In Orlick is concretized all the undefined evil of the Dickens world, that has nourished itself underground and crept along walls, like the ancient stains on the house of Atreus. He is the lawlessness implied in the unnatural conversions of the human into the nonhuman, the retributive death that invades those who have grown lean in life and who have exercised the powers of death over others. He is the instinct of aggression and destruction, the daemonism of sheer external Matter as such; he is pure 'thingness' emerging without warning from the ooze where he has been unconsciously cultivated. As Orlick is one form of spiritual excess – unmotivated hate – Joe Gargery is the opposed form – love without reservation. Given these terms of the spiritual framework, the redemptive act itself could scarcely be anything but grotesque – and it is by a grotesque gesture, one of the most profoundly intuitive symbols in Dickens, that Mrs Joe is redeemed. What is implied by her humble propitiation of the beast Orlick is a recognition of personal guilt in the guilt of others, and of its dialectical relationship with love. The motif reappears in the moment of major illumination in the book. Pip 'bows down', not to Joe Gargery, toward whom he has been privately and literally guilty, but to the wounded, hunted, shackled man, Magwitch, who has been guilty toward himself. It is in this way that the manifold organic relationships among men are revealed, and that the Dickens world – founded in fragmentariness and disintegration – is made whole.

NOTES

1. V. S. Pritchett, *The Living Novel* (New York, 1947).
2. *The Wound and the Bow* (Boston and London, 1941) p. 65.

ROBERT MORSE
Our Mutual Friend (1949)

'In these times of ours, though concerning the exact year there is no need to be precise, a boat of dirty and disreputable appearance, with two figures in it, floated on the Thames, between Southwark Bridge which is of iron, and London Bridge which is of stone, as an autumn evening was closing in.' The sinister search on the water has begun, and the first chapter of Dickens' sinister masterpiece. We find ourselves on the water, and muddy water is to trickle and seep through all the following pages. The two figures in the boat are Gaffer Hexam and his daughter Lizzie. Lizzie shows a strong dislike for her father's occupation, which is that of robbing the pockets of drowned men. Gaffer remonstrates with her in such terms as these: 'How can you be so thankless to your best friend [the river], Lizzie? The very fire that warmed you when you were a baby was picked out of the river alongside the coal barges. The very basket that you slept in, the tide washed ashore. The very rockers that I put it upon to make a cradle of it, I cut out of a piece of wood that drifted from some ship or another.' Such rhetoric from the mouth of a man who is pictured as the roughest of waterside scavengers is likely to seem to us, in our day, as Dickens at his most improbable. And when his daughter answers in speech of even greater refinement and purity of grammar, the question arises: How realistic did the works of Dickens seem to his contemporary Londoners?

It is possible that the question of true-to-life did not arise, and that Dickens' contemporaries accepted his dark vision of England and London and London's creatures as readily as we today accept Raymond Chandler's California with its brutal and neurotic crew of killers and private-eyes – or even the sweet mirage of New York presented by our women's magazines. And yet we have been trained in the modern school of realism where naturalness of dialogue and 'truth' of psychological reaction are the touchstone, and often the only merit.

With the authority of a teller of folk tales, for whom naturalness has no purpose, Dickens simply assures his readers: This is what happened. And for the most part we are pleased to believe him, no matter how arbitrary the sequence of events may seem. The disappointing moments in his novels are just those moments when his persuasive genius fails, and disbelief returns us, in spite of ourselves, to the outer world. Such lapses are often quite grave, at least at first view. It is not easy, for example, to believe that the noble old Jew, Riah, could accept his long bondage to an ugly master and an ugly occupation because of gratitude. Nor is it easy to believe that Florence Dombey, in *Dombey and Son*, could have gone on loving her father so faithfully in the face of his harsh treatment. And yet these feeble motivations are essential to much of the action of these novels. Why did Dickens risk weakening his project? On reflection, it will appear that in both cases he has permitted a conception of moral goodness, of moral right, to prevail over human probability.

Riah's gratitude to the monstrous Fascination Fledgeby is seen as a sacred and unalterable obligation, a noble trait in a noble (if far-fetched) character. It is Gratitude itself. Again, in the case of poor Florence Dombey, a good child *ought* to love her parent, and love him she does in spite of all opposition.

But these rare lapses into disbelief, easy as they are to explain away on various grounds, do little damage to our acceptance of Dickens' world. The writer's art confers on his creations an intensity of existence that makes their fantastic proportions seem the true proportions, and, as we read, we believe – just as we do not doubt the distorted forms of Greek sculpture or of Picasso's *baigneuses*, which if translated into flesh would send us screaming in flight.

Why do these monsters of purity and evil, these ridiculous eccentrics and grotesques, hold our attention? What field of experience does Dickens draw on to make us feel their truth? Do they not live under our own skins, waiting to be given the externalized form of myth and art? Dickens has gone underground to that region where the mists of unnameable anxieties and the smoke of infantile terrors prevail. There, at the edge of the sea of sleep, he has built his London. On the opposite shore dwell the Gorgons, Andromeda and Perseus, the Minotaur in the Cretan maze. The Harpies call across the separating waters to Miss Flite's birds – Hope, Joy, Youth, Peace, Rest, Life, Dust, Ashes, Waste, Want, Ruin, Despair, Madness, Death, Cunning, Folly, Words, Wigs,

Rags, Sheepskin, Plunder, Precedent, Jargon, Gammon, and Spinach. In this underground metropolis (whose visual aspects have been so wonderfully reported by Phiz) no one need be surprised to see Lady Dedlock emerging from Tom-all-alone's, and Quilp creeping into Little Nell's bed, or eating eggs, shell and all, to terrify his wife.

How does Dickens keep the vaulting of his cave-world secure, and stop each chink against skepticism and outer day, of which the least beam would disintegrate Miss Havisham's wedding cake where generations of rats had failed?

Consider first the variety of invention Dickens infuses into every part of his books, an inventiveness which, like the music of Beethoven, sweeps away any apprehension of fatigue with its great mood of boundless improvisation. Each object, each creature, animal or human, must be given personality and a unique vitality. He will play with the description of a tavern sign with such brilliant fancy, so many allusions to unexpected domains, that one scarcely notices that this painted board occupies two pages of the text. The horse, as in *The Old Curiosity Shop*, is characterized as thoroughly as his drivers. Each waiter, coachman, clerk, although perhaps never to be seen again, during his brief appearance is impaled in the bright center of our attention, and we are obliged to see his qualities and failings, ludicrous or sad, before he is released to his invisible life. Dickens is like a medium who bids us look into his crystal ball, and as we see the images form, he keeps a sharp eye on us to see that the spell does not falter, and at the same time urges: Look! Look more closely! Are you sure that you can see it *all*?

In short he can find interest and the material of art in almost anything. Often this liveliness is effected by simple but surprising juxtapositions, by odd angles of vision, by ironic reversals of his meaning (as 'the *divine* Tippins'), by sheer verbal vivacity, by sonorous rhetorical devices of alliteration and repetition – which sometimes indeed embarrass by their excessiveness. But take this: Mr Pecksniff is merely warming his hands at the fire, but he warms them 'as benevolently as though they were somebody else's, not his'. A simple action is made into pure fun, and at the same time the false goodness of Pecksniff is revealed.

The roof of Dickens' cave hangs on a strong ribbing of plot, and here again he shows his invention in a gothic ingenuity. It might be argued that all novels have a plot, but surely *Anna Karenina, For Whom the Bell Tolls, Madame Bovary*, have a kind of narrative structure that differentiates them from *Bleak House, Our Mutual Friend,* or *Great Expectations.* The authors of the first group apply their art to producing an air of naturalness, almost of biography. The 'story' of their books given an over-all social and geographical environment, grows out of the nature of their characters. The complexities are those of psychological interrelations; and although there may be a wealth of naturalistic incident, there is a minimum of the old wills, concealed identities, and dramatic coincidence dear to Dickens. Such novels have the cadence of veracity. At their best, they have no more plot than a true account of human lives – which is no plot at all, compared to the abstract pattern of Cinderella, the Oedipus myth, *Bleak House.*

Except for its survival in certain detective novels, the large interwoven design (manipulated, artificial, if you like) has gone out of fashion with its calculated tangles and calculated unravelings. Perhaps, leaving aside the out-and-out folk tale, its inherent drawbacks can be overcome only by such master novelists as Dumas, Balzac, Dickens. But it is comfortable to begin a 'plot novel', to feel its bulk in the hand, and to know that all those pages to come will be ordered with a felicity and ingenuity beyond the accidents of actual life, just as it is a satisfaction to hear the opening themes of a Haydn sonata and know in advance that they are going to be worked out according to a beautiful law and will come to an end at the precise moment when the sonata form is satisfied. For a plot does not depend primarily on surprise and suspense; it depends on completeness of resolution. The successful plot novel, like an ingenious fairy tale, can be re-read without loss of interest, and we come again to the ritual triumph of hero and heroine over the opposing (or evil) forces with the same sense of moral order. Indeed we often may guess, before we are halfway through our first reading, the main resolution of the plot, because such and such a denouement is precisely what would please us most. Whereas when we begin a novel by Colette or Dorothy Richardson we have no idea what end we shall arrive at – just as the shape of a Strauss tone poem cannot be guessed from its opening measures.

But whoever has read one Dickens novel takes up a second with the happy confidence that the persons he meets there, however remote from each other they may at first appear, will all interlock in a tightening pattern and each make his influence felt by the others, as in a folk tale the ragged old woman casually befriended by the third son is sure to reappear in his hour of need. And it is not surprising in this mythic

England that its inhabitants should be related to each other with a folk-tale coherence.

The major writers of today have been curiously willing to dispense with the advantages of the well-meshed plot. For however mechanical plot may seem, however prefabricated its dovetailing and niceties and knot-tying, it still gives a novelist one of the most obvious means of securing *unity*. Our novelists, like our free-verse poets, have set themselves the appalling task of reaching form by pure intuition – a chancy appeal, at best, to the shifting and unguessable sympathies of their readers.

The author of *Great Expectations* took no such risk. With so much of the eccentric, effervescent, and improbable to impart he could not readily overlook the gross advantages of a unifying plot. But he also used other, more subtle devices to give unity to each novel.

The word 'caricature' is often associated with Dickens, perhaps to some extent because of the brilliant Grand Guignol drawings of Cruikshank and Phiz. The term loses much of its force if we view Dickens' world as the imaginative projection of an inner world underlying actuality. A caricaturist and satirist (unless his motives are those of interested propaganda, political or otherwise) stands in a mundane and moral daylight with Voltaire and Aristophanes, directing his missiles cruel or gay at the stupidities, the pretensions, the evil practices of his less enlightened fellows, and thereby wins them to greater sanity. But what are we to think of a writer who pictures virtue as extravagantly as vice? For are not Little Nell and Tom Pinch and Florence Dombey as monstrously overdrawn as Pecksniff and Mrs Jellyby? Are these caricatures intended as signposts to guide us to more rational and moral behavior, or are they the creations of a sensibility that reveled in the haunts of Dr Groddeck's 'it'? The 'caricature' may be simply the intensification or distortion of dream, but from the point of view of *unity*, if Dickens' people are caricatures they are invoked at an almost identical level of caricature, and once slapped on the back by his masterly hand they rise and breathe the same vigorous air.

Although these characters seem so often to emerge from folk tale and dream, they are not all nightmarish. Sleep has its pleasant apparitions. And among the legendary types we fleetingly detect underlying the personages of Dickens there are many Cinderellas, Jack the Giant Killers, Dick Whittingtons, Fairy Godmothers, and Pucks, as well as the Ogres and Robber Bridegrooms. (Who could Mr and Mrs Small-weed be, by the way, other than Punch and Judy?) But these lay or archetypal figures do not often oppress us with familiarity; they are so richly clothed in borrowed garments of actuality that the smooth, ancient timbers of their limbs rarely peep through. No, it must not be supposed that Dickens' underground London is cut off entirely from its counterpart. The million sights and sounds of outer life drift downward in a kind of sediment, and, as certain jelly-like organisms gather the debris of the sea bottom about them to form a shell, so Dickens' characters crust themselves in these fragments of actuality.

Dickens notoriously used the names and peculiarities of many persons encountered in his own life, as well as the names and features of buildings and places. He kept the sharpest lookout for traits and manners, for little absurd, grotesque, or pathetic ways. Daily he crammed his memory with this loot, and when the time came for the creation of a new tavern, character, or street, he had only to agitate these thousand bits of observation, and administer, as from a salt shaker, the proper seasoning for person or place. In similar fashion he distributes the deeper traits of pride, hypocrisy, cheerfulness, fidelity, greed, and the like – as well as the general attributes of youth, beauty, intelligence, etc., together with hundreds of occupations such as fishing, body snatching, the law. His salt shaker holds them all. How else, beyond plot and uniformity of caricature, does Dickens integrate his novels?

One soon becomes aware that each book arises from a single theme, although the variations are so brilliant and ingenious it is not always easy to arrive at the most basic statement. However, once the most inclusive statement has been found it will be seen that this main theme is the *raison d'être* and the explanation of all parts of the book, and the reader may take a special pleasure in tracing much seemingly incongruous material back to its central source. Each novel, then, is *about* something, and furthermore about something serious. *A Tale of Two Cities*, for example, is built on the solemn theme of resurrection.

Usually, to point and illustrate his main theme, Dickens selects some social or moral situation in need of reform, and attacks it with hot indignation. So, in *Bleak House*, which has for its theme the dead hand of the past, he attacks the Court of Chancery. In *Nicholas Nickleby*, which is about innocent and generous youth's first acquaintance with 'what is called the world – a conventional phrase which, being interpreted, often signifieth all the rascals in it', Dickens attacks the atrocious schools of his day, giving us Dotheboys Hall, a name that even now raises specters of hunger, cold, and injustice. Hypocrisy is the theme of

Martin Chuzzlewit, and, regrettably, the institution chosen for illustration is the young Republic of the United States. *Our Mutual Friend*
deals with Money, and here the Poor Laws are singled out for bitter
rhetoric: 'It is a remarkable Christian improvement, to have made a
pursuing Fury of the Good Samaritan.'

Thus it will be seen that these examples of Dickens' zeal for reform
arise from the fundamental theme of each novel, and must not be
mistaken for the main purpose of his books. They serve merely as
illustrations, much as the bas-reliefs Dante introduces in the *Purgatorio*
typify the faults to be purged at various levels of the Mount.

But beyond the basic theme, certain unifying sub-themes of another,
perhaps more abstract, order can be discovered in these remarkably
constructed books. These sub-themes, moving at right angles to the
major premise, serve to secure the package already firmly corded
lengthwise. Take *Our Mutual Friend* as an example.

Money, to repeat, is the main theme – from the Harmon will, to
the ostentation of the Veneerings, the Lammles' cynical marriage, Mr
Boffin's feigned miserliness, the looting of drowned bodies, and so on.
It is in these drowned bodies that a counter-theme reveals itself. There
are four actual drownings, and three near-drownings, all of them
involving important characters. As an embellishment to this subject,
Dickens adds an almost gloating description of Gaffer's gruesome
wallpaper of police handbills advertising corpses found in the river.
('This is them two young sisters what tied themselves together with
a handkercher.')

Muddy Water might be called a variant of the drowning theme.
We are never far from the Thames and its shipping and its dank
mysteries – and here again we meet the river as a symbol of Life
flowing towards the sea of Death, a symbol constantly recurring in the
writings of Dickens. And, as it has been said of Shakespeare that each
play follows a consistent imagery, it is easy to point out in *Our Mutual
Friend* a poetic revelry in water associations. Here is a description of
Riderhood's headgear: 'an old sodden fur cap, formless and mangy,
that looked like a furry animal, dog or cat, puppy or kitten, drowned
and decaying'. (This example is also an instance of Dickens' skill in
coloring a character by oblique metaphorical methods. Everything
about his personages must reveal and partake of their nature.)

Opposed to Muddy Water is the theme of Dust, with the Harmon
dust heaps for starting-point: 'he grew rich as a Dust Contractor, and

lived in a hollow in a hilly country composed of Dust. On his own small estate the growling old vagabond threw up his own mountain range, like an old volcano, and its geological formation was Dust. Coal-dust, vegetable-dust, bone-dust, crockery-dust, rough dust and sifted dust – all manner of dust.' Scattered through the other novels there are many references to dust as the end of all living things, but here it seems more likely that the dust heaps represent the vanity of amassing wealth, or gold-dust – although our author takes care to leave his 'good' characters well provided for in the end. (Of course with the felt proviso that these 'good' people will use their means nobly towards furthering the great vague cause of Happiness.)

In *Our Mutual Friend* the use of another theme or principle may be observed, a principle which shapes, colors, and binds this novel together no less radically than the theme of money. This may be identified as the principle of *doubleness*. Dickens employs it in much the same way that a composer will unify all the movements of a symphony by repeating the same tone relation, interval, harmonic progression, or family of notes throughout the work. He uses doubleness, although far less simply, as Chopin uses thirds in an étude for thirds, in which the thirds are neither the melody nor the musical significance of the piece, but the necessary medium of both.

To begin with, the characters group naturally into pairs – which is, of course, true of many novels. But where were there ever so many pairs, and pairs of pairs, and new pairs formed after a reshuffling of old pairs?

But this is only one aspect of doubleness. Let us consider the many examples of duplicity, disguise, false claims, hourglass reversals, and dual natures. John Harmon appears under two assumed names. We do not even know who he really is for a great part of the book. He exchanges clothes with a physical double, or *Doppelgänger*, whose corpse is wrongly identified as Harmon. Harmon also puts on false whiskers and a wig in another disguise. Headstone duplicates Riderhood's clothes in order to make him appear Eugene's murderer. Even Sloppy has *his* disguise.

We find further examples of duplicity in Mr Boffin's pretense of turning miser; in the Lammles' deception of each other into marriage on the grounds of imaginary wealth; in Fledgeby's concealed traffic in 'queer bills'; in Riah's enforced false front, etc.

Doubleness appears again as character duality. Charlie, with his mixture of 'uncompleted savagery and uncompleted civilization', provides a good specimen of a divided nature – also Eugene, also Mortimer, among others. Then there is Twemlow, who is meek, downtrodden, and vague until at the end he takes his tremendous stand in defense of the principles that make a gentleman.

The most grotesque use of doubleness is found in reversals of the natural role: Bella calls her Pa her younger brother, 'with a dear venerable chubbiness on him' – although much of the time she patronizes him in an unpleasantly arch and incestuous way as if he were a faithful but unimportant lover; Lizzie loves her brother as a son; Jenny Wren, the Doll's Dressmaker, treats *her* alcoholic father as if he were a bad little boy – but Jenny is all doubleness, with her double life of visions, her crippled legs and vigorous hair, her precocious insight.

It is easy to cite many simpler instances of two-ness, such as the two wills, the two John Harmons, the Boffins' parlor – half of which, to suit Mrs Boffin, is carpeted and fashionably furnished, while the other half reflects Mr Boffin's taste in its resemblance to a tap-room, even to sand and sawdust on the floor.

This unifying sub-theme has been considered in disproportionate detail partly because it is such a curious device in itself, partly because it illumines a little-known aspect of creative writing, and partly because it is the kind of thing that generally goes unnoticed in Dickens' highly artful art.

These then, to summarize, are some of the ways by which Dickens persuades readers to stay in his underground world and to believe, as long as they remain there, that this world is all-inclusive and subject to its own unique law: for the source of emotional vitality he draws on the deepest mythology of mankind, the personages of the myth being presented with a lavishness of minute and general characteristics that rivals the invention of life itself and prevents them from becoming the hollow shapes of folklore, although they embody or demonstrate through their actions the capital-letter categories of sin and virtue or the lesser list of foibles and merits; these personages, since they are all lighted by the same searching but subterranean sun, are all evoked on the same level of 'caricature' (to borrow a word from the upper world) and thus obey the prime law of their creator's art, which is unity; they obey this law still further in their interrelations, which are as imposed and ordered in pattern as the musical forms of the late eighteenth century – or as the arbitrary sequence of folk tale; unity is again established by the author's choice of a single animating theme for each novel, a theme gravely applicable to the common experience of Western man, and wonderfully reflected and varied in the people and events of the book; the basic theme is usually illustrated by some form of abuse, which Dickens attacks fiercely; lesser themes, more abstract, more 'artful', almost *textural*, further the integration of each novel – as the themes of drowning, water-and-dust, and doubleness give coherence to *Our Mutual Friend*, so that wherever the loaf is sliced the same pattern of ingredients is revealed.

If Dickens could read these foregoing sentences, would he be amazed that so much is ascribed to him that he had never intended, and so much that he *had* intended is ignored? An idle question perhaps, but valid enough in an anemic age that squeaks and sips the strong blood of the dead artist. Perhaps our safest answer must be that whoever has made a masterpiece must have known what he was doing, fully as well as his critics. What knowledge we gain of Dickens through his novels reveals a complicated soul, bitterly aware of the causes for despairing, obsessed with death and decay, fascinated by the sordid, the evil, and the grotesque to such an extent that he brings his greatest gusto as a writer to their description. But even to the blackest of these descriptions he gives a tone of wry surface levity, a playfulness of language, that makes the horror of his subject both more ghastly and more supportable. He stands smiling at our elbow and points to the savagery and injustice. Indeed he is almost too *much* at our elbow, warning us what to feel, addressing us in lachrymose or heated perorations, clucking ruefully over his pathetic contrivances. Often he comes very close to spoiling his effects by this intrusion, but the thing to be felt is there, and even he (unlike Thackeray with his thumb in our buttonhole) cannot take it from us.

But, in opposition to the pessimistic darkness, Dickens also exposes an almost childlike faith in Low Church goodness. He sets high value on kindness, patience, the innocence and elation of youth, the power of love to move aside dead mountains, or at least to make their weight bearable. And besides, he is the funniest writer in the world, with more *kinds* of fun than any other, from the broadest burlesque, through all gradations of the comedy of character, situation, manners, speech, parody, cruel and gentle wit, to the final subtlety of the tear-stained smile.

He has many ways of being serious as well, although he never produces in us the exaltation of high tragedy – partly because in these vast, many-peopled entertainments no single character is allowed to reach heroic proportions. The tears are the tears of pathos, and fall for a dying child, for shabby courage and humble fidelity. The tragic issue is simply the general contest of man with his own nature and the nature of things, for Dickens' belief in positive evil is implicit, and all of his characters either struggle against evil, or founder in it, or were born its creatures. But Dickens raises no protagonist of great intellectual, moral, or emotional stature to do battle. Is it because of this that he is usually esteemed in our time as a lesser figure than certain other nineteenth-century novelists? And yet, in its great variety, his work unites almost all of the ingredients to be found in each of these men, so that it is harder to sum up Dickens in a phrase or two than almost any other writer except Shakespeare or Dante. His quality is easily felt, but eludes statement, so that it seems comparatively simple to make some true and basic announcement about Tolstoy, Dostoevsky, or Proust. These three are generally considered 'greater writers', but are they better novelists? Do they fuse their meanings, their intentions, their 'axe to grind' into a single art form – or do they find the confines of the novel too cramping for the largeness of the thing they have to say, and impatiently brush aside the pretext of fiction in order to communicate directly?

Tolstoy shares Dickens' moral fervor, and his underlying themes are perhaps as serious, but even his supreme *War and Peace* is wanting in a kind of weight because of his optimistic ignorance of evil, and his refusal to use material that might sound 'invented'. Dostoevsky, of course, knew as much about sin and the irrational and every conceivable blackness as Dickens, and was often the wildest of comedians, but his immense and stormy vision seems to break out of control, and a Western reader, finding himself swept away on the back of the apocalyptic beast into the night, is likely to wish he might be set down on his own feet again, and find his bearings with the help of his own horn-rimmed spectacles. Yet Dickens has far more in common with Dostoevsky than with Proust, who, for all the sharpness of his scalpels, anatomizes a comparatively narrow segment of experience.

And yet Dickens, although he shares the quality of *excessiveness* which marks the Russians and the Frenchmen as great artists, does not produce in the modern mind the same impression of a great immediate experience. Perhaps the secret lies in the word 'immediate'. We rarely put ourselves in the place of Dickens' characters and feel directly with them. We see them from without, and the romance of Florence Dombey touches us *personally* no more than the lovers in 'The Eve of St Agnes'. We become Little Nell, in our own visceral being, no more than we become Rapunzel; and we suffer the pangs of Lady Dedlock with the same remote pain that the torments of Brunetto Latini communicate from the page of Dante. Who weeps for Peggotty's niece as they weep for Anna Karenina? In short, we are not forced into direct emotional participation, which is the goal of most contemporary writing since Tolstoy and Maupassant. The interest, the meaning, of Dickens' novels lies elsewhere, and if we are moved, we are moved in the serener regions of the spirit where poetry and folk tale make their appeal to understanding. No other major novelist builds his books so frankly by the poet's method.

As a poet he warns of Paul Dombey's death in symbolic terms of the sea's murmurings, for as a poet he deals everywhere in symbols and suggestive images and chanted repetitions and protracted fancies with an abandon denied to the prosier scribes of daily life – and therein lie both the freedom and the *order* of his writing. But as a poet he is far from the sad lyricism of Virginia Woolf or the melomania of D. H. Lawrence, although he touches them both at points; he more nearly resembles Chaucer and the robust poet-dramatists of the Elizabethan age. Yet (since it is hard to say anything 'true' of Dickens) this too is a false picture – for whom does he *not* resemble one way or another?

Perhaps it is because of the detachment of the poetic method that Dickens' novels can be read again without loss of pleasure, for, as in a well-loved poem, the sequence is largely independent of the kind of time in which suspense draws us on. Since we have never been invited to identify ourselves passionately with the fate of the characters, and have not lived through their story as if it were our own, we do not return to Dickens as we are likely to return even to Tolstoy, with a sense of chill, of lost magic and shrunken dimension. For there are certain books as difficult to recapture in their essence as an old love, as difficult to relive as a passage in our past, simply because they *were* our love and our past, and their truth for us has been assimilated and has actually modified our present. Dickens' books are not of this kind; like a sonnet, or Jack and the Beanstalk, their rewards belong to a perpetual present.

JAMES WRIGHT

The Mystery of Edwin Drood (1961)

The Mystery of Edwin Drood is the last of Dickens' novels. In accordance with his practice, it first appeared in six monthly parts from April to September in 1870; and it was first published as a volume in the same year. The first three parts were issued by Dickens himself before his death, and thereafter the remaining parts were issued by his friend and biographer, John Forster. Although there have been occasional speculations about the possible length of the completed novel, the testimony of Forster and others indicates that Dickens planned to finish it in twelve monthly numbers. It is true, of course, that the novelist had not always been averse to changing his plans right in the middle of a novel. For example, he interrupted the course of *Martin Chuzzlewit* by sending his hero to America, because the regular issues of the novel were not selling enough copies to satisfy Dickens, and he wished to capitalize on the popularity of his previous writings on the United States. He also modified the plan of *Master Humphrey's Clock* in such a way as to produce *The Old Curiosity Shop*; and the reader can see that amazing and neglected novel taking shape before his very eyes. However, both *Martin Chuzzlewit* and *The Old Curiosity Shop* are comparatively early works, written during the years when Dickens' methods of composition, for all their astonishing fertility, were still more or less improvisational. By the time he came to write *Edwin Drood*, he had learned to plan and to control both the plots and the imaginative visions of his novels from beginning to end. And there can be no doubt that Dickens, of all people, would have ended his novel within the limits which he planned, and that his conclusion would have been as imaginatively audacious as the first half, that haunting and broken vision which we possess.

The vision, of course, is one of the most tantalizing of all Dickensian attractions. There is the rather obvious attraction of the mystery plot concocted by a master who lives just long enough to ask all of the most tempting questions and then dies at the very moment when, in the ordinary course of things, he would have begun to present the answers. But the book is attractive – one might almost say seductive – in other ways, too. The meaning which it promises and never quite has time to reveal is not merely the mechanical solution to a mystery; it is also a meaning of a poetic or imaginative kind. It is this second meaning which is able to speak to those of us whose interest in the book may not depend on a taste for mystery stories in general.

Nevertheless, the problem of the plot itself remains important. After all, the novel is a mystery story, a popular kind of writing in which Dickens became interested largely through his association with Wilkie Collins. Dickens and Collins had collaborated on a few literary projects; and Dickens published, in his own magazine, several of Collins' mysteries, notably *The Woman in White* and *The Moonstone*. His interest in the craft of the mystery story is only another manifestation of the fact that Dickens was a popular writer in the strict sense of the word. His concern for the response of his public is an essential fact about him, however one may wish to interpret it. Let us turn, then, to this popular mystery story itself, in order to see what its mechanical problems are, and how they might have been solved if Dickens had lived long enough to dazzle his audience at the conclusion with some peculiarly Dickensian combination of storytelling virtuosity and poetic insight.

Traditional discussions of the plot and attempts to unravel it have involved such problems as the following: the fate of Edwin Drood; the identity of Datchery, that 'stranger who appeared in Cloisterham' after Drood's disappearance; and the identity of the opium-peddling hag sometimes called the 'Princess Puffer', who administers the narcotic to John Jasper and then pursues him in sinister fashion at times when he is not even aware of her. Further problems arise with regard to the mechanical relationship between these various characters, in terms of the bare solution of the plot itself.

A number of subsequent authors have written their own continuations and solutions of *Edwin Drood*. Perhaps this sort of thing was to be expected. Such continuations do not seem worth discussing at any length. I do not mean to imply that they are arrogant. As noted, Dickens himself was a popular author, and probably would not have objected to a widespread technical interest in a plot which he himself had tried so hard to make interesting in the first place. On the other hand, I do not believe that the continuations of the novel possess any interest beyond the merely technical. And technique, taken alone, is trivial. What matters in Dickens' novel, as in the work of any great author, is the illumination of meaning which the technique is made to serve.

There have been more responsible Dickensians, however, among those whose concern is to understand, if possible, just what it was that Dickens himself intended to do with his half-finished plot. Noteworthy among such investigators has been W. Robertson Nicoll, who in 1912 published his book *The Problem of 'Edwin Drood': A Study in the Methods of Dickens*. In this careful and scholarly work, Mr Nicoll gathered all of the relevant external evidence (remarks made by Dickens to his associates and to members of his family, testimony by his illustrator, and so on) which might contribute to a solution of the plot. He also succinctly reviewed the most intelligible and probable suggestions for a solution. Other scholars, in the responsible tradition of Mr Nicoll, have been at work on the novel more or less constantly since Dickens' death. This is not the place to review their work, but it has had one remarkably important result: the conclusive identification of John Jasper as a criminal.

Now, defining the kind of criminal Jasper turns out to be is the occasion for long and difficult research, the chief results of which have been brilliantly summarized by Edgar Johnson in his distinguished biography, *Charles Dickens: His Tragedy and Triumph*. Jasper is a murderer. He has murdered Edwin Drood and, perhaps, concealed the body somehow in the Sapsea monument. Datchery, the stranger with the stagy white hair and the fluttering, ill-concealed hands, is generally conceded to be the fearless and resourceful Helena Landless. The exact identity and function of the opium-dispensing Princess Puffer is not clear, and it will probably remain for ever a matter for speculation, whether scholarly or amateur. The story is told of a medium who claimed to have been in touch with Dickens during a seance. When she asked him what sort of thing he did to while away the time over there, he answered, in an acutely uncomfortable voice, that he was still trying to solve the complete mystery of Edwin Drood.

But whether or not the mystery itself can be solved, the very identification of John Jasper as a criminal is a matter of the greatest significance. For it was not the mystery itself, conceived as the mere unraveling of a plot, that engaged the attention, as it were, of Dickens' entire poetic imagination. It is characteristic of Dickens throughout his career that he was able to use a variety of literary conventions for the fulfillment of some deeper imaginative intention, whether he was adapting the convention of the sporting story (as it was written by Surtees) in order to arrive finally at *Pickwick*, or the convention of the mystery story in order to arrive at the character of John Jasper. Dickens' ability to shape popular conventions toward his own artistic ends is illuminated in a passage from an article that appeared in the *Pall Mall Magazine* in June 1906, some thirty-five years after Dickens' death. The article is called 'Edwin Drood and the Last Days of Charles Dickens, by his younger daughter Kate Perugini'. After summarizing the external evidence for the view that Edwin Drood is murdered by his uncle John Jasper, Mrs Perugini writes the following:

> If those who are interested in the subject will carefully read what I have quoted, they will not be able to detect any word or hint from my father that it was upon the Mystery alone that he relied for the interest and originality of his idea. The originality was to be shown, as he tells us, in what we may call the psychological description the murderer gives us of his temptations, temperament, and character, as if told by another. . . . I do not mean to imply that the mystery itself had no strong hold on my father's imagination; but, greatly as he was interested in the intricacies of that tangled skein, the information he voluntarily gave to Mr Forster, from whom he had withheld nothing for thirty-three years, certainly points to the fact that he was quite as deeply fascinated and absorbed in the study of the criminal Jasper, as in the dark and sinister crime that has given the book its title. . . . It was not, I imagine, for the intricate working out of his plot alone that my father cared to write this story; but it was through his wonderful observation of character, and his strange insight into the tragic secrets of the human heart, that he desired his greatest triumph to be achieved.

It seems to me that Dickens' daughter, one of the most intelligent as well as one of the most audacious and independent of his many children, has placed the emphasis where it belongs. It is true that Dickens was interested in the intricacies of his plot in *Edwin Drood*; but this is just a way of saying that he was Dickens. The man was probably capable of being interested in anything whatever; and that is one reason why he is so precious to us, for he is capable of explaining to us, with incomparable intensity and humor, just why it is that the chimney pots on the London roofs are more fantastically strange than the wildest minarets in the most far-off Orient, and why and how it is that an ill-clothed and vicious ragamuffin like Deputy is actually a poetic genius, and how it comes about that a meanly skilled pickpocket and cutpurse like Jack Dawkins in *Oliver Twist* has a more intelligent and more generous grasp of human justice than any official interpreter of the whole British Constitution. It is always Dickens' capacity for being interested that leads him to his greatest artistic illuminations. His American biographer, Mr Johnson, tells us that, though Dickens was not a 'glittering conversationalist', he was 'better than a brilliant talker, he was a brilliant listener, who stimulated others to their best, filled everyone with the conviction that Dickens delighted in his company, and allowed no man to be a bore'. And just as this genius for being fascinated by other human beings leads Dickens to the creation of a multitude of characters whose extent and variety staggers the imagination, so the same powers of interest led him from his initial concern with the intricacies of a mystery plot *per se* to a deeper concern with the more profound and genuinely terrible intricacies of his chief character, John Jasper the criminal.

Jasper's being a criminal, a murderer addicted to the habit of opium, is a fact of both psychological and social significance. Both meanings are related to the equally important fact of his being a highly respected citizen of his community, an admired organist in the Cloisterham Cathedral. Dickens had always been deeply absorbed in the phenomena of crime and criminals, both in his travels and in his fiction. In one of the letters which he wrote to his friend Forster during his first visit to America in 1842, he speaks of visiting a prison in Pennsylvania, and reflects with horror and fascination on the supposed meditations of the prisoners who are compelled to undergo solitary confinement. Again, during the time when he was at work on the opening chapters of *Edwin Drood*, he escorted some visiting friends through some dangerous criminal haunts in London, and did not neglect the opium dens. As for his exploration of criminal themes in his fiction, a number of characters come to mind at once: Bill Sykes, whose ghastly murder of his mistress Nancy in *Oliver Twist* Dickens was reading to large audiences of hysterical women at the very time when he was working on *Edwin Drood*; Jonas Chuzzlewit, whose flight from the police in the closing pages of *Martin Chuzzlewit* is very nearly hallucinatory (to use Taine's term) in its dreadful intensity, which is rarely surpassed by Dostoevski himself. And there are the gloomy scenes in Fleet Prison, following the trial scene, in *Pickwick Papers*. Even though that first of his works is justly considered to be pervaded by sunlight, it nevertheless contains the awareness of crime, the peculiar Dickensian darkness which is a feature of his work from the beginning to the end.

And Jasper himself is a man who embodies the Dickensian darkness perhaps more thoroughly than any previous character. As mentioned, the mere fact of his being a criminal has an interest that is both psychological and social. That is, Jasper is simultaneously a solid representative of his society and a rather bitter critical comment upon it.

The psychological interest of his character has to do with the division within and against himself. Jasper is the respectable choir member in a perfectly respectable English cathedral town. The very opening lines of the book mention 'an ancient English Cathedral tower'. Immediately there is the question, 'how can the ancient English Cathedral tower be here?' Then, within a few more lines, Dickens evokes a world of nightmare, and we realize finally that we are not in the midst of one of those charmingly picturesque little places, so often and mistakenly associated with the name of Dickens, in which Scrooge is perpetually handing out Christmas turkeys to the Deserving Poor and the Cheeryble Brothers are forever frightening children out of their wits by throwing money at them; no, we are placed in the nightmare more directly at the beginning of *Edwin Drood*. Without wasting a single breath, Dickens has mentioned the cathedral town and then plunged us into one of its deepest meanings. We are in the opium nightmare of the choir member. When next we see Jasper, he is perfectly in control of himself, and he enjoys the regard of his fellow townsmen. But the secret is out. Or, rather, we are in on it; and, as far as the book goes, the reader never quite escapes from the divided darkness of Jasper's nature.

It seems of crucial importance, moreover, that we should note Jasper's sincerity of feeling. That is, he is not a hypocrite. If he had been a mere liar, an actor whose feeling for his nephew Edwin Drood was only a pretense assumed for the benefit of the public, then Jasper would be nothing much. What makes him remarkable is not only the sincerity, but the almost inexpressible intensity, of his feeling for Edwin and for everything else. And if his love for Edwin is as genuine as we have every right to believe, then the murder becomes a kind of suicide also – as perhaps all personal murders are. Oscar Wilde's startling lines are appropriate to Jasper's case: killing Edwin, he had certainly killed the thing he loved, 'and so he had to die'. Thus divided against himself, Jasper is always searching for ways to forget and lose that self, and he never succeeds. He tries music, opium, love: and all three lead him further into terror. Perhaps his inner division has become so intense and unbearable that it has reappeared in his external actions; perhaps he has himself reappeared in the external world as two distinct persons. It is a weird speculation, but Dickens himself has given us the hint. In the third chapter of the novel – where Dickens is describing, of all things, Miss Twinkleton's Seminary for Young Ladies – there is the following sentence:

> As, in some cases of drunkenness, and in others of animal magnetism, there are two states of consciousness which never clash, but each of which pursues its separate course as though it were continuous instead of broken (thus, if I hide my watch when I am drunk, I must be drunk again before I can remember where), so Miss Twinkleton has two distinct and separate phases of being.

Perhaps Miss Twinkleton is not the only one.

And perhaps Jasper also is not alone in his self-division. If he is a representative of his society, then that society is also divided against itself, so that often there is no sane relation between its words and its actions. And, indeed, Dickens' novel bears out such a reading. The first example who comes to mind is the terrifying philanthropist, Mr Honeythunder. There is no point in quoting him. He would shout me down in any case. In addition to this monster, however, there are less obvious instances of division between word and action, between deeds of light and deeds of darkness. For example, there is the Dean's refusal to offer further sanctuary to the persecuted Neville Landless. There is the almost literally insane epitaph which Mr Sapsea composed for his wife's tomb – an epitaph which is indeed as stupefyingly funny as Chesterton says it is, and which is also one of the most frightening evidences of spiritual blindness and cruelty ever recorded. The entire book, or what we have of the book, is riddled with these pretenses and divisions. Dickens' opening evocation of the opium den, with its nightmare of character embodied in Jasper himself, establishes both the tone and the meaning of his artistic vision with complete mastery. Jasper himself is English society, the society for whom and to whom Dickens wrote. It is a society capable of much feeling, even of love sometimes. But it is also divided against itself; it hides its indifference to women's feelings under fantastic self-adulatory words; it shouts about philanthropy through the voice of Mr Honeythunder while the small ragamuffins stone the drunken Durdles home after dark.

Through what Jasper is and what he does, Dickens might have been speaking to his public in the words of the Apocalypse: 'Thou sayest, I am rich; I have everything and need nothing; but thou knowest not that thou art miserable and poor and beggarly and blind and naked. . . .'

EDGAR JOHNSON

Epilogue (1952)

DICKENS'S whole career and achievement were singularly consistent. Though he grew and developed, he never lost the living sympathies that lie at the heart of his greatness. Those sympathies were rooted in an almost endless relish for the richness and variety of life and of human nature, a love of experience that exulted in the pure vividness with which things are themselves. Dickens liked and disliked people; he was never merely indifferent. He loved and laughed and derided and despised and hated; he never patronized or sniffed. He could be desperately unhappy; he was never only bored. He had no fastidious shrinkings, no snobberies, no dogmatic rejections.

These are the qualities that give his world such intensity. He was as fascinated by the decaying cabbage-stalks of Covent Garden, or by the fishy smell of Mr Peggotty's outhouse where crabs and lobsters never left off pinching one another, as he was by the Cratchits' goose in its hissing hot gravy. The grime and foul gutters of Saffron Hill interested him as much as the clowns and spangle-skirted bareback riders of Astley's Circus, the hemp and tangled masts of Limehouse Hole, the shadowy rafters of Westminster Hall, the salt reaches of Cooling Marsh, the dripping urns of Chesney Wold, Boffin's dust-heaps, and the polluted air of the Old Bailey. He was not repelled by a lively scoundrel like Mr Jingle or revolted by Jo's malodorous body and verminous rags; he felt no scorn for chuckleheaded Mr Toots or the shabby and bibulous Newman Noggs; even for the merry and black-hearted Fagin in his greasy thieves' kitchen Dickens had a gleam of sympathy.

In his comprehensive delight in all experience Dickens resembles Walt Whitman, but he was innocent of that nebulous transcendental-ism that blurred Whitman's universe into vast misty panoramas and left him, for all his huge democratic vistas, unable to tell a story or paint a single concrete human being. Dickens saw the brilliant individual quality of each person and experience in its comic or pathetic or dramatic essence, and in so doing he surprisingly realized Walter Pater's aspiration toward 'a life of constant and eager observation'. Though he burned with a warm and tender, rather than a 'hard, gem-like flame', surely Dickens far more than Pater vibrated with the very pulsations 'of a variegated, dramatic life'. If he fell short of Pater's exquisite sensibility in the rendering of nuance, his grasp was the more muscular because he was vigorously free from the strangulated refine-ment that made Pater a chambered aesthetic nautilus quivering away in his shell from all contact with coarseness and vulgarity. It is the welter of existence that Dickens embraced, not a delicately selected part of it.

But for all the enthusiasm with which he welcomed the multiplicity of experience, Dickens did not fail in a just discrimination of black and white. His very sympathy with life's thronging variety made him stern to whatever impoverished and destroyed. From the hypocritical Stiggins in *Pickwick* to the bullying Honeythunder in *Edwin Drood*, he abominated those who sought to reduce it to a dispirited gray or to subordinate others to their own desire for power. He hated the gloomy and ferocious self-righteousness of the Murdstones. He derided the woolly-mindedness of Mrs Jellyby, neglecting the poor of London's slums and even her own family while she worried about the natives of Borioboola-Gha, and detested the domineering presumption of Mrs Pardiggle, pushing her way into the cottages of the poor with useless and arrogant advice. He saw England plundered by Boodle and Coodle, controlled by the landed aristocracy of Sir Leicester Dedlock, the selfish commercialism of Mr Dombey, the industrial greed of Mr Bounderby, and the slippery financial machinations of Mr Merdle; and helplessly obstructed by the Circumlocution Office while Mr Gradgrind sifted the ashes of the national dust-heap and formulated the dogmas of political economy. Meanwhile, he beheld with loathing how this dreadful structure of iniquity and suffering spawned a host of lesser parasites, vermin, and beasts of prey, the Fagins, Bumbles, Artful Dodgers, Fangs, Squeerses, Hawks, Tiggs, Slymes, Pecksniffs, Scrooges, Smallweeds, Vholeses, Casbys, Barnacles, Weggs, Lammles, and Fledgebys, all sucking or bludgeoning their own advantage out of their victims.

Not primarily a systematic thinker, but a man of feeling, intuitive and emotional, Dickens had nevertheless a sharp intelligence which pierced through the complexities of the social scene to a comprehension of its shocking realities that was essentially true. His instinctive sympathy with the fruitful and creative enabled him to see how the generous potentialities of human nature were crippled, and he felt his way step by step to a realization of the forces that blighted men's health and happiness. As a young reporter, he watched the landowners resisting to the last ditch the abolition of the rotten boroughs. As a mature man he saw the slum landlords rack-renting their tenants and breeding the cholera by their determination not to spend a penny on sanitary improvement, observed the factory owners mutilating their workers with unfenced machinery, heard them screaming that they would be ruined by a ten-hour day and a living wage. He could put two and two together, and he did. By the time he had reached the middle of his career he understood capitalist industrialism at least as well as most nineteenth-century political economists.

He understood it with unwavering hostility. Every book he produced was not only a celebration of the true wealth of life; it was an attack on the forces of cruelty and selfishness. His heart seized the sword of a sharp and witty logic that slashed contemptuously through innumerable varieties of logical humbug and rationalist special pleading. He had no patience with statistical abstractions and economic theories that ignored the welfare of flesh-and-blood human beings, or with metaphysical systems remote from the hopes and fears of the human heart. Unlike so many of the lovers of humanity who are bitterly unable to love human beings, it was not an abstract humanity constructed in his mind that Dickens loved, but men, women, and children, with all their frailties and absurdities. His hatreds sprang full-armed out of that love.

Select Bibliography

THE Dickens bibliography is now enormous. The following selection consists of books and substantial articles only. It represents my own choice of the most stimulating criticism, and has no claim to be anything more than this. An excellent long bibliography with commentary has been compiled by Ada Nisbet, and will be found on pages 44–153 of *Victorian Fiction: A Guide to Research*, ed. Lionel Stevenson (Harvard U.P., 1964). There is also a select bibliography, much fuller than this, on pages 387–410 of *The Dickens Critics*, ed. George H. Ford and Lauriat Lane, Jr. (Cornell U.P., 1961).

BOOKS (ARRANGED BY CHRONOLOGY)

G. K. Chesterton, *Charles Dickens* (Methuen, 1906).

George Orwell, 'Charles Dickens' (1939). Available in *Critical Essays* (Secker & Warburg, 1954) and elsewhere.

Edmund Wilson, 'Dickens: The Two Scrooges', in *The Wound and the Bow* (Houghton Mifflin and W. H. Allen, 1941; also Methuen paperbacks).

Humphry House, *The Dickens World* (Oxford U.P., 1941).

Jack Lindsay, *Charles Dickens: A Biographical and Critical Study* (Dakers, 1950).

Edgar Johnson, *Charles Dickens: His Tragedy and Triumph*, 2 vols. (Simon & Schuster, 1952; Gollancz, 1953).

George H. Ford, *Dickens and His Readers: Aspects of Novel-criticism since 1836*. (Princeton, 1955; Norton Library paperback, 1965).

John Butt and Kathleen Tillotson, *Dickens at Work* (Methuen, 1957).

J. Hillis Miller, *Charles Dickens: The World of his Novels* (Harvard U.P., 1958; Oxford U.P., 1959).

Monroe Engel, *The Maturity of Dickens* (Harvard U.P., 1959; Oxford U.P., 1959).

A. O. J. Cockshut, *The Imagination of Charles Dickens* (Collins, 1961).

Philip Collins, *Dickens and Crime* (Macmillan, 1962, 2nd ed. 1964; St. Martin's Press, 1962; now in paperback).

Mark Spilka, *Dickens and Kafka* (Indiana U.P., 1963; Dennis Dobson, 1963).

Earle Davis, *The Flint and the Flame* (University of Missouri P., 1963; Gollancz, 1964).

Philip Collins, *Dickens and Education* (Macmillan, 1963; St Martin's Press, 1964; now in paperback).

Steven Marcus, *Dickens: from Pickwick to Dombey* (Chatto, 1965).

Robert Garis, *The Dickens Theatre: A Reassessment of the Novels* (Oxford U.P., 1965).

Taylor Stoehr, *Dickens: The Dreamer's Stance* (Cornell U.P., 1965).

William F. Axton, *Circle of Fire: Dickens' Vision and Style and the Popular Victorian Theatre* (University of Kentucky P., 1966).

Ross H. Dabney, *Love and Property in the Novels of Dickens* (Chatto, 1967).

ARTICLES

Many of the best articles are collected in *The Dickens Critics*, ed. George H. Ford and Lauriat Lane, Jr. (Cornell U.P., 1961). In addition to the pieces by Graham Greene, Lionel Trilling, Angus Wilson and Robert Morse, which have also been included here, I particularly recommend: Dorothy Van Ghent on 'The Dickens World: A View from Todgers's', Arnold Kettle on *Oliver Twist*, V. S. Pritchett on 'The Comic World of Dickens', Morton D. Zabel on *Bleak House*, George Bernard Shaw on *Hard Times*, and George Santayana on 'Dickens'.

A collection called *Dickens and the Twentieth Century* edited by John Gross and Gabriel Pearson was published by Routledge in 1962. The quality of this is variable, but there are articles on all of the major novels, by an impressive array of critics.

Notes on Contributors

C. B. Cox is Professor of English at the University of Manchester, and co-editor of the *Critical Quarterly*. His book *The Free Spirit* was published by Oxford U.P. in 1963.

A. E. Dyson is Senior Lecturer in English at the University of East Anglia, and co-editor of the *Critical Quarterly*. His book *The Crazy Fabric* was published by Macmillan in 1965.

Monroe Engel is Professor of English at Harvard. His Book *The Maturity of Dickens* was published by the Harvard University Press in 1959.

Dorothy Van Ghent is Professor of English at the State University of New York, Buffalo. Her book *The English Novel: Form and Function* was published by Rinehart & Co., N.Y., 1953.

Graham Greene is one of the best known and most celebrated modern novelists.

John Gross has become widely known among younger British critics.

W. J. HARVEY was Professor of English at the Queen's University, Belfast. His book *Character and the Novel* was published by Chatto & Windus in 1965.

HUMPHRY HOUSE died in 1955 at the age of forty-six, soon after he had started to edit Dickens's letters. His best-known book was *The Dickens World* (Oxford U.P., 1941).

EDGAR JOHNSON is Professor of English at the City College of New York. His famous biography *Charles Dickens: His Tragedy and Triumph* was first published in 1952.

STEVEN MARCUS is Professor of English at Columbia University, New York. In addition to *Dickens from Pickwick to Dombey* (Chatto, 1965) – in my view, the best critical book yet published on Dickens – he has recently become famous as the author of *The Other Victorians* (Chatto, 1966), a study of Victorian pornography.

J. HILLIS MILLER teaches English at the Johns Hopkins University. In addition to *Charles Dickens: The World of his Novels* (Harvard U.P., 1958), he has published *The Disappearance of God* (Harvard and Oxford U.P., 1963), and is becoming recognized as one of the best critics of his generation.

MARK SPILKA is Professor of English at Brown University. In addition to *Dickens and Kafka* (Indiana U.P. and Dennis Dobson, 1963), he is the author of *The Love Ethic of D. H. Lawrence*.

KATHLEEN TILLOTSON is Professor of English at Bedford College, London. In addition to *Novels of the Eighteen-Forties* (Oxford U.P., 1954), she is the author, with the late John Butt, of *Dickens at Work* (Methuen, 1957).

LIONEL TRILLING is Professor of English at Columbia University, New York, and one of the most famous of modern critics.

ANGUS WILSON is the well-known British novelist, who is now also Professor of English at the University of East Anglia.

JAMES WRIGHT teaches in the University of Minnesota.

Index